DATABASE MODELING AND DESIGN

DATABASE MODELING AND DESIGN
Logical Design

Fifth Edition

TOBY TEOREY
SAM LIGHTSTONE
TOM NADEAU
H. V. JAGADISH

AMSTERDAM • BOSTON • HEIDELBERG • LONDON
NEW YORK • OXFORD • PARIS • SAN DIEGO
SAN FRANCISCO • SINGAPORE • SYDNEY • TOKYO
Morgan Kaufmann Publishers is an imprint of Elsevier

Acquiring Editor: Rick Adams
Development Editor: David Bevans
Project Manager: Sarah Binns
Designer: Joanne Blank

Morgan Kaufmann Publishers is an imprint of Elsevier.
30 Corporate Drive, Suite 400, Burlington, MA 01803, USA

This book is printed on acid-free paper.

Library of Congress Cataloging-in-Publication Data
Database modeling and design : logical design / Toby Teorey ... [et al.]. – 5th ed.
    p. cm.
  Rev. ed. of: Database modeling & design / Tobey Teorey, Sam Lightstone, Tom Nadeau. 4th ed. 2005.
  ISBN 978-0-12-382020-4
  1. Relational databases. 2. Database design. I. Teorey, Toby J. Database modeling & design.
  QA76.9.D26T45 2011
  005.75′6–dc22
                        2010049921

British Library Cataloguing-in-Publication Data
A catalogue record for this book is available from the British Library.

For information on all Morgan Kaufmann publications,
visit our Web site at www.mkp.com or www.elsevierdirect.com

Printed in the United States of America
11 12 13 14 15   5 4 3 2 1

To Julie, for her wonderful support
                    —Toby Teorey

To my wife and children, Elisheva, Hodaya, and Avishai
                              —Sam Lightstone

To Carol, Paula, Mike, and Lagi
                    —Tom Nadeau

To Aradhna, Siddhant, and Kamya
                    —H V Jagadish

CONTENTS

PREFACE

Database design technology has undergone significant evolution in recent years, although business applications continue to be dominated by the relational data model and relational database systems. The relational model has allowed the database designer to separately focus on logical design (defining the data relationships and tables) and physical design (efficiently storing data onto and retrieving data from physical storage). Other new technologies such as data warehousing, OLAP, and data mining, as well as object-oriented, spatial, and Web-based data access, have also had an important impact on database design.

In this fifth edition, we continue to concentrate on techniques for database design in relational database systems. However, because of the vast and explosive changes in new physical database design techniques in recent years, we have reorganized the topics into two separate books: *Database Modeling and Design: Logical Design* (5th Edition) and *Physical Database Design: The Database Professional's Guide* (1st Edition)

Logical database design is largely the domain of application designers, who design the logical structure of the database to suit application requirements for data manipulation and structured queries. The definition of database tables for a particular vendor is considered to be within the domain of logical design in this book, although many database practitioners refer to this step as physical design.

Physical database design, in the context of these two books, is performed by the implementers of the database servers, usually database administrators (DBAs) who must decide how to structure the database for a particular machine (server), and optimize that structure for system performance and system administration. In smaller companies these communities may in fact be the same people, but for large enterprises they are very distinct.

We start the discussion of logical database design with the entity-relationship (ER) approach for data requirements specification and conceptual modeling. We then take a detailed look at another dominating data modeling approach, the Unified Modeling Language (UML). Both approaches are used throughout the text for all the data modeling examples, so the user can select either one (or both) to help follow the logical design methodology. The discussion of basic principles is supplemented with common examples that are based on real-life experiences.

Organization

The database life cycle is described in Chapter 1. In Chapter 2, we present the most fundamental concepts of data modeling and provide a simple set of notational constructs (the Chen notation for the ER model) to represent them. The ER model has traditionally been a very popular method of conceptualizing users' data requirements. Chapter 3 introduces the UML notation for data modeling. UML (actually UML-2) has become a standard method of modeling large-scale systems for object-oriented languages such as C++ and Java, and the data modeling component of UML is rapidly becoming as popular as the ER model. We feel it is important for the reader to understand both notations and how much they have in common.

Chapters 4 and 5 show how to use data modeling concepts in the database design process. Chapter 4 is devoted to direct application of conceptual data modeling in logical database design. Chapter 5 explains the transformation of the conceptual model to the relational model, and to Structured Query Language (SQL) syntax specifically.

Chapter 6 is devoted to the fundamentals of database normalization through third normal form and its variation, Boyce-Codd normal form, showing the functional equivalence between the conceptual model (both ER and UML) and the relational model for third normal form.

The case study in Chapter 7 summarizes the techniques presented in Chapters 1 through 6 with a new problem environment.

Chapter 8 illustrates the basic features of object-oriented database systems and how they differ from relational database systems. An "impedance mismatch" problem often arises due to data being moved between tables in a relational database and objects in an application program. Extensions made to relational systems to handle this problem are described.

Chapter 9 looks at Web technologies and how they impact databases and database design. XML is perhaps the best known Web technology. An overview of XML is given, and we explore database design issues that are specific to XML.

Chapter 10 describes the major logical database design issues in business intelligence - data warehousing, online analytical processing (OLAP) for decision support systems, and data mining.

Chapter 11 discusses three of the currently most popular software tools for logical design: IBM's Rational Data Architect, Computer Associates' AllFusion ERwin Data Modeler, and Sybase's PowerDesigner. Examples are given to demonstrate how each of these tools can be used to handle complex data modeling problems.

The Appendix contains a review of the basic data definition and data manipulation components of the relational database query language SQL (SQL-99) for those readers who lack familiarity with database query languages. A simple example database is used to illustrate the SQL query capability.

The database practitioner can use this book as a guide to database modeling and its application to database design for business and office environments and for well-structured scientific and engineering databases. Whether you are a novice database user or an experienced professional, this book offers new insights into database modeling and the ease of transition from the ER model or UML model to the relational model, including the building of standard SQL data definitions. Thus, no matter whether you are using IBM's DB2, Oracle, Microsoft's SQL Server, Access, or MySQL for example, the design rules set forth here will be applicable. The case studies used for the examples throughout the book are from real-life databases that were designed using the principles formulated here. This book can also be used by the advanced undergraduate or beginning graduate student to supplement a course textbook in introductory database management, or for a stand-alone course in data modeling or database design.

Typographical Conventions

For easy reference, entity and class names (Employee, Department, and so on) are capitalized from Chapter 2 forward. Throughout the book, relational table names (**product**, **product_count**) are set in boldface for readability.

Acknowledgments

We wish to acknowledge colleagues that contributed to the technical continuity of this book: James Bean, Mike Blaha, Deb Bolton, Joe Celko, Jarir Chaar, Nauman Chaudhry, David Chesney, David Childs, Pat Corey, John DeSue, Yang Dongqing, Ron Fagin, Carol Fan, Jim Fry, Jim Gray, Bill Grosky, Wei Guangping, Wendy Hall, Paul Helman, Nayantara Kalro, John Koenig, Ji-Bih Lee, Marilyn Mantei Tremaine, Bongki Moon, Robert Muller, Wee-Teck Ng, Dan O'Leary, Kunle Olukotun, Dorian Pyle, Dave Roberts, Behrooz Seyed-Abbassi, Dan Skrbina, Rick Snodgrass, Il-Yeol Song, Dick Spencer, Amjad Umar, and Susanne Yul. We also wish to thank the Department of Electrical Engineering and Computer Science (EECS), especially Jeanne Patterson, at the University of Michigan for providing resources for writing and revising. Finally, thanks for the generosity of our wives and children that has permitted us the time to work on this text.

Solutions Manual

A solutions manual to all exercises is available. Contact the publisher for further information.

ABOUT THE AUTHORS

Toby Teorey is Professor Emeritus in the Computer Science and Engineering Division (EECS Department) at the University of Michigan, Ann Arbor. He received his B.S. and M.S. degrees in electrical engineering from the University of Arizona, Tucson, and a Ph.D. in computer science from the University of Wisconsin, Madison. He was chair of the 1981 ACM SIGMOD Conference and program chair of the 1991 Entity–Relationship Conference. Professor Teorey's current research focuses on database design and performance of computing systems. He is a member of the ACM.

Sam Lightstone is a Senior Technical Staff Member and Development Manager with IBM's DB2 Universal Database development team. He is the cofounder and leader of DB2's autonomic computing R&D effort. He is also a member of IBM's Autonomic Computing Architecture Board, and in 2003 he was elected to the Canadian Technical Excellence Council, the Canadian affiliate of the IBM Academy of Technology. His current research includes numerous topics in autonomic computing and relational DBMSs, including automatic physical database design, adaptive self-tuning resources, automatic administration, benchmarking methodologies, and system control. He is an IBM Master Inventor with over 25 patents and patents pending, and he has published widely on autonomic computing for relational database systems. He has been with IBM since 1991.

Tom Nadeau is a Senior Database Software Engineer at the American Chemical Society. He received his B.S. degree in computer science and M.S. and Ph.D. degrees in electrical engineering and computer science from the University of Michigan, Ann Arbor. His technical interests include data warehousing, OLAP, data mining, text mining, and machine learning. He won the best paper award at the 2001 IBM CASCON Conference.

H. V. Jagadish is the Bernard A. Galler Collegiate Professor of Electrical Engineering and Computer Science at the University of Michigan. He received a Ph.D. from Stanford in 1985 and worked many years for AT&T, where he eventually headed the database department. He also taught at the University of Illinois. He currently leads research in databases in the context of the Internet and in biomedicine. His research team built a native XML store, called TIMBER, a hierarchical database for storing and querying XML data. He is Editor-in-Chief of the *Proceedings of the Very Large Data Base Endowment* (PVLDB), a member of the Board of the Computing Research Association (CRA), and a Fellow of the ACM.

1

INTRODUCTION

Database technology has evolved rapidly in the past three decades since the rise and eventual dominance of relational database systems. While many specialized database systems (object-oriented, spatial, multimedia, etc.) have found substantial user communities in the sciences and engineering, relational systems remain the dominant database technology for business enterprises.

Relational database design has evolved from an art to a science that has been partially implementable as a set of software design aids. Many of these design aids have appeared as the database component of computer-aided software engineering (CASE) tools, and many of them offer interactive modeling capability using a simplified data modeling approach. Logical design—that is, the structure of basic data relationships and their definition in a particular database system—is largely the domain of application designers. The work of these designers can be effectively done with tools such as the ERwin Data Modeler or Rational Rose with Unified Modeling Language (UML), as well as with a purely manual approach. Physical design—the creation of efficient data storage and retrieval mechanisms on the computing platform you are using—is typically the domain of the database administrator (DBA). Today's DBAs have a variety of vendor-supplied tools available to help design the most efficient databases. This book is devoted to the logical design methodologies and tools most popular for relational databases today. Physical design methodologies and tools are covered in a separate book.

In this chapter, we review the basic concepts of database management and introduce the role of data modeling and database design in the database life cycle.

Data and Database Management

The basic component of a file in a file system is a *data item*, which is the smallest named unit of data that has meaning in the real world—for example, last name, first name, street address, ID number, and political party. A group of related data items treated as a unit by an application is called a *record*. Examples of types of records are order, salesperson, customer, product, and department. A *file* is a collection of records of a single type. Database systems have built upon and expanded these definitions: In a relational database, a data item is called a *column* or *attribute*, a record is called a *row* or *tuple*, and a file is called a *table*.

A *database* is a more complex object; it is a collection of interrelated stored data that serves the needs of multiple users within one or more organizations—that is, an interrelated collection of many different types of tables. The motivation for using databases rather than files has been greater availability to a diverse set of users, integration of data for easier access and update for complex transactions, and less redundancy of data.

A *database management system* (DBMS) is a generalized software system for manipulating databases. A DBMS supports a logical view (schema, subschema); physical view (access methods, data clustering); data definition language; data manipulation language; and important utilities such as transaction management and concurrency control, data integrity, crash recovery, and security. Relational database systems, the dominant type of systems for well-formatted business databases, also provide a greater degree of data independence than the earlier hierarchical and network (CODASYL) database management systems. *Data independence* is the ability to make changes in either the logical or physical structure of the database without requiring reprogramming of application programs. It also makes database conversion and reorganization much easier. Relational DBMSs provide a much higher degree of data independence than previous systems; they are the focus of our discussion on data modeling.

Database Life Cycle

The database life cycle incorporates the basic steps involved in designing a global schema of the logical database, allocating data across a computer network, and defining local DBMS-specific schemas. Once the design is completed, the life cycle continues with database implementation and maintenance. This chapter contains an overview of the database life cycle, as shown in Figure 1.1. In succeeding chapters we will focus on the database design process from the modeling of requirements through logical design (Steps I and II below). We illustrate the result of each step of the life cycle with a series of diagrams in Figure 1.2. Each diagram shows a possible form of the output of each step so the reader can see the progression of the design process from an idea to an actual database implementation. These forms are discussed in much more detail in Chapters 2–6.

I. *Requirements analysis.* The database requirements are determined by interviewing both the producers and users of data and using the information to produce a formal requirements specification. That specification includes the data required for processing, the natural data relationships, and the software platform for the database implementation. As an example, Figure 1.2 (Step I) shows the concepts of products, customers, salespersons, and orders being formulated in the mind of the end user during the interview process.

II. *Logical design.* The *global schema*, a conceptual data model diagram that shows all the data and their relationships, is developed using techniques such as entity-relationship (ER) or UML. The data model constructs must be ultimately transformed into tables.

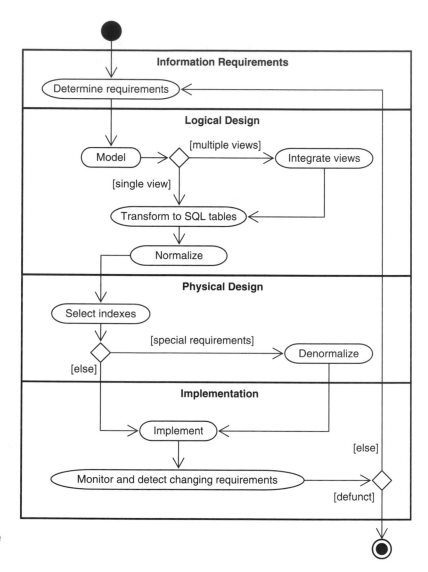

Figure 1.1 The database life cycle.

a. *Conceptual data modeling.* The data requirements are analyzed and modeled by using an ER or UML diagram that includes many features we will study in Chapters 2 and 3, for example, semantics for optional relationships, ternary relationships, supertypes, and subtypes (categories). Processing requirements are typically specified using natural language expressions or SQL commands along with the frequency of occurrence. Figure 1.2 (Step II.a) shows a possible ER

Database Life Cycle

Step I Information Requirements (reality)

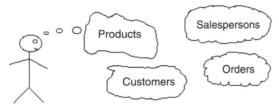

Step II Logical design

Step II.a Conceptual data modeling

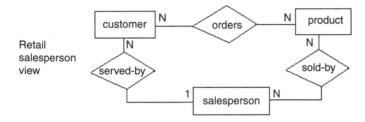

Step II.b View integration

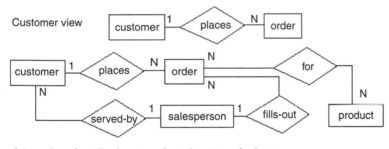

Integration of retail salesperson's and customer's views

Figure 1.2 Life cycle results, step by step (continued on following page).

model representation of the product/customer database in the mind of the end user.

b. *View integration.* Usually, when the design is large and more than one person is involved in requirements analysis, multiple views of data and relationships occur, resulting in inconsistencies due to variance in taxonomy, context, or perception. To eliminate redundancy and inconsistency from the model, these views must

Step II.c Transformation of the conceptual data model to SQL tables

Customer

cust-no	cust-name	....

Product

prod-no	prod-name	qty-in-stock

Salesperson

sales-name	addr	dept	job-level	vacation-days

Order

order-no	sales-name	cust-no

Order-product

order-no	prod-no

```
create table customer
    (cust_no integer,
    cust_name char(15),
    cust_addr char(30),
    sales_name char(15),
    prod_no integer,
    primary key (cust_no),
    foreign key (sales_name)
        references salesperson,
    foreign key (prod_no)
        references product):
```

Step II.d Normalization of SQL tables

Decomposition of tables and removal of update anomalies.

Salesperson

sales-name	addr	dept	job-level

SalesVacations

job-level	vacation-days

Step III Physical Design

Indexing
Clustering
Partitioning
Materialized views
Denormalization

Figure 1.2, cont'd
Further life cycle results, step by step.

be "rationalized" and consolidated into a single global view. View integration requires the use of ER semantic tools such as identification of synonyms, aggregation, and generalization. In Figure 1.2 (Step II.b), two possible views of the product/customer database are merged into a single global view based on common data for customer and order. View integration is also important when applications have to be integrated, and each may be written with its own view of the database.

c. *Transformation of the conceptual data model to SQL tables.* Based on a categorization of data modeling constructs and a set of mapping rules, each relationship and its associated entities are transformed into a set of DBMS-specific candidate relational tables. We will show these transformations in standard SQL in Chapter 5. Redundant tables are eliminated as part of this process. In our example, the tables in Step II.c of Figure 1.2 are the result of transformation of the integrated ER model in Step II.b.

d. *Normalization of tables.* Given a table (R), a set of attributes (B) is functionally dependent on another set of attributes (A) if, at each instant of time, each A value is associated with exactly one B value. Functional dependencies (FDs) are derived from the conceptual data model diagram and the semantics of data relationships in the requirements analysis. They represent the dependencies among data elements that are unique identifiers (keys) of entities. Additional FDs, which represent the dependencies between key and nonkey attributes within entities, can be derived from the requirements specification. Candidate relational tables associated with all derived FDs are normalized (i.e., modified by decomposing or splitting tables into smaller tables) using standard normalization techniques. Finally, redundancies in the data that occur in normalized candidate tables are analyzed further for possible elimination, with the constraint that data integrity must be preserved. An example of normalization of the Salesperson table into the new Salesperson and SalesVacations tables is shown in Figure 1.2 from Step II.c to Step II.d.

We note here that database tool vendors tend to use the term *logical model* to refer to the conceptual data model, and they use the term *physical model* to refer to the DBMS-specific implementation model (e.g., SQL tables). We also note that many conceptual data models are obtained not from scratch, but from the process of *reverse engineering* from an existing DBMS-specific schema (Silberschatz et al., 2010).

III. *Physical design.* The physical design step involves the selection of indexes (access methods), partitioning, and clustering of data. The logical design methodology in Step II simplifies the approach to designing large relational databases by reducing the number of data dependencies that need to be analyzed. This is accomplished by inserting the conceptual data modeling and integration steps (Steps II.a and II.b of Figure 1.2) into the traditional relational design approach. The objective of these steps is an accurate representation of reality. Data integrity is preserved through normalization of the candidate tables created when the conceptual data model is transformed into a relational model. The purpose of physical design is to then optimize performance. As part of the physical design, the global schema can sometimes be refined in limited ways to reflect processing (query and transaction) requirements if there are obvious large gains to be made in efficiency. This is called *denormalization*. It consists of selecting dominant processes on the basis of high frequency, high volume, or explicit priority; defining simple extensions to tables that will improve query performance; evaluating total cost for query, update, and storage; and considering the side effects, such as possible loss of integrity. This is particularly important for online analytical processing (OLAP) applications.

IV. *Database implementation, monitoring, and modification.* Once the design is completed, the database can be created through implementation of the formal schema using the data definition language (DDL) of a DBMS. Then the data manipulation language (DML) can be used to query and update the database, as well as to set up indexes and establish constraints, such as referential integrity. The language SQL contains both DDL and DML constructs; for example, the *create table* command represents DDL, and the *select* command represents DML.
As the database begins operation, monitoring indicates whether performance requirements are being met. If they are not being satisfied, modifications should be made to improve performance. Other modifications may be necessary when requirements change or end

user expectations increase with good performance. Thus, the life cycle continues with monitoring, redesign, and modifications. In the next two chapters we look first at the basic data modeling concepts; then, starting in Chapter 4, we apply these concepts to the database design process.

Conceptual Data Modeling

Conceptual data modeling is the driving component of logical database design. Let us take a look of how this important component came about and why it is important. Schema diagrams were formalized in the 1960s by Charles Bachman. He used rectangles to denote record types and directed arrows from one record type to another to denote a one-to-many relationship among instances of records of the two types. The *entity-relationship* (ER) approach for conceptual data modeling, one of the two approaches emphasized in this book, and described in detail in Chapter 2, was first presented in 1976 by Peter Chen. The Chen form of ER models uses rectangles to specify entities, which are somewhat analogous to records. It also uses diamond-shaped objects to represent the various types of relationships, which are differentiated by numbers or letters placed on the lines connecting the diamonds to the rectangles.

The Unified Modeling Language (UML) was introduced in 1997 by Grady Booch and James Rumbaugh and has become a standard graphical language for specifying and documenting large-scale software systems. The data modeling component of UML (now UML-2) has a great deal of similarity with the ER model, and will be presented in detail in Chapter 3. We will use both the ER model and UML to illustrate the data modeling and logical database design examples throughout this book.

In conceptual data modeling, the overriding emphasis is on simplicity and readability. The goal of conceptual schema design, where the ER and UML approaches are most useful, is to capture real-world data requirements in a simple and meaningful way that is understandable by both the database designer and the end user. The end user is the person responsible for accessing the database and executing queries and updates through the use of DBMS software, and therefore has a vested interest in the database design process.

Summary

Knowledge of data modeling and database design techniques is important for database practitioners and application developers. The database life cycle shows what steps are needed in a methodical approach to designing a database, from logical design, which is independent of the system environment, to physical design, which is based on the details of the database management system chosen to implement the database. Among the variety of data modeling approaches, the ER and UML data models are arguably the most popular in use today because of their simplicity and readability.

Tips and Insights for Database Professionals

Tip 1. Work methodically through the steps of the life cycle. Each step is clearly defined and has produced a result that can serve as a valid input to the next step.

Tip 2. Correct design errors as soon as possible by going back to the previous step and trying new alternatives. The later you wait, the more costly the errors and the longer the fixes.

Tip 3. Separate the logical and physical design completely because you are trying to satisfy completely different objectives.

Logical design. The objective is to obtain a feasible solution to satisfy all known and potential queries and updates. There are many possible designs; it is not necessary to find a "best" logical design, just a feasible one. Save the effort for optimization for physical design.

Physical design. The objective is to optimize performance for known and projected queries and updates.

Literature Summary

Much of the early data modeling work was done by Bachman (1969, 1972), Chen (1976), Senko et al. (1973), and others. Database design textbooks that adhere to a significant portion of the relational database life cycle described in this chapter are Teorey and Fry (1982), Muller (1999), Stephens and Plew (2000), Silverston (2001), Harrington (2002), Bagui (2003), Hernandez and Getz (2003), Simsion and Witt (2004), Powell (2005), Ambler and Sadalage (2006), Scamell and Umanath (2007), Halpin and Morgan (2008), Mannino (2008), Stephens (2008), Churcher (2009), and Hoberman (2009).

Temporal (time-varying) databases are defined and discussed in Jenson and Snodgrass (1996) and Snodgrass (2000). Other well-used approaches for conceptual data modeling include IDEF1X (Bruce, 1992; IDEF1X, 2005) and the data modeling component of the Zachmann Framework (Zachmann, 1987; Zachmann Institute for Framework Advancement, 2005). Schema evolution during development, a frequently occurring problem, is addressed in Harriman, Hodgetts, and Leo (2004).

2

THE ENTITY–RELATIONSHIP MODEL

This chapter defines all the major entity–relationship (ER) concepts that can be applied to the conceptual data modeling phase of the database life cycle.

The ER model has two levels of definition—one that is quite simple and another that is considerably more complex. The simple level is the one used by most current design tools. It is quite helpful to the database designer who must communicate with end users about their data requirements. At this level you simply describe, in diagram form, the entities, attributes, and relationships that occur in the system to be conceptualized, using semantics that are definable in a data dictionary. Specialized constructs, such as "weak" entities or mandatory/optional existence notation, are also usually included in the simple form. But very little else is included, in order to avoid cluttering up the ER diagram while the designer's and end user's understandings of the model are being reconciled.

An example of a simple form of ER model using the Chen notation is shown in Figure 2.1. In this example we want to keep track of videotapes and customers in a video store. Videos and customers are represented as entities Video and Customer, and the relationship "rents" shows a many-to-many association between them. Both Video and Customer entities have a few attributes that describe their characteristics, and the relationship "rents" has an attribute due date that represents the date that a particular video rented by a specific customer must be returned.

From the database practitioner's standpoint, the simple form of the ER model (or UML) is the preferred form for both data modeling and end user verification. It is easy to learn and applicable to a wide variety of design problems that might be encountered in industry and small businesses. As we will demonstrate, the simple form is easily translatable into SQL data definitions, and thus it has an immediate use as an aid for database implementation.

The complex level of ER model definition includes concepts that go well beyond the simple model. It includes concepts from the semantic models of artificial intelligence and from competing conceptual data models. Data modeling at this level helps the database designer capture more semantics without having to resort to narrative explanations. It is also useful to the database application

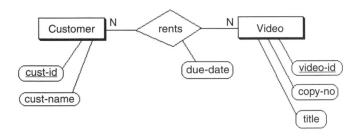

Figure 2.1 A simple form of the ER model using the Chen notation.

programmer, because certain integrity constraints defined in the ER model relate directly to code—code that checks range limits on data values and null values, for example. However, such detail in very large data model diagrams actually detracts from end user understanding. Therefore, the simple level is recommended as the basic communication tool for database design verification.

In the next section, we will look at the simple level of ER modeling described in the original work by Chen and extended by others. The following section presents the more advanced concepts that are less generally accepted but useful to describe certain semantics that cannot be constructed with the simple model.

Fundamental ER Constructs

Basic Objects: Entities, Relationships, Attributes

The basic ER model consists of three classes of objects: entities, relationships, and attributes.

Entities

Entities are the principal data objects about which information is to be collected; they usually denote a person, place, thing, or event of informational interest. A particular occurrence of an entity is called an *entity instance*, or sometimes an *entity occurrence*. In our example, Employee, Department, Division, Project, Skill, and Location are all examples of entities (for easy reference, entity names will be capitalized throughout this text). The entity construct is a rectangle as depicted in Figure 2.2. The entity name is written inside the rectangle.

Relationships

Relationships represent real-world associations among one or more entities, and as such, have no physical or conceptual existence other than that which depends upon their entity associations. Relationships are described in terms of degree, connectivity, and existence. These terms are defined in the sections that follow. The most common meaning associated with the term *relationship* is indicated by the

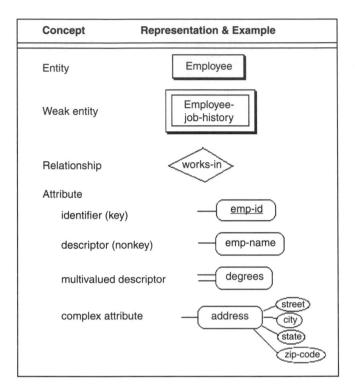

Concept	Representation & Example
Entity	Employee
Weak entity	Employee-job-history
Relationship	works-in
Attribute	
identifier (key)	emp-id
descriptor (nonkey)	emp-name
multivalued descriptor	degrees
complex attribute	address — street, city, state, zip-code

Figure 2.2 The basic ER model.

connectivity between entity occurrences: one-to-one, one-to-many, and many-to-many. The relationship construct is a diamond that connects the associated entities, as shown in Figure 2.2. The relationship name can be written inside or just outside the diamond.

A *role* is the name of one end of a relationship when each end needs a distinct name for clarity of the relationship. In most of the examples given in Figure 2.3, role names are not required because the entity names combined with the relationship name clearly define the individual roles of each entity in the relationship. However, in some cases role names should be used to clarify ambiguities. For example, in the first case in Figure 2.3, the recursive binary relationship "manages" uses two roles, "manager" and "subordinate," to associate the proper connectivities with the two different roles of the single entity. Role names are typically nouns. In this diagram one role of an employee is to be the "manager" of up to n other employees. The other role is for a particular "subordinate" to be managed by exactly one other employee.

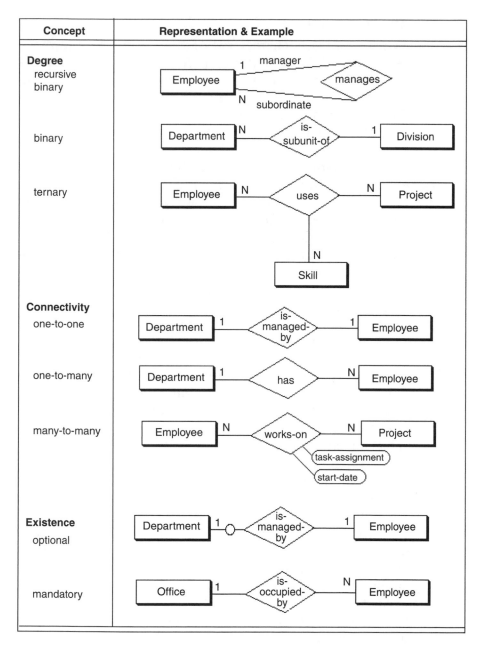

Figure 2.3 Degrees, connectivity, and attributes of a relationship.

Attributes and Keys

Attributes are characteristics of entities that provide descriptive detail about them. A particular instance (or occurrence) of an attribute within an entity or relationship is called an *attribute value*. Attributes of an entity such as Employee may include emp-id, emp-name, emp-address, phone-no, fax-no, job-title, and so on. The attribute construct is an ellipse with the attribute name inside (or oblong as shown in Figure 2.2). The attribute is connected to the entity it characterizes.

There are two types of attributes: identifiers and descriptors. An *identifier* (or key) is used to uniquely determine an instance of an entity. For example, an identifier or key of Employee is emp-id; each instance of Employee has a different value for emp-id, and thus there are no duplicates of emp-id in the set of Employees. Key attributes are underlined in the ER diagram, as shown in Figure 2.2. We note, briefly, that you can have more than one identifier (key) for an entity, or you can have a set of attributes that compose a key (see the "Superkeys, Candidate Keys, and Primary Keys" section in Chapter 6).

A *descriptor* (or nonkey attribute) is used to specify a non-unique characteristic of a particular entity instance. For example, a descriptor of Employee might be emp-name or job-title; different instances of Employee may have the same value for emp-name (two John Smiths) or job-title (many Senior Programmers).

Both identifiers and descriptors may consist of either a single attribute or some composite of attributes. Some attributes, such as specialty-area, may be multivalued. The notation for multivalued attributes is shown with a double attachment line, as shown in Figure 2.2. Other attributes may be complex, such as an address that further subdivides into street, city, state, and zip code.

Keys may also be categorized as either primary or secondary. A primary key fits the definition of an identifier given in this section in that it uniquely determines an instance of an entity. A secondary key fits the definition of a descriptor in that it is not necessarily unique to each entity instance. These definitions are useful when entities are translated into SQL tables and indexes are built based on either primary or secondary keys.

Weak Entities

Entities have internal identifiers or keys that uniquely determine each entity occurrence, but weak entities are entities that derive their identity from the key of a connected "parent" entity. Weak entities are often depicted with a double-bordered rectangle (see Figure 2.2), which denotes that all instances (occurrences) of that entity are dependent for their existence in the database on an associated entity. For example, in Figure 2.2, the weak entity Employee-job-history is related to the entity Employee. The Employee-job-history for a particular employee only can exist if there exists an Employee entity for that employee.

Degree of a Relationship

The degree of a relationship is the number of entities associated in the relationship. Binary and ternary relationships are special cases where the degree is 2 and 3, respectively. An n-ary relationship is the general form for any degree n. The notation for degree is illustrated in Figure 2.3. The binary relationship, an association between two entities, is by far the most common type in the natural world. In fact, many modeling systems use only this type. In Figure 2.3 we see many examples of the association of two entities in different ways: Department and Division, Department and Employee, Employee and Project, and so on. A binary recursive relationship (e.g., "manages" in Figure 2.3) relates a particular Employee to another Employee by management. It is called recursive because the entity relates only to another instance of its own type. The binary recursive relationship construct is a diamond with both connections to the same entity.

A ternary relationship is an association among three entities. This type of relationship is required when binary relationships are not sufficient to accurately describe the semantics of the association. The ternary relationship construct is a single diamond connected to three entities as shown in Figure 2.3. Sometimes a relationship is mistakenly modeled as ternary when it could be decomposed into two or three equivalent binary relationships. When this occurs, the ternary relationship should be eliminated to achieve both simplicity and semantic purity. Ternary relationships are discussed in greater detail in the "Ternary Relationships" section below and in Chapter 5.

An entity may be involved in any number of relationships, and each relationship may be of any degree. Furthermore, two entities may have any number of binary relationships between them, and so on for any *n* entities (see *n*-ary relationships defined in the "General *n*-ary Relationships" section below).

Connectivity of a Relationship

The *connectivity* of a relationship describes a constraint on the connection of the associated entity occurrences in the relationship. Values for connectivity are either "one" or "many." For a relationship between entities Department and Employee, a connectivity of one for Department and many for Employee means that there is at most one entity occurrence of Department associated with many occurrences of Employee. The actual count of elements associated with the connectivity is called the *cardinality* of the relationship connectivity; it is used much less frequently than the connectivity constraint because the actual values are usually variable across instances of relationships. Note that there are no standard terms for the connectivity concept, so the reader is admonished to look at the definition of these terms carefully when using a particular database design methodology.

Figure 2.3 shows the basic constructs for connectivity for binary relationships: one-to-one, one-to-many, and many-to-many. On the "one" side, the number 1 is shown on the connection between the relationship and one of the entities, and on the "many" side, the letter N is used on the connection between the relationship and the entity to designate the concept of many.

In the one-to-one case, the entity Department is managed by exactly one Employee, and each Employee manages exactly one Department. Therefore, the minimum and maximum connectivities on the "is-managed-by" relationship are exactly one for both Department and Employee.

In the one-to-many case, the entity Department is associated with ("has") many Employees. The maximum connectivity is given on the Employee (many) side as the unknown value N, but the minimum connectivity is known as one. On the Department side the minimum and maximum connectivities are both one—that is, each Employee works within exactly one Department.

In the many-to-many case, a particular Employee may work on many Projects and each Project may have many Employees. We see that the maximum connectivity for Employee and Project is N in both directions, and the minimum connectivities are each defined (implied) as one.

Some situations, though rare, are such that the actual maximum connectivity is known. For example, a professional basketball team may be limited by conference rules to 12 players. In such a case, the number 12 could be placed next to an entity called Team Members on the many side of a relationship with an entity Team. Most situations, however, have variable connectivity on the many side, as shown in all the examples of Figure 2.3.

Attributes of a Relationship

Attributes can be assigned to certain types of relationships as well as to entities. An attribute of a many-to-many relationship such as the "works-on" relationship between the entities Employee and Project (Figure 2.3) could be "task-assignment" or "start-date." In this case, a given task assignment or start date only has meaning when it is common to an instance of the assignment of a particular Employee to a particular Project via the relationship "works-on."

Attributes of relationships are typically assigned only to binary many-to-many relationships and to ternary relationships. They are not normally assigned to one-to-one or one-to-many relationships because of potential ambiguities. For example, in the one-to-one binary relationship "is-managed-by" between Department and Employee, an attribute start-date could be applied to Department to designate the start date for that department. Alternatively, it could be applied to Employee to be an attribute for each Employee instance to designate the employee's start date as the manager of that department. If, instead, the relationship is many-to-many, so that an employee can manage many departments over time, then the attribute start-date must shift to the relationship so each instance of the relationship that matches one employee with one department can have a unique start date for that employee as the manager of that department.

Existence of an Entity in a Relationship

Existence of an entity occurrence in a relationship is defined as either mandatory or optional. If an occurrence of either the "one" or "many" side entity must always exist for the entity to be included in the relationship, then it is mandatory. When an occurrence of that entity need not always exist, it is considered optional. For example, in Figure 2.3 the entity Employee may or may not be the manager of any Department, thus making the entity Department in the "is-managed-by" relationship between Employee and Department optional.

Optional existence, defined by a 0 on the connection line between an entity and a relationship, defines a minimum connectivity of zero. *Mandatory existence* defines a minimum connectivity of one. When existence is unknown, we assume the minimum connectivity is one—that is, mandatory.

Maximum connectivities are defined explicitly on the ER diagram as a constant (if a number is shown on the ER diagram next to an entity) or a variable (by default if no number is shown on the ER diagram next to an entity). For example, in Figure 2.3 the relationship "is-occupied-by" between the entity Office and Employee implies that an Office may house from zero to some variable maximum (N) number of Employees, but an Employee must be housed in exactly one Office—that is, it is mandatory.

Existence is often implicit in the real world. For example, an entity Employee associated with a dependent (weak) entity, Dependent, cannot be optional, but the weak entity is usually optional. Using the concept of optional existence, an entity instance may be able to exist in other relationships even though it is not participating in this particular relationship.

Alternative Conceptual Data Modeling Notations

At this point we need to digress briefly to look at other conceptual data modeling notations that are commonly used today and compare them with the Chen approach. A popular alternative form for one-to-many and many-to-many relationships uses "crow's foot" notation for the "many" side (see Figure 2.4a). This form was used by some CASE tools, such as KnowledgeWare's Information Engineering Workbench (IEW). Relationships have no explicit construct but are implied by the connection line between entities and a relationship name on the connection line. Minimum connectivity is specified by either a 0 (for zero) or perpendicular line (for one) on the connection lines between entities. The term *intersection entity* is used to designate a weak entity, especially an entity that is equivalent to a many-to-many relationship. Another popular form used today is the IDEF1X notation (IDEF1X, 2005), conceived by Robert G. Brown (Bruce, 1992). The similarities with the Chen notation are obvious from Figure 2.4(b). Fortunately, any of these forms is reasonably easy to learn and read, and their equivalence for the basic ER concepts is obvious from the diagrams. Without a clear standard for the ER model, however, many other constructs are being used today in addition to the three types shown here.

Advanced ER Constructs

Generalization: Supertypes and Subtypes

The original ER model has been effectively used for communicating fundamental data and relationship definitions with the end user for a long time. However, using it to develop and integrate conceptual models with different end user views was severely limited until it could be extended to include database abstraction concepts such as *generalization*. The generalization relationship specifies that several types of entities with certain common attributes can be generalized into a higher-level entity type—a generic or superclass entity, which is more commonly known as a *supertype* entity. The lower levels of

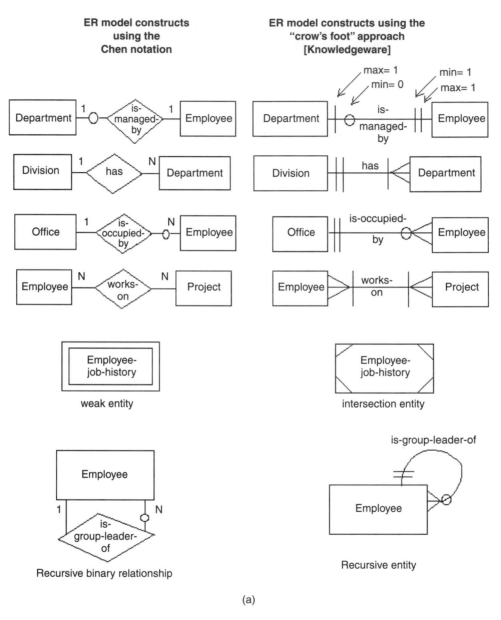

Figure 2.4 Conceptual data modeling notations (a) Chen vs. "crow's foot" notation, and

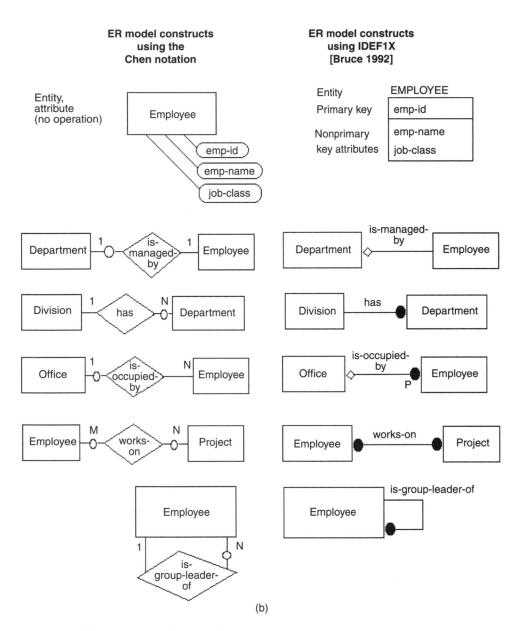

(b)

Figure 2.4, cont'd (b) Chen vs. IDEF1X notation.

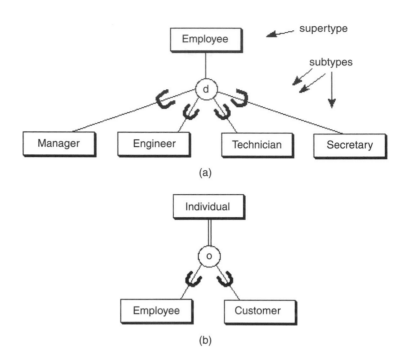

Figure 2.5 Supertypes and subtypes: (a) generalization with disjoint subtypes, and (b) generalization with overlapping subtypes and completeness constraint.

entities—*subtypes* in a generalization hierarchy—can be either disjoint or overlapping subsets of the supertype entity. As an example, in Figure 2.5 the entity Employee is a higher-level abstraction of Manager, Engineer, Technician, and Secretary, all of which are disjoint types of Employee. The ER model construct for the generalization abstraction is the connection of a supertype entity with its subtypes, using a circle and the subset symbol on the connecting lines from the circle to the subtype entities. The circle contains a letter specifying a disjointness constraint (see the following discussion). *Specialization*, the reverse of generalization, is an inversion of the same concept; it indicates that subtypes specialize the supertype.

A supertype entity in one relationship may be a subtype entity in another relationship. When a structure comprises a combination of supertype/subtype relationships, that structure is called a *supertype/subtype hierarchy*, or *generalization hierarchy*. Generalization can also be described in terms of inheritance, which specifies that all the attributes of a supertype are propagated down the hierarchy to entities of a lower type. Generalization may occur when a generic entity, which we call the supertype entity, is partitioned by different values of a common attribute. For example, in Figure 2.5, the entity Employee is a generalization of Manager, Engineer, Technician, and Secretary over the attribute job-title in Employee.

Generalization can be further classified by two important constraints on the subtype entities: *disjointness* and *completeness*. The disjointness constraint requires the subtype entities to be mutually exclusive. We denote this type of constraint by the letter "d" written inside the generalization circle (Figure 2.5a). Subtypes that are not disjoint (i.e., that overlap) are designated by using the letter "o" inside the circle. As an example, the supertype entity Individual has two subtype entities, Employee and Customer; these subtypes could be described as overlapping or not mutually exclusive (Figure 2.5b). Regardless of whether the subtypes are disjoint or overlapping, they may have additional special attributes in addition to the generic (inherited) attributes from the supertype.

The completeness constraint requires the subtypes to be all-inclusive of the supertype. Thus, subtypes can be defined as either total or partial coverage of the supertype. For example, in a generalization hierarchy with supertype Individual and subtypes Employee and Customer, the subtypes may be described as all-inclusive or total. We denote this type of constraint by a double line between the supertype entity and the circle. This is indicated in Figure 2.5(b), which implies that the only types of individuals to be considered in the database are employees and customers.

Aggregation

Aggregation is a form of abstraction between a supertype and subtype entity that is significantly different from the generalization abstraction. Generalization is often described in terms of an "is-a" relationship between the subtype and the supertype—for example, an Employee is an Individual. Aggregation, on the other hand, is the relationship between the whole and its parts and is described as a "part-of" relationship—for example, a report and a prototype software package are both parts of a deliverable for a contract. Thus,

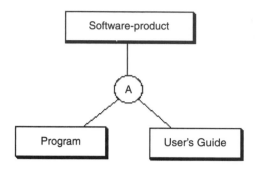

Figure 2.6 Aggregation.

in Figure 2.6 the entity Software-product is seen to consist of component parts Program and User's Guide. The construct for aggregation is similar to generalization in that the supertype entity is connected with the subtype entities with a circle; in this case, the letter A is shown in the circle. However, there are no subset symbols because the "part-of" relationship is not a subset. Furthermore, there are no inherited attributes in aggregation; each entity has its own unique set of attributes.

Ternary Relationships

Ternary relationships are required when binary relationships are not sufficient to accurately describe the semantics of an association among three entities. Ternary relationships are somewhat more complex than binary relationships, however. The ER notation for a ternary relationship is shown in Figure 2.7 with three entities attached to a single relationship diamond, and the connectivity of each entity is designated as either "one" or "many." An entity in a ternary relationship is considered to be "one" if only one instance of it can be associated with one instance of each of the other two associated entities. It is "many" if more than one instance of it can be associated with one instance of each of the other two associated entities. In either case, it is assumed that one instance of each of the other entities is given.

As an example, the relationship "manages" in Figure 2.7(c) associates the entities Manager, Engineer, and Project. The entities Engineer and Project are considered "many"; the entity Manager is considered "one." This is represented by the following assertions:

Assertion 1: One engineer, working under one manager, could be working on many projects.

Assertion 2: One project, under the direction of one manager, could have many engineers.

Assertion 3: One engineer, working on one project, must have only a single manager.

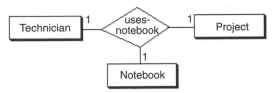

A technician uses exactly one notebook for each project. Each notebook belongs to one technician for each project. Note that a technician may still work on many projects and maintain different notebooks for different projects.

Functional dependencies
emp-id, project-name -> notebook-no
emp-id, notebook-no -> project-name
project-name, notebook-no -> emp-id

(a)

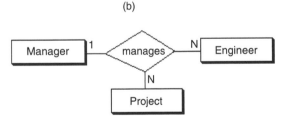

Each employee assigned to a project works at only one location for that project, but can be at different locations for different projects. At a particular location, an employee works on only one project. At a particular location, there can be many employees assigned to a given project.

Functional dependencies

emp-id, loc-name -> project-name
emp-id, project-name -> loc-name

(b)

Each engineer working on a particular project has exactly one manager, but each manager of a project may manage many engineers, and each manager of an engineer may manage that engineer on many projects.

Functional dependency

project-name, emp-id -> mgr-id

(c)

Figure 2.7 Ternary relationships: (a) one-to-one-to-one ternary relationship, (b) one-to-one-to-many ternary relationship, (c) one-to-many-to-many ternary relationship, and

(Continued)

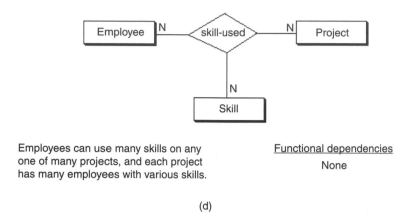

Employees can use many skills on any
one of many projects, and each project
has many employees with various skills.

Functional dependencies
None

(d)

Figure 2.7, cont'd (d) many-to-many-to-many ternary relationship.

Assertion 3 could also be written in another form, using an arrow (->) in a kind of shorthand called a *functional dependency.* For example:

emp-id, project-name -> mgr-id

where emp-id is the key (unique identifier) associated with the entity Engineer, project-name is the key associated with the entity Project, and mgr-id is the key of the entity Manager. In general, for an *n*-ary relationship, each entity considered to be a "one" has its key appearing on the right side of exactly one functional dependency (FD). No entity considered "many" ever has its key appear on the right side of an FD.

All four forms of ternary relationships are illustrated in Figure 2.7. In each case the number of "one" entities implies the number of FDs used to define the relationship semantics, and the key of each "one" entity appears on the right side of exactly one FD for that relationship.

Ternary relationships can have attributes in the same way as many-to-many binary relationships can. The values of these attributes are uniquely determined by some combination of the keys of the entities associated with the relationship. For example, in Figure 2.7(d) the relationship "skill-used" might have the attribute "tool" associated with a given employee using a particular skill on a certain project, indicating that a value for tool is uniquely determined by the combination of employee, skill, and project.

General *n*-ary Relationships

Generalizing the ternary form to higher-degree relationships, an *n*-ary relationship that describes some association among *n* entities is represented by a single relationship diamond with *n* connections, one to each entity (Figure 2.8). The meaning of this form can best be described in terms of the func

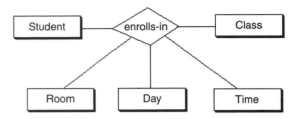

Figure 2.8 *n*-ary relationships.

tional dependencies among the keys of the *n* associated entities. There can be anywhere from zero to *n* FDs, depending on the number of "one" entities. The collection of FDs that describe an *n*-ary relationship must each have *n* components: $n - 1$ on the left side (determinant) and 1 on the right side. A ternary relationship ($n = 3$), for example, has two components on the left and one on the right, as we saw in the example in Figure 2.7. In a more complex database, other types of FDs may also exist within an *n*-ary relationship. When this occurs, the ER model does not provide enough semantics by itself, and it must be supplemented with a narrative description of these dependencies.

Exclusion Constraint

The normal, or default, treatment of multiple relationships is the *inclusive OR*, which allows any or all of the entities to participate. In some situations, however, multiple relationships may be affected by the *exclusive OR* (exclusion) constraint, which allows at most one entity instance among several entity types to participate in the relationship with a single root entity. For example, in Figure 2.9 suppose the root entity Work-task has two associated entities,

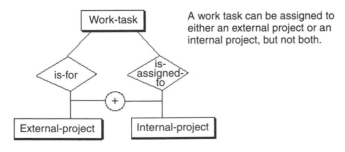

A work task can be assigned to either an external project or an internal project, but not both.

Figure 2.9 Exclusion constraint.

External-project and Internal-project. At most, one of the associated entity instances could apply to an instance of Work-task.

Foreign Keys and Referential Integrity

A *foreign key* is an attribute of an entity or an equivalent SQL table, which may be either an identifier or a descriptor. A foreign key in one entity (or table) is taken from the same domain of values as the (primary) key in another (parent) table in order for the two tables to be connected to satisfy certain queries on the database. *Referential integrity* requires that for every foreign key instance that exists in a table, the row (and thus the key instance) of the parent table associated with that foreign key instance must also exist. The referential integrity constraint has become integral to relational database design and is usually implied as a requirement for the resulting relational database implementation. (Chapter 5 illustrates the SQL implementation of referential integrity constraints.)

Summary

The basic concepts of the ER model and their constructs are described in this chapter. An entity is a person, place, thing, or event of informational interest. Attributes are objects that provide descriptive information about entities. Attributes may be unique identifiers or nonunique descriptors. Relationships describe the connectivity between entity instances: one-to-one, one-to-many, or many-to-many. The degree of a relationship is the number of associated entities: two (binary), three (ternary), or any n (n-ary). The role (name), or relationship name, defines the function of an entity in a relationship.

The concept of existence in a relationship determines whether an entity instance must exist (mandatory) or not (optional). So, for example, the minimum connectivity of a binary relationship—that is, the number of entity instances on one side that are associated with one instance on the other side—can either be zero, if optional, or one, if mandatory. The concept of generalization allows for the implementation of supertype and subtype abstractions.

This simple form of ER models is used in most design tools and is easy to learn and apply to a variety of industrial and business applications. It is also a very useful tool for communicating with the end user about the conceptual model and for verifying the assumptions made in the modeling process.

A more complex form, a superset of the simple form, is useful for the more experienced designer who wants to capture greater semantic detail in diagram form, while avoiding having to write long and tedious narrative to explain certain requirements and constraints. The more advanced constructs in ER diagrams are sporadically used and have no generally accepted form as yet. They include ternary relationships, which we define in terms of the FD concept of relational databases; constraints on exclusion; and the implicit constraints from the relational model such as referential integrity.

Tips and Insights for Database Professionals

Tip 1. ER is a much better level of abstraction than specifying individual data items or functional dependencies, and it is easier to use to develop a conceptual model for large databases. The main advantages of ER modeling are that it is easy to learn, easy to use, and very easy to transform to SQL table definitions.

Tip 2. Identify entities first, then relationships, and finally the attributes of entities.

Tip 3. Identify binary relationships first whenever possible. Only use ternary relationships as a last resort.

Tip 4. ER model notations are all very similar. Pick the notation that works best for you unless your client or boss prefers a specific notation for their purposes. Remember that ER notation is the primary tool for communicating data concepts with your client.

Tip 5. Keep the ER model simple. Too much detail wastes time and is harder to communicate to your client.

Literature Summary

Most of the notation in this chapter is from Chen's original ER definition (1976). The concept of data abstraction was first proposed by Smith and Smith (1977) and applied to the ER model by Scheuermann, Scheffner, and Weber (1980), Elmasri and Navathe (2010), Bruce (1992), and IDEF1X (2005), among others. The application of the semantic network model to conceptual schema design was shown by Bachman (1977), McLeod and King (1979), Hull and King (1987), and Peckham and Maryanski (1988).

3

THE UNIFIED MODELING LANGUAGE

The Unified Modeling Language (UML) is a graphical language for communicating design specifications for software. The object-oriented software development community created UML to meet the special needs of describing object-oriented software design. UML has grown into a standard for the design of digital systems in general.

There are a number of different types of UML diagrams serving various purposes (Rumbaugh et al., 2005). The *class* and the *activity* diagram types are particularly useful for discussing database design issues. UML class diagrams capture the structural aspects found in database schemas. UML activity diagrams facilitate discussion on the dynamic processes involved in database design. This chapter is an overview of the syntax and semantics of the UML class and activity diagram constructs used in this book. These same concepts are useful for planning, documenting, discussing, and implementing databases. We are using UML 2.0, although for the purposes of the class diagrams and activity diagrams shown in this book, if you are familiar with UML 1.4 or 1.5 you will probably not see any differences.

UML class diagrams and entity–relationship (ER) models (Chen, 1976; Chen, 1987) are similar in both form and semantics. The original creators of UML point out the influence of ER models on the origins of class diagrams (Rumbaugh et al., 2005). The influence of UML has in turn affected the database community. Class diagrams now appear frequently in the database literature to describe database schemas.

UML activity diagrams are similar in purpose to flow charts. Processes are partitioned into constituent activities along with control flow specifications.

This chapter is organized into three main sections. The first section presents class diagram notation, along with examples. The next section covers activity diagram notation, along with illustrative examples. Finally, the last section concludes with a few tips for UML usage.

Class Diagrams

A class is a descriptor for a set of *objects* that share some attributes and/or operations. We conceptualize classes of objects in our everyday lives. For example, a car has attributes, such as a vehicle identification number (VIN) and mileage. A car also has operations, such as accelerate and brake. All cars have these attributes and operations. Individual cars differ in the details. A given car has a value for the VIN and mileage. For example, a given car might have a VIN of 1NXBR32ES3Z126369 with a mileage of 22,137 miles. Individual cars are objects that are instances of the Car class.

Classes and objects are a natural way of conceptualizing the world around us. The concepts of classes and objects are also the paradigms that form the foundation of object-oriented programming. The development of object-oriented programming led to the need for a language to describe object-oriented design, giving rise to UML.

There is a close correspondence between class diagrams in UML and ER diagrams. Classes are analogous to entities.

Database schemas can be diagrammed using UML. It is possible to conceptualize a database table as a class. The columns in the table are the attributes, and the rows are objects of that class. For example, we could have a table named **Car** with columns named "vin" and "mileage" (note that we put table names in boldface throughout the book for readability). Each row in the table would have values for these columns, representing an individual car. A given car might be represented by a row with the value 1NXBR32ES3Z126369 in the vin column, and 22,137 in the mileage column.

The major difference between classes and entities is the lack of operations in entities. Note that the term *operation* is used here in the UML sense of the word. Stored procedures, functions, triggers, and constraints are forms of named behavior that can be defined in databases; however, these are not associated with the behavior of individual rows. The term *operations* in UML refers to the methods inherent in classes of objects. These behaviors are not stored in the definition of rows within the database. There are no operations named "accelerate" or "brake" associated with rows in our **Car** table in Figure 3.1. Classes can be shown with attributes and no operations in UML, which is the typical usage for database schemas.

Basic Class Diagram Notation

The top of Figure 3.1 illustrates the UML syntax for a class, showing both *attributes* and *operations*. It is also possible to include user-defined named compartments, such as "responsibilities." We will focus on the class name, attributes, and operations compartments. The UML icon for a class is a rectangle. When the class is shown with attributes and operations, the rectangle is subdivided into three horizontal compartments. The top compartment contains the class name, centered in boldface, beginning with a capital letter. Typically, class names are nouns. The middle compartment contains attribute names, left justified in regular face, beginning with a lowercase letter. The bottom compartment contains operation names, left justified in regular face, beginning with a lowercase letter, ending with parentheses. The parenthesis may contain arguments for the operation.

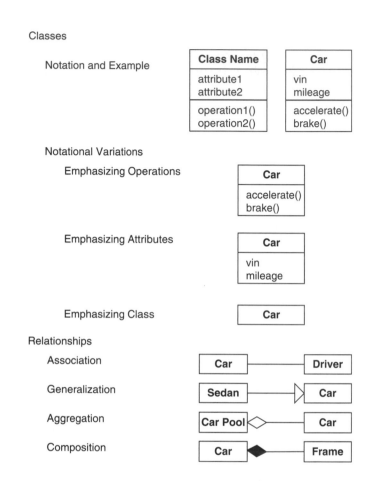

Figure 3.1 Basic UML class diagram constructs.

The class notation has some variations, reflecting emphasis. Classes can be written without the attribute compartment and/or the operations compartment. Operations are important in software. If the software designer wishes to focus on the operations, the class can be shown with only the class name and operations compartments. Showing operations and hiding attributes is a very common syntax used by software designers. Database designers, on the other hand, do not generally deal with class operations; however, the attributes are of paramount importance. The needs of the database designer can be met by writing the class with only the class name and attribute compartments showing. Hiding operations and showing attributes is an uncommon syntax for a software designer, but it is common for database design. Lastly, in high-level diagrams, it is often desirable to illustrate the relationships of the classes without becoming entangled in the details of the attributes and operations. Classes can be written with just the class name compartment when simplicity is desired.

Various types of relationships may exist between classes. *Associations* are one type of relationship. The most generic form of association is drawn with a line connecting two classes. For example, in Figure 3.1 there is an association between the Car class and the Driver class.

A few types of associations, such as *aggregation* and *composition*, are very common. UML has designated symbols for these associations. Aggregation indicates "part of" associations, where the parts have an independent existence. For example, a Car may be part of a Car Pool. The Car also exists on its own, independent of any Car Pool. Another distinguishing feature of aggregation is that the part may be shared among multiple objects. For example, a Car may belong to more than one Car Pool. The aggregation association is indicated with a hollow diamond attached to the class that holds the parts. Figure 3.1 indicates that a Car Pool aggregates Cars.

Composition is another "part of" association, where the parts are strictly owned, not shared. For example, a Frame is part of a single Car. The notation for composition is an association adorned with a solid black diamond attached to the class that owns the parts. Figure 3.1 indicates that a Frame is part of the composition of a Car.

Generalization is another common relationship. For example, Sedan is a type of car. The Car class is more general than the Sedan class. Generalization is indicated by a solid line adorned with a hollow arrowhead pointing to the more general class. Figure 3.1 shows generalization from the Sedan class to the Car class.

Class Diagrams for Database Design

The reader may be interested in the similarities and differences between UML class diagrams and ER models. Figures 3.2 through 3.5 are parallel to some of the figures in Chapter 2, allowing for easy comparisons. We then turn our attention to capturing primary key information in

Figure 3.6. We conclude this section with an example database schema of the music industry, illustrated by Figures 3.7 through 3.10.

Figure 3.2 illustrates UML constructs for relationships with various degrees of association and multiplicities. These examples are parallel to the ER models shown in Figure 2.3. You may refer back to Figure 2.3 if you wish to contrast the UML constructs with ER constructs.

Associations between classes may be reflexive, binary, or *n*-ary. *Reflexive association* is a term we are carrying over from ER modeling. It is not a term defined in UML, although it is worth discussing. Reflexive association

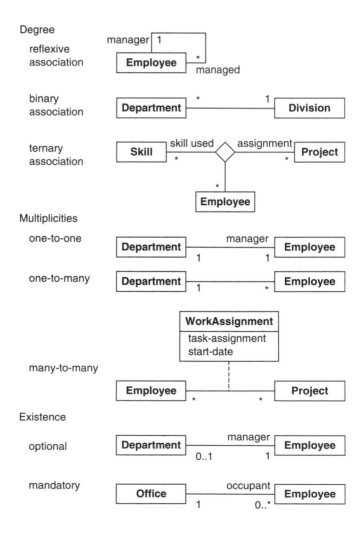

Figure 3.2 Selected UML relationship types (parallel to Figure 2.3).

relates a class to itself. The reflexive association in Figure 3.2 means an Employee in the role of manager is associated with many managed Employees. The roles of classes in a relationship may be indicated at the ends of the relationship. The number of objects involved in the relationship, referred to as *multiplicity*, may also be specified at the ends of the relationship. An asterisk indicates that many objects take part in the association at that end of the relationship. The multiplicities of the reflexive association example in Figure 3.2 indicate that an Employee is associated with one manager, and a manager is associated with many managed Employees.

A binary association is a relationship between two classes. For example, one Division has many Departments. Notice the solid black diamond at the Division end of the relationship. The solid diamond is an adornment to the association that indicates composition. The Division is composed of Departments.

The ternary relationship in Figure 3.2 is an example of an *n*-ary association—an association that relates three or more classes. All classes partaking in the association are connected to a hollow diamond. Roles and/or multiplicities are optionally indicated at the ends of the *n*-ary association. Each end of the ternary association example in Figure 3.2 is marked with an asterisk, signifying many. The meaning of each multiplicity is isolated from the other multiplicities. Given a class, if you have exactly one object from every other class in the association, the multiplicity is the number of associated objects for the given class. One Employee working on one Project assignment uses many Skills. One Employee uses one Skill on many Project assignments. One Skill used on one Project is fulfilled by many Employees.

The next three class diagrams in Figure 3.2 show various combinations of multiplicities. The illustrated one-to-one association specifies that each Department is associated with exactly one Employee acting in the role of manager, and each manager is associated with exactly one Department. The diagram with the one-to-many association means that each Department has many Employees, and each Employee belongs to exactly one Department.

The many-to-many example in Figure 3.2 means each Employee associates with many Projects, and each Project associates with many Employees. This example also illustrates the use of an association class. If an association has attributes, these are written in a class that is attached to the association with a dashed line. The association class named WorkAssignment in Figure 3.2 contains two association attributes named task-assignment and start-date. The association and the class together form an association class.

Multiplicity can be a range of integers, written with the minimum and maximum values separated by two periods. The asterisk by itself carries the same meaning as the range [0..*]. Also, if the minimum and maximum values are the same number, then the multiplicity can be written as a single number. For example, [1..1] means the same as [1]. Optional existence can be specified using a zero. The [0..1] in the optional existence example of Figure 3.2 means an Employee in the role of manager is associated with either no Department (e.g., upper management) or one Department.

Mandatory existence is specified whenever a multiplicity begins with a positive integer. The example of mandatory existence in Figure 3.2 means an Employee is an occupant of exactly one Office. One end of an association can indicate mandatory existence, while the other end may use optional existence. This is the case in the example, where an Office may have any number of occupants, including zero.

Generalization is another type of relationship. A superclass is a generalization of a subclass. Specialization is the opposite relationship of generalization. A subclass is a specialization of the superclass. The generalization relationship in UML is written with a hollow arrow pointing from the subclass to the generalized superclass. The top example in Figure 3.3 shows four subclasses: Manager, Engineer, Technician, and Secretary. These four subclasses are all specializations of

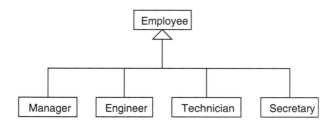

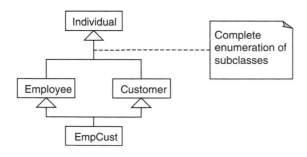

Figure 3.3 UML generalization constructs (parallel to Figure 2.4).

the more general superclass, Employee—that is, Managers, Engineers, Technicians, and Secretaries are types of Employees.

Notice the four relationships share a common arrowhead. Semantically, these are still four separate relationships. The sharing of the arrowhead is permissible in UML, to improve the clarity of the diagrams.

The bottom example in Figure 3.3 illustrates that a class can act as both a subclass in one relationship and a superclass in another relationship. The class named Individual is a generalization of the Employee and Customer classes. The Employee and Customer classes are in turn superclasses of the EmpCust class. A class can be a subclass in more than one generalization relationship. The meaning in the example is that an EmpCust object is both an Employee and a Customer.

You may occasionally find that UML doesn't supply a standard symbol for what you are attempting to communicate. UML incorporates some extensibility to accommodate user needs, such as a *note*. A note in UML is written as a rectangle with a dog-eared upper-right corner. The note can attach to the pertinent element(s) with a dashed line(s). Write briefly in the note what you wish to convey. The bottom diagram in Figure 3.3 illustrates a note, which describes the Employee and Customer classes as the "Complete enumeration of subclasses."

The distinction between composition and aggregation is sometimes elusive for those new to UML. Figure 3.4 shows an example of each, to help clarify. The top diagram means that a Program and Electronic Documentation both contribute to the composition of a Software Product. The composition signifies that the parts do not exist without the Software Product (there is no software pirating in our ideal world). The bottom diagram specifies that a Teacher and a Textbook are aggregated by a course. The aggregation signifies that the Teacher and the Textbook are part of the Course, but they also exist separately. If a course is canceled, the Teacher and the Textbook continue to exist.

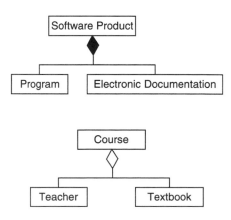

Figure 3.4 UML aggregation constructs (parallel to Figure 2.6).

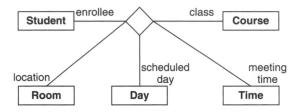

Figure 3.5 UML *n*-ary relationship (parallel to Figure 2.8).

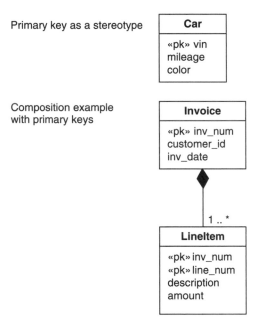

Figure 3.6 UML constructs illustrating primary keys.

Figure 3.5 illustrates another example of an *n*-ary relationship. The *n*-ary relationship may be clarified by specifying roles next to the participating classes. A Student is an enrollee in a class, associated with a given Room location and a scheduled Day and meeting Time.

The concept of a primary key arises in the context of database design. Often, each row of a table is uniquely identified by the values contained in one or more columns designated as the primary key. Objects in software are not typically identified in this fashion. As a result, UML does not have an icon representing a primary key. However, UML is extensible. The meaning of an element in UML may be extended with a *stereotype*. Stereotypes are depicted with a short natural language word or phrase, enclosed in guillemets: « and ». We take advantage of this extensibility, using a stereotype «pk» to designate primary key attributes. Figure 3.6 illustrates the stereotype mechanism. The vin attribute is specified as the primary key for Cars. This means that a given VIN identifies a specific Car. A noteworthy rule of thumb for primary keys: When a composition relationship exists, the primary key of the part includes the primary key of the owning object. The second diagram in Figure 3.6 illustrates this point.

Example from the Music Industry

Large database schemas may be introduced with high-level diagrams. Details can be broken out in additional diagrams. The overall goal is to present ideas in a clear, organized fashion. UML offers notational variations and an organizational mechanism. You will sometimes find there are multiple ways of representing the same material in UML. The decisions you make with regard to your representation depend in part on your purpose for a given diagram. Figures 3.7 through 3.10 illustrate some of the possibilities with an example drawn from the music industry.

Packages may be used to organize classes into groups. Packages may themselves also be grouped into packages. The goal of using packages is to make the overall design of a system more comprehensible. One use for packages is to represent a schema. You can then show multiple schemas concisely. Another use for packages is to group related classes together within a schema, and present the schema clearly. Given a set of classes, different people may conceptualize different groupings. The division is a design decision, with no right or wrong answer. Whatever decisions are made, the result should enhance readability. The notation for a package is a folder icon, and the contents of a package can be optionally shown in the body of the folder. If the contents are shown, then the name of the package is placed in the tab. If the contents are elided, then the name of the package is placed in the body of the icon.

If the purpose is to illustrate the relationships of the packages, and the classes are not important at the moment, then it is better to illustrate with the contents elided. Figure 3.7 illustrates the notation with the music industry example at a very high level. Music is created and placed on Media. The Media is then distributed. There is an association between the Music and the Media, and between the Media and Distribution.

Let us look at the organization of the classes. The music industry is illustrated in Figure 3.8 with the classes listed. The Music package contains classes that are responsible for creating the music. Examples of Groups are the Beatles and the Bangles. Sarah McLachlan and Sting are Artists. Groups and Artists are involved in creating the music. We will look shortly at the other classes and how they are

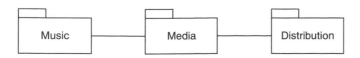

Figure 3.7 Example of related packages.

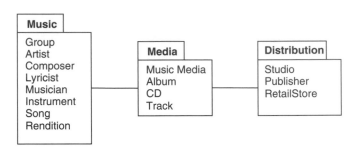

Figure 3.8 Example illustrating classes grouped into packages.

related. The Media package contains classes that physically hold the recordings of the music. The Distribution package contains classes that bring the media to you.

The contents of a package can be expanded into greater detail. The relationships of the classes within the Music package are illustrated in Figure 3.9. A Group is an aggregation of two or more Artists. As indicated by the multiplicity between Artist and Group [0..*], an Artist may or may not be in a Group, and may be in more than one Group. Composers, Lyricists, and Musicians are different types of Artists. A Song is associated with one or more Composers. A Song may not have any Lyricist, or any number of Lyricists. A Song may have any number of Renditions. A Rendition is associated with exactly one Song. A Rendition is associated with Musicians and Instruments. A given Musician–Instrument combination is associated with any number of Renditions. A specific Rendition–Musician combination may be associated with any number of

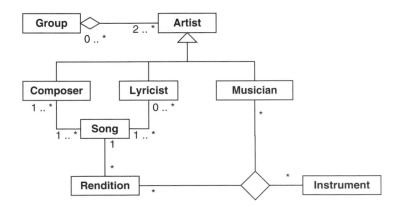

Figure 3.9 Relationships between classes in the Music package.

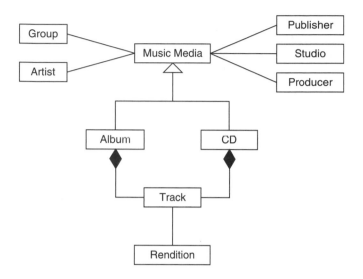

Figure 3.10 Classes of the Media package, and related classes.

Instruments. A given Rendition–Instrument combination is associated with any number of Musicians.

A system may be understood more easily by shifting focus to each package in turn. We turn our attention now to the classes and relationships in the Media package, shown in Figure 3.10. The associated classes from the Music and Distribution packages are also shown, detailing how the Media package is related to the other two packages. The Music Media is associated with the Group and Artist classes, which are contained in the Music package shown in Figure 3.8. The Music Media is also associated with the Publisher, Studio, and Producer classes, which are contained in the Distribution package shown in Figure 3.8. Albums and CDs are types of Music Media. Albums and CDs are both composed of Tracks. Tracks are associated with Renditions.

Activity Diagrams

UML has a full suite of diagram types, each of which fulfills a need for describing a view of the design. UML *activity diagrams* are used to specify the activities and the flow of control in a process. The process may be a workflow followed by people, organizations, or other physical things. Alternatively, the process may be an algorithm implemented in software. The syntax and the semantics of UML constructs are the same, regardless of the process described. Our examples draw from workflows that are followed by people and organizations, since these are more useful for the logical design of databases.

Activity Diagram Notation Description

Activity diagrams include notation for nodes, control flow, and organization. The icons we are describing here are outlined in Figure 3.11. The notation is further clarified by example in the "Activity Diagrams for Workflow" section.

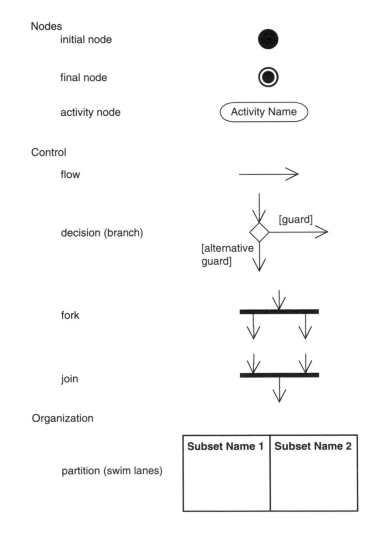

Figure 3.11 UML activity diagram constructs.

The nodes include the *initial node*, *final nodes*, and *activity nodes*. Any process begins with control residing in the initial node, represented as a solid black circle. The process terminates when control reaches a final node, represented with a solid black circle surrounded by a concentric circle (i.e., a bull's-eye). Activity nodes are states where specified work is processed. For example, an activity might be named "Generate quote." The name of an activity is typically a descriptive verb or short verb phrase, written inside a lozenge shape. Control resides in an activity until that activity is completed. Then control follows the outgoing flow.

Control flow icons include *flows*, *decisions*, *forks*, and *joins*. A flow is drawn with an arrow. Control flows in the direction of the arrow. Decision nodes are drawn as a hollow diamond with multiple outgoing flows. Each flow from a decision node must have a *guard condition*. A guard condition is written within square brackets next to the flow. Control flows in exactly one direction from a decision node, and only follows a flow if the guard condition is true. The guard conditions associated with a decision node must be mutually exclusive, to avoid non-deterministic behavior. There can be no ambiguity as to which direction the control follows. The guards must cover all possible test conditions, so that control is not blocked at the decision node. One path may be guarded with [else]. If a path is guarded with [else], then control flows in that direction only if all the other guards fail. Forks and joins are both forms of synchronization written with a solid bar. The fork has one incoming flow, and multiple outgoing flows. When control flows to a fork, the control concurrently follows all the outgoing flows. These are referred to as concurrent threads. Joins are the opposite of forks; the join construct has multiple incoming flows and one outgoing flow. Control flows from a join only when control has reached the join from each of the incoming flows.

Activity diagrams may be further organized using partitions, also known as swim lanes. Partitions split activities into subsets, organized by responsible party. Each subset is named and enclosed with lines.

Activity Diagrams for Workflow

Figure 3.12 illustrates the UML activity diagram constructs used for the publication of this book. This diagram is partitioned into two subsets of activities, organized by responsible party. The left subset contains Customer activities, and the right subset contains Manufacturer activities. Activity partitions may be arranged vertically, horizontally, or in a grid. Curved dividers may be used, although this is atypical. Activity diagrams can also be written without a partition. The construct is organizational, and doesn't carry inherent

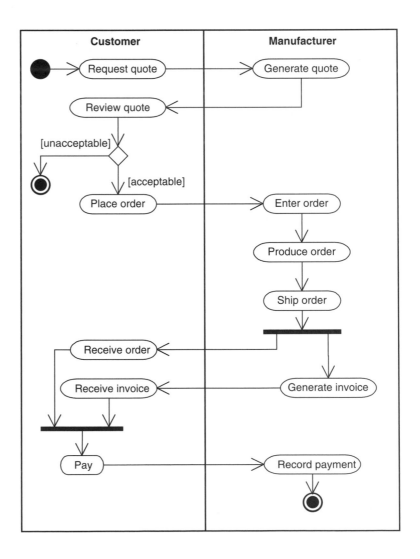

Figure 3.12 UML activity diagram, manufacturing example.

semantics. The meaning is suggested by your choice of subset names.

Control begins in the initial state, represented by the solid dot in the upper-left corner of Figure 3.12. Control flows to the first activity, where the customer requests a quote (Request quote). Control remains in an activity until that activity is completed; then the control follows the outgoing arrow. When the request for the quote is complete, the Manufacturer generates a quote (Generate quote). Then the Customer reviews the quote (Review quote).

The next construct is a branch, represented by a diamond. Each outgoing arrow from a branch has a guard. The guard represents a condition that must be true in order for control to flow along that path. Guards are written as short condition descriptions enclosed in brackets. After the customer finishes reviewing the quote in Figure 3.12, if it is unacceptable the process reaches a final state and terminates. A final state is represented with a target (the bull's-eye). If the quote is acceptable, then the Customer places an order (Place order). The Manufacturer enters (Enter order), produces (Produce order), and ships the order (Ship order).

At a fork, control splits into multiple concurrent threads. The notation is a solid bar with one incoming arrow and multiple outgoing arrows. After the order ships in Figure 3.12, control reaches a fork and splits into two threads. The Customer receives the order (Receive order). In parallel to the Customer receiving the order, the Manufacturer generates an invoice (Generate invoice), and then the customer receives the invoice (Receive invoice). The order of activities between threads is not constrained. Thus, the Customer may receive the order before or after the Manufacturer generates the invoice, or even after the Customer receives the invoice.

At a join, multiple threads merge into a single thread. The notation is a solid bar with multiple incoming arrows and one outgoing arrow. In Figure 3.12, after the customer receives the order and the invoice, then the customer will pay (Pay). All incoming threads must complete before control continues along the outgoing arrow.

Finally, in Figure 3.12, the Customer pays, the Manufacturer records the payment (Record payment), and then a final state is reached. Notice that an activity diagram may have multiple final states. However, there can only be one initial state.

There are at least two uses for activity diagrams in the context of database design. Activity diagrams can specify the interactions of classes in a database schema. Class diagrams capture structure, and activity diagrams capture behavior. The two types of diagrams can present complementary aspects of the same system. For example, one can easily imagine that Figure 3.12 illustrates the usage of classes named Quote, Order, Invoice, and Payment. Another use for activity diagrams in the context of database design is to illustrate processes surrounding the database. For example, database life cycles can be illustrated using activity diagrams.

Summary

UML is a graphical language that is currently very popular for communicating design specifications for software and, in particular, for logical database designs via class diagrams. The similarity between UML and the ER model is shown through some common examples, including ternary relationships and generalization. UML activity diagrams are used to specify the activities and flow of control in processes.

Tips and Insights for Database Professionals

Tip 1. The advantages of UML modeling are that it is widely used in industry, more standardized than other conceptual models, and more connected to object-oriented applications. Use UML if these match your priorities.

Tip 2. Decide what you wish to communicate first (usually classes), and then focus your description. Illustrate the details that further your purpose, and omit the rest. UML is like any other language in that you can immerse yourself in excruciating detail and lose your purpose. Be concise.

Tip 3. Keep each UML diagram to one page. Diagrams are easier to understand if they can be seen in one glance. This is not to say that you must restrict yourself, rather you should divide and organize your content into reasonable, understandable portions. Use packages to organize your presentation. If you have many brilliant ideas to convey (of course you do!), begin with a high-level diagram that paints the broad picture. Then follow up with a diagram dedicated to each of your ideas.

Tip 4. Use UML when it is useful. Don't feel compelled to write a UML document just because you feel you need a UML document. UML is not an end in itself, but it is an excellent design tool for appropriate problems.

Tip 5. Accompany your diagrams with textual descriptions, thereby clarifying your intent. Additionally, remember that some people are oriented verbally, others visually. Combining natural language with UML is effective.

Tip 6. Take care to clearly organize each diagram. Avoid crossing associations. Group elements together if there is a connection in your mind. Two UML diagrams can contain the exact same elements and associations, and one might be a jumbled mess, while the other is elegant and clear. Both convey the same meaning in UML, but clearly the elegant version will be more successful at communicating design issues.

Literature Summary

The definitive reference manual for UML is Rumbaugh, Jacobson, and Booch (2005). Use Muller (1999) for more detailed UML database modeling. Other useful UML texts are Naiburg and Maksimchuk (2001), Quatrani (2003), and Rumbaugh, Jacobson, and Booch (2004).

4

REQUIREMENTS ANALYSIS AND CONCEPTUAL DATA MODELING

This chapter shows how the entity–relationship (ER) and Unified Modeling Language (UML) approaches can be applied to the database life cycle, particularly in Steps I through II.b (as defined in Chapter 1), which include the requirements analysis and conceptual data modeling stages of logical database design. The example introduced in Chapter 2 is used again to illustrate the ER modeling principles developed in this chapter.

Introduction

Logical database design is accomplished with a variety of approaches, including the top-down, bottom-up, and combined methodologies. The traditional approach, particularly for relational databases, has been a low-level, bottom-up activity, synthesizing individual data elements into normalized tables after careful analysis of the data element interdependencies defined by the requirements analysis. Although the traditional process has been somewhat successful for small- to medium-size databases, when used for large databases its complexity can be overwhelming to the point where practicing designers do not bother to use it with any regularity. In practice, a combination of the top-down and bottom-up approaches is used; in most cases, tables can be defined directly from the requirements analysis.

The conceptual data model has been most successful as a tool for communication between the designer and the end user during the requirements analysis and logical design phases. Its success is due to the fact that the model, using either ER or UML, is easy to understand and convenient to represent. Another reason for its effectiveness is that it is a top-down approach using the concept of abstraction. The number of entities in a database is typically far fewer than the number of individual data elements because data elements usually represent the attributes. Therefore, using entities as an abstraction for data elements and focusing on the relationships between entities greatly reduces the number of objects under consideration and simplifies the analysis. Though it is still necessary to represent data elements by attributes of entities at the conceptual level, their dependencies are normally confined to the other attributes within the entity or, in some cases, to those attributes associated with other entities with a direct relationship to their entity.

The major interattribute dependencies that occur in data models are the dependencies between the *entity keys*, the unique identifiers of different entities that are captured in the conceptual data modeling process. Special cases, such as dependencies among data elements of unrelated entities, can be handled when they are identified in the ensuing data analysis.

The logical database design approach defined here uses both the conceptual data model and the relational model in successive stages. It benefits from the simplicity and ease of use of the conceptual data model and the structure and associated formalism of the relational model. In order to facilitate this approach, it is necessary to build a framework for transforming the variety of conceptual data model constructs into tables that are already normalized or can be normalized with a minimum of transformation. The beauty of this type of transformation is that it results in normalized or nearly normalized SQL tables from the start; frequently, further normalization is not necessary.

Before we do this, however, we need to first define the major steps of the relational logical design methodology in the context of the database life cycle.

Requirements Analysis

Step I, requirements analysis, is an extremely important step in the database life cycle and is typically the most labor intensive. The database designer must interview the end user population and determine exactly what the database is to be used for and what it must contain. The basic objectives of requirements analysis are:

- To delineate the data requirements of the enterprise in terms of basic data elements.
- To describe the information about the data elements and the relationships among them needed to model these data requirements.
- To determine the types of transactions that are intended to be executed on the database and the interaction between the transactions and the data elements.
- To define any performance, integrity, security, or administrative constraints that must be imposed on the resulting database.

- To specify any design and implementation constraints, such as specific technologies, hardware and software, programming languages, policies, standards, or external interfaces.
- To thoroughly document all of the preceding in a detailed requirements specification. The data elements can also be defined in a data dictionary system, often provided as an integral part of the database management system.

The conceptual data model helps designers to accurately capture the real data requirements because it requires them to focus on semantic detail in the data relationships, which is greater than the detail that would be provided by functional dependencies alone.

Conceptual Data Modeling

Let us now look more closely at the basic data elements and relationships that should be defined during requirements analysis and conceptual design. These two life cycle steps are often done simultaneously.

Consider the substeps in Step II.a, conceptual data modeling, using the ER model:

- Classify entities and attributes (classify classes and attributes in UML).
- Identify the generalization hierarchies (for both the ER model and UML).
- Define relationships (define associations and association classes in UML).

The remainder of this section discusses the tasks involved in each substep.

Classify Entities and Attributes

Though it is easy to define entity, attribute, and relationship constructs, it is not as easy to distinguish their roles in modeling the database. What makes a data element an entity, an attribute, or even a relationship? For example, project headquarters are located in cities. Should "city" be an entity or an attribute? A vita is kept for each employee. Is "vita" an entity or a relationship?

The following guidelines for classifying entities and attributes will help the designer's thoughts converge to a normalized relational database design:

- Entities should contain descriptive information.
- Multivalued attributes should be classified as entities.
- Attributes should be attached to the entities they most directly describe.

Now we examine each guideline in turn.

Entity Contents

Entities should contain descriptive information. If there is descriptive information about a data element, the data element should be classified as an entity. If a data element requires only an identifier and does not have relationships, it should be classified as an attribute. With city, for example, if there is some descriptive information such as country and population for cities, then city should be classified as an entity. If only the city name is needed to identify a city, then city should be classified as an attribute associated with some entity, such as Project. The exception to this rule is that if the identity of the value needs to be constrained by set membership, you should create it as an entity. For example, "state" is much the same as city, but you probably want to have a State entity that contains all the valid State instances. Examples of other data elements in the real world that are typically classified as entities include Employee, Task, Project, Department, Company, Customer, and so on.

Multivalued Attributes

A multivalued attribute of an entity is an attribute that can have more than one value associated with the key of the entity. For example, a large company could have many divisions, some of them possibly in different cities. In this case, division or division-name would be classified as a multivalued attribute of the Company entity (and its key, company-name). The headquarters-address attribute of the company, on the other hand, would normally be a single-valued attribute.

Classify multivalued attributes as entities. In this example, the multivalued attribute division-name should be reclassified as an entity Division with division-name as its identifier (key) and division-address as a descriptor attribute. If attributes are restricted to be single valued only, the later design and implementation decisions will be simplified.

Attribute Attachment

Attach attributes to the entities they most directly describe. For example, the attribute office-building-name should normally be an attribute of the entity Department, rather than the entity Employee. The procedure of identifying entities and attaching attributes to entities is iterative. Classify some data elements as entities and attach identifiers and descriptors to them. If you find some violation of the preceding guidelines, change some data elements from entity to attribute (or from attribute to entity), attach attributes to the new entities, and so forth.

Identify the Generalization Hierarchies

If there is a generalization hierarchy among entities, then put the identifier and generic descriptors in the supertype entity and put the same identifier and specific descriptors in the subtype entities.

For example, suppose five entities were identified in the ER model shown in Figure 2.5(a):

- Employee, with identifier empno and descriptors empname, address, and date-of-birth.
- Manager, with identifier empno and descriptors empname and jobtitle.
- Engineer, with identifier empno and descriptors empname, highest-degree, and jobtitle.
- Technician, with identifier empno, and descriptors empname and specialty.
- Secretary, with identifier empno, and descriptors empname and best-skill.

Let's say we determine, through our analysis, that the entity Employee could be created as a generalization of Manager, Engineer, Technician, and Secretary. Then we put identifier empno and generic descriptors empname, address, and date-of-birth in the supertype entity Employee; identifier empno and specific descriptor jobtitle in the subtype entity Manager; identifier empno and specific descriptor highest-degree and jobtitle in the subtype entity Engineer; etc. Later, if we decide to eliminate Employee as an entity, the original identifiers and generic attributes can be redistributed to all the subtype entities.

Define Relationships

We now deal with data elements that represent associations among entities, which we call relationships. Examples of typical relationships are works-in, works-for, purchases, drives, or any verb that connects entities. For every relationship the following should be specified: degree (binary, ternary, etc.), connectivity (one-to-many, etc.), optional or mandatory existence, and any attributes that are associated with the relationship and not the entities. The following are some guidelines for defining the more difficult types of relationships.

Redundant Relationships

Analyze redundant relationships carefully. Two or more relationships that are used to represent the same concept are considered to be redundant. Redundant relationships are more likely to result in unnormalized tables when transforming the ER model into relational schemas. Note that two or more relationships are allowed between the same two entities as long as those relationships have different meanings. In this case they are not considered redundant. One important case of nonredundancy is shown in Figure 4.1(a) for the ER model and Figure 4.1(c) for UML. If "belongs-to" is a one-to-many relationship between Employee and Professional-association, if "located-in" is a one-to-many relationship between Professional-association and City, and if "lives-in" is a one-to-many relationship between Employee and City, then "lives-in" is not redundant because the relationships are unrelated. However, consider the situation shown in Figure 4.1(b) for the ER model and Figure 4.1(d) for UML. The employee works on a project located in a city, so the "works-in" relationship between Employee and City is redundant and can be eliminated.

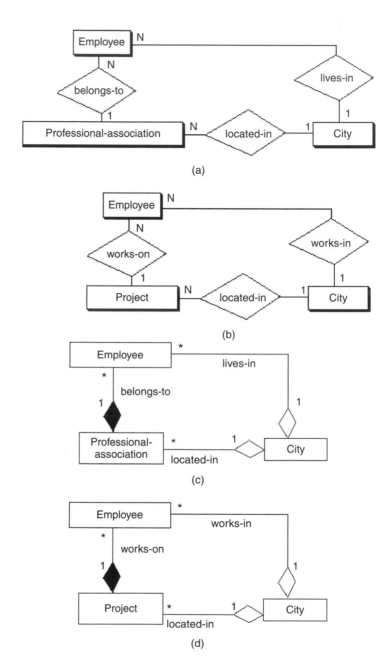

Figure 4.1 Examples of redundant and nonredundant relationships: (a) nonredundant relationships, (b) redundant relationships using transitivity, (c) nonredundant associations, and (d) redundant associations using transitivity.

Ternary Relationships

Define ternary relationships carefully. We define a ternary relationship among three entities only when the concept cannot be represented by several binary relationships among those entities. For example, let us assume there is some association among entities Technician, Project, and Note-book. If each technician can be working on any of several pro-jects and using the same notebooks on each project, then three many-to-many binary relationships can be defined (see Figure 4.2(a) for the ER model and Figure 4.2(c) for UML). If, however, each technician is constrained to use exactly one notebook for each project and that notebook belongs to only one technician, then a one-to-one-to-one ter-nary relationship should be defined (see Figure 4.2(b) for the ER model and Figure 4.2(d) for UML). The approach to take in ER modeling is to first attempt to express the associations in terms of binary relationships; if this is impossible because of the constraints of the associations, try to express them in terms of a ternary relationship.

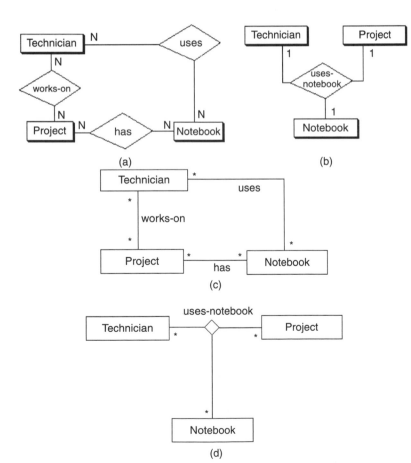

(a)

(b)

(c)

(d)

Figure 4.2 Comparison of binary and ternary relationships: (a) binary relationships, (b) different meaning using a ternary relationship, (c) binary associations, and (d) different meaning using a ternary association.

The meaning of connectivity for ternary relationships is important. Figure 4.2(b) shows that for a given pair of instances of Technician and Project, there is only one corresponding instance of Notebook; for a given pair of instances of Technician and Notebook, there is only one corresponding instance of Project; and for a given pair of instances of Project and Notebook, there is only one instance of Technician. In general, we know by our definition of ternary relationships that if a relationship among three entities can only be expressed by a functional dependency involving the keys of all three entities, then it cannot be expressed using only binary relationships, which only apply to associations between two entities. Object-oriented design provides arguably a better way to model this situation (Muller, 1999).

Example of Data Modeling: Company Personnel and Project Database

ER Modeling of Individual Views Based on Requirements

Let us suppose it is desirable to build a company-wide database for a large engineering firm that keeps track of all full-time personnel, their skills and projects assigned, department (and divisions) worked in, engineer professional associations belonged to, and engineer desktop computers allocated. During the requirements collection process—that is, interviewing the end users—we obtain three views of the database.

The first view, a management view, defines each employee as working in a single department, and defines a division as the basic unit in the company, consisting of many departments. Each division and department has a manager, and we want to keep track of each manager. The ER model for this view is shown in Figure 4.3(a).

The second view defines each employee as having a job title: engineer, technician, secretary, manager, and so on. Engineers typically belong to professional associations and might be allocated an engineering workstation (or computer). Secretaries and managers are each allocated a desktop computer. A pool of desktops and workstations is maintained for potential allocation to new employees and

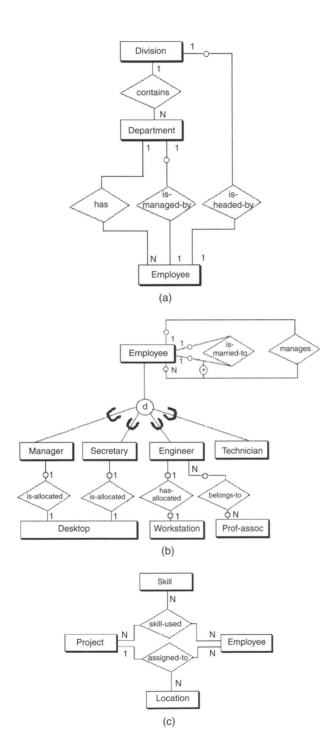

Figure 4.3 Example of data modeling: (a) management view, (b) employee view, (c) employee assignment view, and

Continued

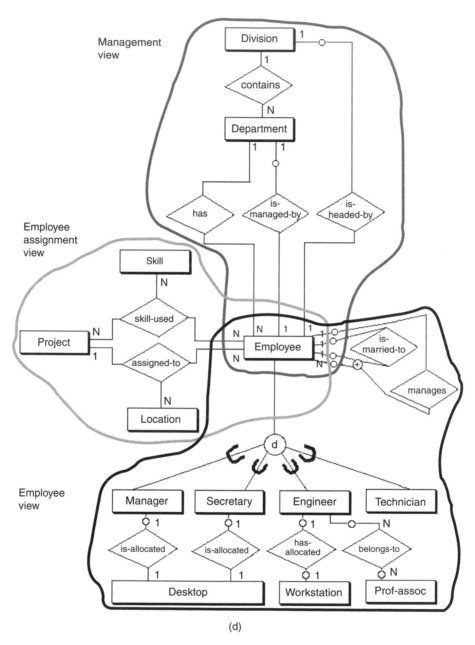

(d)

Figure 4.3, cont'd (d) global ER schema.

for loans while an employee's computer is being repaired. Any employee may be married to another employee, and we want to keep track of this relationship to avoid assigning an employee to be managed by his or her spouse. This view is illustrated in Figure 4.3(b).

The third view, shown in Figure 4.3(c), involves the assignment of employees, mainly engineers and technicians, to projects. Employees may work on several projects at one time, and each project could be headquartered at different locations (cities). However, each employee at a given location works on only one project at that location. Employee skills can be individually selected for a given project, but no individual has a monopoly on skills, projects, or locations.

Global ER Schema

A simple integration of the three views just defined over the entity Employee results in the global ER schema (diagram) in Figure 4.3(d), which becomes the basis for developing the normalized tables. Each relationship in the global schema is based on a verifiable assertion about the actual data in the enterprise, and analysis of those assertions leads to the transformation of these ER constructs into candidate SQL tables, as Chapter 5 shows.

Note that equivalent views and integration could be done for a UML conceptual model over the class Employee. We will use the ER model for the examples in the rest of this chapter, however.

The diagram shows examples of binary, ternary, and binary recursive relationships; optional and mandatory existence in relationships; and generalization with the disjointness constraint. Ternary relationships "skill-used" and "assigned-to" are necessary because binary relationships cannot be used for the equivalent notions. For example, one employee and one location determine exactly one project (a functional dependency). In the case of "skill-used," selective use of skills to projects cannot be represented with binary relationships.

The use of optional existence, for instance, between Employee and Division or between Employee and Department, is derived from our general knowledge that most employees will not be managers of any division or department. In another example of optional existence, we show that the allocation of a workstation to an engineer may not always occur, nor will all desktops or workstations necessarily be allocated to someone at all times. In general, all relationships, optional existence constraints, and generalization constructs need to be verified with the end user before the ER model is transformed to SQL tables.

In summary, the application of the ER model to relational database design offers the following benefits:

- Use of an ER approach focuses end users' discussions on important relationships between entities. Some applications are characterized by counterexamples affecting a small number of instances, and lengthy consideration of these instances can divert attention from basic relationships.
- A diagrammatic syntax conveys a great deal of information in a compact, readily understandable form.
- Extensions to the original ER model, such as optional and mandatory membership classes, are important in many relationships. Generalization allows entities to be grouped for one functional role or to be seen as separate subtypes when other constraints are imposed.
- A complete set of rules transforms ER constructs into mostly normalized SQL tables, which follow easily from real-world requirements.

View Integration

A critical part of the database design process is Step II.b, the integration of different user views into a unified, non-redundant global schema. The individual end user views are represented by conceptual data models, and the integrated conceptual schema results from sufficient analysis of the end user views to resolve all differences in perspective and terminology. Experience has shown that nearly every situation can be resolved in a meaningful way through integration techniques.

Schema diversity occurs when different users or user groups develop their own unique perspectives of the world or, at least, of the enterprise to be represented in the database. For instance, the marketing division tends to have the whole product as a basic unit for sales, but the engineering division may concentrate on the individual parts of the whole product. In another case, one user may view a project in terms of its goals and progress toward meeting those goals over time, but another user may view a project in terms of the resources it needs and the personnel involved. Such differences cause the conceptual models to seem to have incompatible relationships and terminology. These differences show up in conceptual data models as different levels of abstraction, connectivity of relationships (one-to-many, many-to-many, and so on), or as the same concept being modeled as an entity, attribute, or relationship, depending on the user's perspective.

As an example of the latter case, in Figure 4.4 we see three different perspectives of the same real-life situation—the placement of an order for a certain product. The result is a variety of schemas. The first schema (Figure 4.4a) depicts Customer, Order, and Product as entities and "places" and "for-a" as relationships. The second schema (Figure 4.4b), however, defines "orders" as a relationship between Customer and Product and omits Order as an entity altogether. Finally, in the third case (Figure 4.4c), the relationship "orders" has been replaced by another relationship "purchases"; order-no, the identifier (key) of an order, is designated as an attribute of the relationship "purchases." In other words, the concept of order has been variously represented as an entity, a relationship, and an attribute, depending on perspective.

There are three basic steps needed for conceptual schema integration:

1. Comparison of schemas and identifying conflicts.
2. Conformation of schemas and resolving conflicts.
3. Merging and restructuring of schemas.

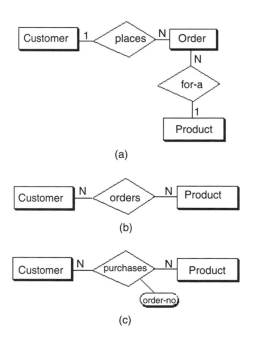

(a)

(b)

(c)

Figure 4.4 Schemas: placement of an order: (a) the concept of order as an entity, (b) the concept of order as a relationship, and (c) the concept of order as an attribute.

Comparison of Schemas: Identifying Conflicts

In the first step, comparison of schemas, the designer looks at how entities correspond and detects conflicts arising from schema diversity—that is, from user groups adopting different viewpoints in their respective schemas.

Naming conflicts include synonyms and homonyms. Synonyms occur when different names are given for the same concept. These can be detected by scanning the data dictionary, if one has been established for the database. For example, the entities Product and Item are often found to be synonyms, and one of them can be renamed to fit the other. Homonyms occur when the same name is used for different concepts. They can often be detected by scanning different schemas and looking for common names. For instance, among the attributes for the entity Product, product-number in one schema may refer to the model number and in another schema it may refer to the serial number. These differences need to be resolved as soon as possible.

Structural conflicts occur in the schema structure itself. Type conflicts involve using different constructs to model the same concept. In Figure 4.4, for example, an entity, a relationship, or an attribute can be used to model the concept of order in a business database.

Key conflicts occur when different keys are assigned to the same entity in different views. For example, a key conflict occurs if an employee's full name, employee ID number, and social security number are all assigned as keys. When this occurs, modify the keys to maintain consistency.

Dependency conflicts result when users specify different levels of connectivity (one-to-many, etc.) for similar or even the same concepts. One resolution of such conflicts might be to use only the most general connectivity—for example, many-to-many. If that is not semantically correct, change the names of entities so that each type of connectivity has a different set of entity names.

As an example of schema comparison, let us look at two different views of overlapping data in Figure 4.5. The views are based on two separate interviews of end users. We adapt the interesting example cited by Batini et al. (1986) to a hypothetical situation related to our example. In Figure 4.5(a) we have a view that focuses on reports and

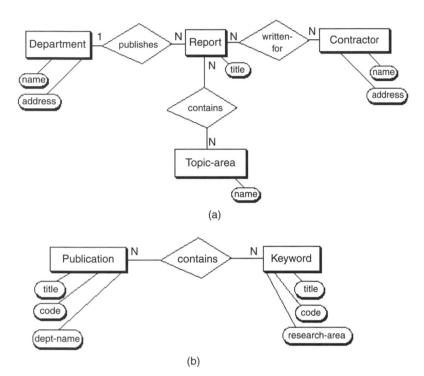

(a)

(b)

Figure 4.5 View integration: find meaningful ways to integrate: (a) original schema 1, focused on reports, and (b) original schema 2, focused on publications.

includes data on departments that publish the reports, topic areas in reports, and contractors for whom the reports are written. Figure 4.5(b) shows another view, with publications as the central focus and keywords on publications as the secondary data. Our objective is to find meaningful ways to integrate the two views.

We first look for synonyms and homonyms, particularly among the entities. Note that a synonym exists between the entities Topic-area in schema 1 and Keyword in schema 2, even though the attributes do not match. Next we look for structural conflicts between schemas. A type conflict is found to exist between the entity Department in schema 1 and the attribute dept-name in schema 2. The resolution of these conflicts occurs in the second step: conformation of schemas.

Conformation of Schemas: Resolving Conflicts

The resolution of conflicts often requires user and designer interaction. The basic goal of the second step is to align or conform schemas to make them compatible for integration. The entities as well as the key attributes may need to be renamed. Conversion may be required so that concepts that are modeled as entities, attributes, or relationships are conformed to be only one of them. Relationships with equal degree, roles, and connectivity constraints are easy to merge. Those with differing characteristics are more difficult and, in some cases, impossible to merge. In addition, relationships that are not consistent—for example, a relationship using generalization in one place and the exclusive-OR in another—must be resolved. Finally, assertions may need to be modified so that integrity constraints are consistent.

Techniques used for view integration include abstraction, such as generalization and aggregation, to create new super-types or subtypes, or even the introduction of new relationships. As an example, the generalization of Individual over different values of the descriptor attribute job-title could represent the consolidation of two views of the database—one based on an individual as the basic unit of personnel in the organization, and another based on the classification of individuals by job titles and special characteristics within those classifications.

For the example in Figure 4.5, the resolution of the conflicts is shown in Figure 4.6. For the synonyms Topic-area in schema 1 and Keyword in schema 2, we find that the attributes, while having different names, are compatible and can be consolidated. This is shown in Figure 4.6(a), which presents a revised schema, schema 2.1. In schema 2.1, Keyword has been replaced by Topic-area. The type conflict between the entity Department

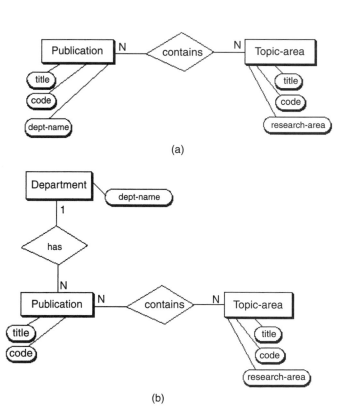

Figure 4.6 View integration: type conflict: (a) schema 2.1, in which Keyword has been replaced by Topic-area and (b) schema 2.2, in which the attribute dept-name has been changed to an attribute and an entity.

in schema 1 and the attribute dept-name in schema 2 is resolved by keeping the stronger entity type, Department, and moving the attribute type dept-name under Publication in schema 2 to the new entity, Department, in schema 2.2 (see Figure 4.6b).

Merging and Restructuring of Schemas

The third step consists of the merging and restructuring of schemas. This step is driven by the goals of completeness, minimality, and understandability. Completeness requires all component concepts to appear semantically intact in the global schema. Minimality requires the designer to remove all redundant concepts in the global schema. Examples of redundant concepts are overlapping entities and truly semantically redundant relationships. An example of overlapping entities might be Ground-Vehicle and Automobile. A redundant relationship might occur between Instructor and Student. The relationships "direct-research" and "advise" may or may not represent the same activity or relationship, so further investigation is required to determine whether they are redundant or not. Understandability requires that the global schema make sense to the user.

Component schemas are first merged by superimposing the same concepts and then restructuring the resulting integrated schema for understandability. For instance, if a supertype/subtype combination is defined as a result of the merging operation, the properties of the subtype can be dropped from the schema because they are automatically provided by the supertype entity.

Continuing our example in Figures 4.5 and 4.6, at this point we have sufficient commonality between schemas to attempt a merge. In schemas 1 and 2.2 we have two sets of common entities, Department and Topic-area. Other entities do not overlap and must appear intact in the superimposed, or merged, schema. The merged schema, schema 3, is shown in Figure 4.7(a). Because the common entities are truly equivalent, there are no bad side effects of the merge due to existing relationships involving those entities in one schema and not in the other (such a relationship that remains intact exists in schema 1 between Topic-area and Report, for example). If true equivalence

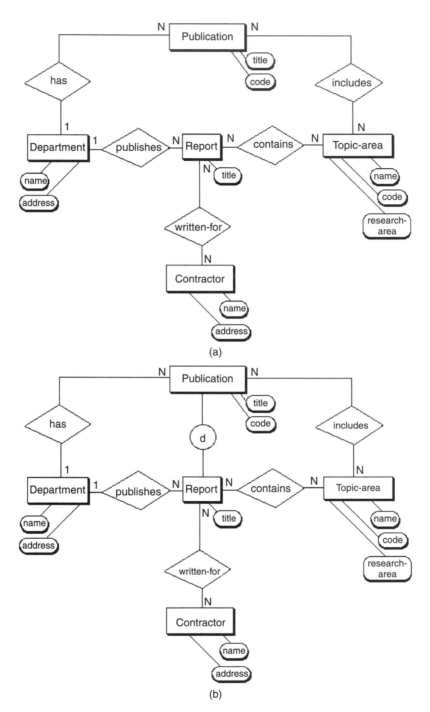

Figure 4.7 View integration: the merged schema: (a) schema 3, the result of merging schema 1 and schema 2.2, (b) schema 3.1, the creation of a generalization relationship, and

Continued

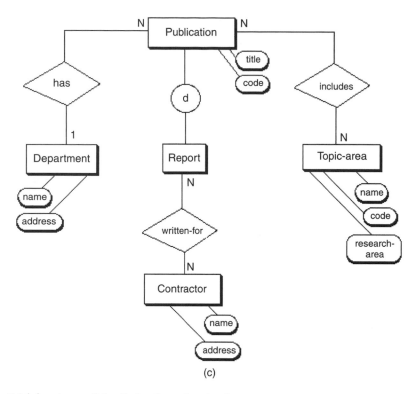

(c)

Figure 4.7, cont'd (c) schema 3.2, elimination of redundancy.

cannot be established, the merge may not be possible in the existing form.

In Figure 4.7(a), there is some redundancy between Publication and Report in terms of the relationships with Department and Topic-area. Such a redundancy can be eliminated if there is a supertype/subtype relationship between Publication and Report, which does in fact occur in this case because Publication is a generalization of Report. In schema 3.1 (Figure 4.7b) we see the introduction of this generalization from Report to Publication. Then in schema 3.2 (Figure 4.7c) we see that the redundant relationships between Report and Department and Topic-area have been dropped. The attribute title has been eliminated as an attribute of Report in Figure 4.7(c) because title already appears as an attribute of Publication at a higher level of abstraction; title is inherited by the sub-type Report.

The final schema, in Figure 4.7(c), expresses completeness because all the original concepts (report, publication, topic area, department, and contractor) are kept intact. It expresses minimality because of the transformation of dept-name from an attribute in schema 1 to an entity and attribute in schema 2.2, and the merger between schema 1 and schema 2.2 to form schema 3, and because of the elimination of title as an attribute of Report and of Report relationships with Topic-area and Department. Finally, it expresses understandability in that the final schema actually has more meaning than the individual original schemas.

The view integration process is one of continual refinement and reevaluation. It should also be noted that minimality may not always be the most efficient way to proceed. If, for example, the elimination of the redundant relationships "publishes" and/or "contains" from schema 3.1 to 3.2 causes the time to do certain queries to be excessively long, it may be better from a performance viewpoint to leave them in. This decision could be made during the analysis of the transactions on the database or the testing phase of the fully implemented database.

Entity Clustering for ER Models

This section presents the concept of entity clustering, which abstracts the ER schema to such a degree that the entire schema can appear on a single sheet of paper or a single computer screen. This has happy consequences for the end user and database designer in terms of developing a mutual understanding of the database contents and formally documenting the conceptual model.

An entity cluster is the result of a grouping operation on a collection of entities and relationships. Entity clustering is potentially useful for designing large databases. When the scale of a database or information structure is large and includes a large number of interconnections among its different components, it may be very difficult to understand the semantics of such a structure and to manage it, especially for the end users or managers. In an ER diagram with 1000 entities, the overall structure will probably not be very clear, even to a well-trained database analyst. Clustering is

therefore important because it provides a method to organize a conceptual database schema into layers of abstraction,
and it supports the different views of a variety of end users.

Clustering Concepts

One should think of grouping as an operation that combines entities and their relationships to form a higher-level
construct. The result of a grouping operation on simple
entities is called an *entity cluster*. A grouping operation
on entity clusters or on combinations of elementary
entities and entity clusters results in a higher-level entity
cluster. The highest-level entity cluster, representing the
entire database conceptual schema, is called the *root entity
cluster*.

Figure 4.8(a) illustrates the concept of entity clustering
in a simple case where (elementary) entities R-sec (report

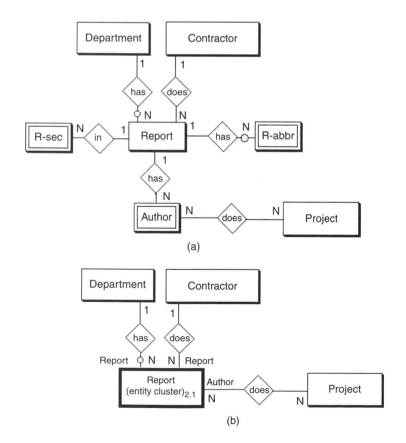

(a)

(b)

Figure 4.8 Entity clustering
concepts: (a) ER model
before clustering and (b) ER
model after clustering.

section), R-abbr (report abbreviation), and Author are naturally bound to (dominated by) the entity Report; and entities Department, Contractor, and Project are not dominated. (Note that to avoid unnecessary detail, we do not include the attributes of entities in the diagrams.) In Figure 4.8(b) the dark-bordered box around the entity Report and the entities it dominates defines the entity cluster Report. The dark-bordered box is called the EC box to represent the idea of entity cluster. In general, the name of the entity cluster need not be the same as the name of any internal entity; however, when there is a single dominant entity, the names are often the same. The EC box number in the lower-right corner is a clustering-level number used to keep track of the sequence in which clustering is done. The number 2.1 signifies that the entity cluster Report is the first entity cluster at level 2. Note that all the original entities are considered to be at level 1.

The higher-level abstraction, the entity cluster, must maintain the same relationships between entities inside and outside the entity cluster as occur between the same entities in the lower-level diagram. Thus, the entity names inside the entity cluster should appear just outside the EC box along the path of their direct relationship to the appropriately related entities outside the box, maintaining consistent interfaces (relationships) as shown in Figure 4.8(b). For simplicity, we modify this rule slightly: If the relationship is between an external entity and the dominant internal entity (for which the entity cluster is named), the entity cluster name need not be repeated outside the EC box. Thus, in Figure 4.8(b), we could drop the name Report both places it occurs outside the Report box, but we must retain the name Author, which is not the name of the entity cluster.

Grouping Operations

The grouping operations are the fundamental components of the entity clustering technique. They define what collections of entities and relationships comprise higher-level objects, the entity clusters. The operations are heuristic in nature and include (see Figure 4.9):

- Dominance grouping.
- Abstraction grouping.

- Constraint grouping.
- Relationship grouping.

These grouping operations can be applied recursively or used in a variety of combinations to produce higher-level entity clusters—that is, clusters at any level of abstraction. An entity or entity cluster may be an object that is subject to combinations with other objects to form the next higher level. That is, entity clusters have the properties of entities and can have relationships with any other objects at any equal or lower level. The original relationships among entities are preserved after all grouping operations, as illustrated in Figure 4.8.

Dominant objects or entities normally become obvious from the ER diagram or the relationship definitions. Each dominant object is grouped with all its related non-

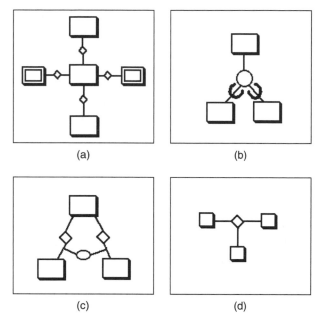

Figure 4.9 Grouping operations: (a) dominance, (b) abstraction, (c) constraint, and (d) relationship grouping.

dominant objects to form a cluster. Weak entities can be attached to an entity to make a cluster. Multilevel data objects using such abstractions as generalization and aggregation can be grouped into an entity cluster. The supertype or aggregate entity name is used as the entity cluster name. Constraint-related objects that extend the ER model to incorporate integrity constraints such as the exclusive-OR can be grouped into an entity cluster. Also, ternary or higher-degree relationships can potentially be grouped into an entity cluster. The cluster represents the relationship as a whole.

Clustering Technique

The grouping operations and their order of precedence determine the individual activities needed for clustering. We can now learn how to build a root entity cluster from the elementary entities and relationships defined in the ER modeling process. This technique assumes that a top-down analysis has been performed as part of the database requirements analysis and that the analysis has been documented so that the major functional areas and subareas are identified. Functional areas are often defined by an enterprise's important organizational units, business activities, or, possibly, by dominant applications for processing information. As an example, recall Figure 4.3, which can be thought of as having three major functional areas: company organization (management view); project management (employee assignment view); and employee data (employee view). Note that the functional areas are allowed to overlap. Figure 4.3 uses an ER diagram resulting from the database requirements analysis to show how clustering involves a series of bottom-up steps using the basic grouping operations. The following list explains these steps.

1. *Define points of grouping within functional areas.* Locate the dominant entities in a functional area through the natural relationships, local *n*-ary relationships, integrity constraints, abstractions, or just the central focus of many simple relationships. If such points of grouping do not exist within an area, consider a functional grouping of a whole area.

2. *Form entity clusters.* Use the basic grouping operations on elementary entities and their relationships to form higher-level objects, or entity clusters. Because entities may belong to several potential clusters, we need to have a set of priorities for forming entity clusters. The following set of rules, listed in priority order, defines the set that is most likely to preserve the clarity of the conceptual model.

    a. Entities to be grouped into an entity cluster should exist within the same functional area—that is, the entire entity cluster should occur within the boundary of a functional area. For example, in Figure 4.3, the relationship between Department and Employee should not be clustered unless Employee is included in the company organization functional area with Department and Division. In another example, the relationship between the supertype Employee and its subtypes could be clustered within the employee data functional area.

b. If a conflict in choice between two or more potential entity clusters cannot be resolved (e.g., between two constraint groupings at the same level of precedence), leave these entity clusters ungrouped within their functional area. If that functional area remains cluttered with unresolved choices, define functional subareas in which to group unresolved entities, entity clusters, and their relationships.

3. *Form higher-level entity clusters.* Apply the grouping operations recursively to any combination of elementary entities and entity clusters to form new levels of entity clusters (higher-level objects). Resolve conflicts using the same set of priority rules given in Step 2. Continue the grouping operations until all the entity representations fit on a single page without undue complexity. The root entity cluster is then defined.

4. *Validate the cluster diagram.* Check for consistency of the interfaces (relationships) between objects at each level of the diagram. Verify the meaning of each level with the end users.

The result of one round of clustering is shown in Figure 4.10, where each of the clusters is shown at level 2.

Summary

Conceptual data modeling, using either the ER or UML approach, is particularly useful in the early steps of the database life cycle, which involve requirements analysis and logical design. These two steps are often done simultaneously, particularly when requirements are determined from interviews with end users and modeled in terms of data-to-data relationships and process-to-data relationships. The conceptual data modeling step (ER approach) involves the classification of entities and attributes first, then identification of generalization hierarchies and other abstractions, and finally the definition of all relationships among entities. Relationships may be binary (the most common), ternary, and higher-level *n*-ary. Data modeling of individual requirements typically involves creating a different view for each end user's requirements. Then the designer must integrate those views into a global schema so that the entire

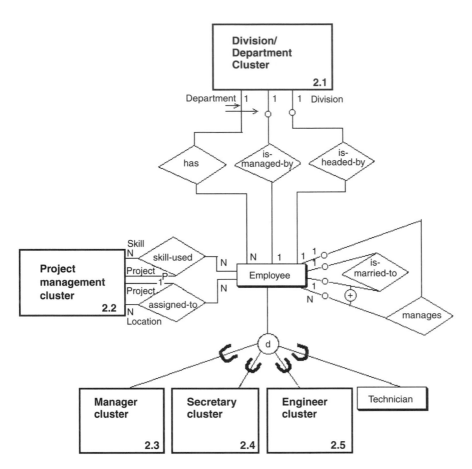

Figure 4.10 Clustering results.

database is pictured as an integrated whole. This helps to eliminate needless redundancy—such elimination is particularly important in logical design. Controlled redundancy can be created later, at the physical design level, to enhance database performance.

Finally, an entity cluster is a grouping of entities and their corresponding relationships into a higher-level abstract object. Clustering promotes the simplicity that is vital for fast end user comprehension. In Chapter 5 we take the global schema produced from the conceptual data modeling and view integration steps and transform it into

SQL tables. The SQL format is the end product of logical design, which is still independent of any particular database management system.

Tips and Insights for Database Professionals

Tip 1. Clearly state the database requirements before doing any ER/UML (conceptual) modeling. Describe what goes into the database (requirements coverage), what comes out of the database (queries), and flexibility for future possible usage.

Tip 2. Best order of ER modeling—entities first, then relationships, then attributes for entities, and finally attributes for relationships when appropriate. You can iterate on relationships and attributes.

Tip 3. Identify binary relationships first whenever possible. Only use ternary relationships as a last resort. Avoid modeling n-ary relationships (n greater than 2), whenever possible, by using equivalent binary relationships. If you can't avoid this, follow the strict rules of functional dependencies to model appropriately.

Tip 4. Keep the conceptual model simple. Too much detail wastes time and is harder to convey to your client.

Tip 5. Interact often with the end user (client), if possible, to make sure all assumptions you make are also true for the client's view of the database.

Tip 6. Entity clustering is optional. Only consider it when the ER diagram is massive and there is a need to increase the level of abstraction to more clearly convey the basic concepts (relationships) in the database.

Literature Summary

Conceptual data modeling is defined in Tsichritzis and Lochovsky (1982), Brodie, Mylopoulos, and Schmidt (1984), Nijssen and Halpin (1989), and Batini, Ceri, and Navathe (1992). Discussion of the requirements data collection process can be found in Martin (1982), Teorey and Fry (1982), and Yao (1985). View integration has progressed from a representation tool (Smith and Smith, 1977) to heuristic algorithms (Batini, Lenzerini, and Navathe, 1986; Elmasri and Navathe, 2010). These algorithms are typically interactive, allowing the database designer to make decisions based on suggested alternative integration actions. A variety of entity clustering models have been defined that provide a useful foundation for the clustering technique shown here (Feldman and Miller, 1986; Dittrich, Gotthard, and Lockemann, 1986; Teorey et al., 1989).

5

TRANSFORMING THE CONCEPTUAL DATA MODEL TO SQL

This chapter focuses on the database life cycle step that is of particular interest when designing relational databases: transformation of the conceptual data model to candidate tables and their definition in SQL (Step II.c). There is a natural evolution from the entity–relationship (ER) and Unified Modeling Language (UML) data models to a relational schema. The evolution is so natural, in fact, that it supports the contention that conceptual data modeling is an effective early step in relational database development. This contention has been proven to some extent by the widespread commercialization and use of software design tools that support not only conceptual data modeling but also the automatic conversion of these models to vendor-specific SQL table definitions and integrity constraints.

Transformation Rules and SQL Constructs

Let's first look at the ER and UML modeling constructs in detail to see how the rules about transforming the conceptual data model to SQL tables are defined and applied. Our example is drawn from the company personnel and project conceptual schemas illustrated in Figure 4.3 (see Chapter 4).

The basic transformations can be described in terms of the three types of tables they produce:

- *SQL table with the same information content as the original entity from which it is derived.* This transformation always occurs for entities with binary relationships (associations) that are many-to-many, one-to-many on the "one" (parent) side, or one-to-one on either side (see Figures 5.1 and 5.2); entities with binary recursive relationships that are many-to-many (see Figures 5.3 and 5.4); and entities with any ternary or higher-degree relationship (see Figures 5.5 and 5.6), or a generalization hierarchy (see Figures 5.7 and 5.8).
- *SQL table with the embedded foreign key of the parent entity.* This transformation always occurs for entities with binary relationships that are one-to-many for the entity on the "many" (child) side (see Figures 5.1 and 5.2), for one-to-one relationships for one of the entities (see Figures 5.1 and 5.2), and for each entity with a binary recursive relationship that is one-to-one or one-to-many (see Figures 5.3 and 5.4). This is one of the two most common ways design tools handle relationships, by prompting the user to define a foreign key in the child table that matches a primary key in the parent table.
- *SQL table derived from a relationship, containing the foreign keys of all the entities in the relationship.* This transformation always occurs for relationships that are

binary and many-to-many (see Figures 5.1f and 5.2f), relationships that are binary recursive and many-to-many, (see Figures 5.3c and 5.4c), and all relationships that are of ternary or higher degree (see Figures 5.5 and 5.6). This is the other most common way design tools handle relationships in the ER and UML models. A many-to-many relationship can only be defined in terms of a table that contains foreign keys that match the primary keys of the two associated entities. This new table may also contain attributes of the original relationship—for example, a relationship "enrolled-in" between two entities Student and Course might have the attributes term and grade, which are associated with a particular enrollment of a student in a particular course.

The following rules apply to handling SQL null values in these transformations:

- Nulls are allowed in an SQL table for foreign keys of associated (referenced) optional entities.
- Nulls are not allowed in an SQL table for foreign keys of associated (referenced) mandatory entities.
- Nulls are not allowed for any key in an SQL table derived from a many-to-many relationship because only complete row entries are meaningful in the table.

Figures 5.1 through 5.8 show how SQL-created table statements can be derived from each type of ER or UML model construct. Note that in each SQL table definition, the term *primary key* represents the key of the table that is to be used for indexing and searching for data.

Binary Relationships

A one-to-one binary relationship between two entities is illustrated in Figure 5.1(a)–(c). Note that the UML-equivalent binary association is given in Figure 5.2(a)–(c).

When both entities are mandatory (Figure 5.1a), each entity becomes a table, and the key of either entity can appear in the other entity's table as a foreign key. One of the entities in an optional relationship (see Department in Figure 5.1b) should contain the foreign key of the other entity in its transformed table. Employee, the other entity in Figure 5.1(b), could also contain a foreign key (dept_no) with nulls allowed, but this would require more storage

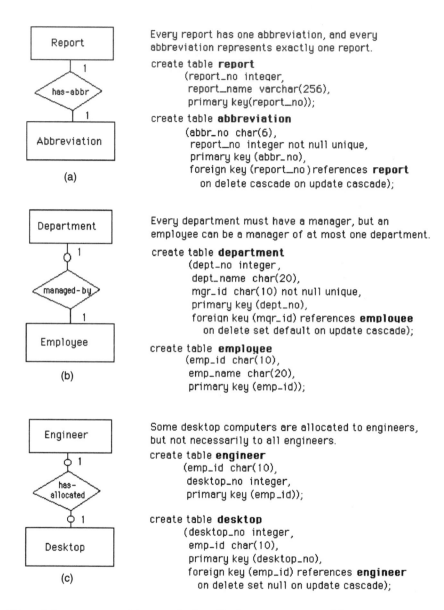

Every report has one abbreviation, and every abbreviation represents exactly one report.

```
create table report
        (report_no integer,
         report_name varchar(256),
         primary key(report_no));
create table abbreviation
        (abbr_no char(6),
         report_no integer not null unique,
         primary key (abbr_no),
         foreign key (report_no)references report
            on delete cascade on update cascade);
```

Every department must have a manager, but an employee can be a manager of at most one department.

```
create table department
        (dept_no integer,
         dept_name char(20),
         mgr_id char(10) not null unique,
         primary key (dept_no),
         foreign key (mgr_id) references employee
            on delete set default on update cascade);
create table employee
        (emp_id char(10),
         emp_name char(20),
         primary key (emp_id));
```

Some desktop computers are allocated to engineers, but not necessarily to all engineers.

```
create table engineer
        (emp_id char(10),
         desktop_no integer,
         primary key (emp_id));
create table desktop
        (desktop_no integer,
         emp_id char(10),
         primary key (desktop_no),
         foreign key (emp_id) references engineer
            on delete set null on update cascade);
```

Figure 5.1 ER model: one-to-one binary relationship between two entities:
(a) one-to-one, both entities mandatory, (b) one-to-one, one entity optional, one mandatory,
(c) one-to-one, both entities optional,

space because of the much greater number of Employee entity instances than Department instances. When both entities are optional (Figure 5.1c), either entity can contain the embedded foreign key of the other entity, with nulls allowed in the foreign keys.

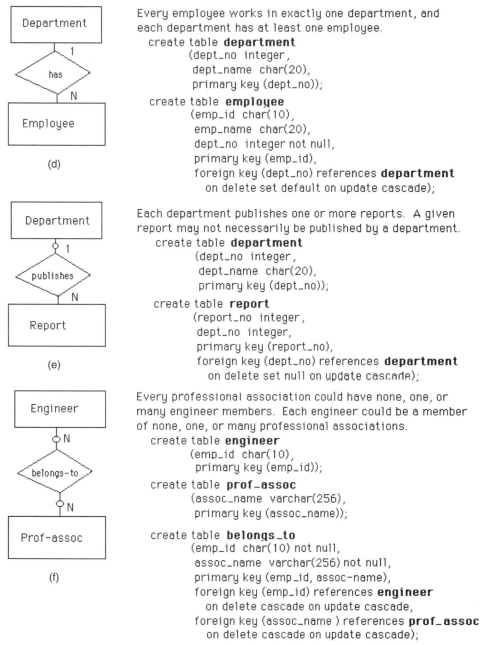

Every employee works in exactly one department, and each department has at least one employee.

```
create table department
        (dept_no  integer,
         dept_name  char(20),
         primary key (dept_no));
create table employee
        (emp_id  char(10),
         emp_name  char(20),
         dept_no  integer not null,
         primary key (emp_id),
         foreign key (dept_no) references department
            on delete set default on update cascade);
```

Each department publishes one or more reports. A given report may not necessarily be published by a department.

```
create table department
        (dept_no  integer,
         dept_name  char(20),
         primary key (dept_no));

create table report
        (report_no  integer,
         dept_no  integer,
         primary key (report_no),
         foreign key (dept_no) references department
            on delete set null on update cascade);
```

Every professional association could have none, one, or many engineer members. Each engineer could be a member of none, one, or many professional associations.

```
create table engineer
        (emp_id  char(10),
         primary key (emp_id));
create table prof_assoc
        (assoc_name  varchar(256),
         primary key (assoc_name));

create table belongs_to
        (emp_id  char(10) not null,
         assoc_name  varchar(256) not null,
         primary key (emp_id, assoc-name),
         foreign key (emp_id) references engineer
            on delete cascade on update cascade,
         foreign key (assoc_name ) references prof_assoc
            on delete cascade on update cascade);
```

Figure 5.1, cont'd. (d) one-to-many, both entities mandatory, (e) one-to-many, one entity mandatory, one optional, and (f) many-to-many, both entities optional.

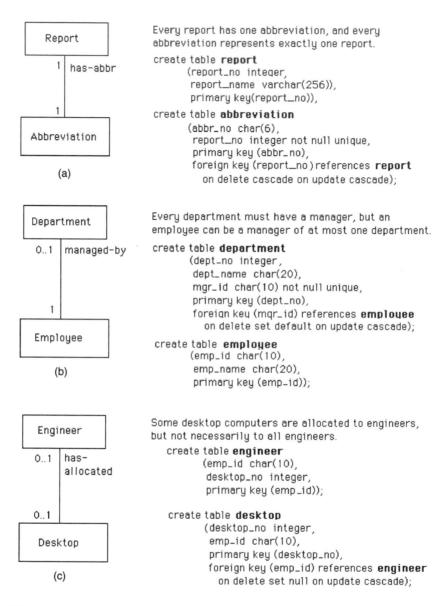

Every report has one abbreviation, and every abbreviation represents exactly one report.

```
create table report
        (report_no integer,
         report_name varchar(256)),
         primary key(report_no)),
create table abbreviation
        (abbr_no char(6),
         report_no integer not null unique,
         primary key (abbr_no),
         foreign key (report_no) references report
            on delete cascade on update cascade);
```

Every department must have a manager, but an employee can be a manager of at most one department.

```
create table department
        (dept_no integer,
         dept_name char(20),
         mgr_id char(10) not null unique,
         primary key (dept_no),
         foreign key (mgr_id) references employee
            on delete set default on update cascade);
create table employee
        (emp_id char(10),
         emp_name char(20),
         primary key (emp_id));
```

Some desktop computers are allocated to engineers, but not necessarily to all engineers.

```
create table engineer
        (emp_id char(10),
         desktop_no integer,
         primary key (emp_id));
create table desktop
        (desktop_no integer,
         emp_id char(10),
         primary key (desktop_no),
         foreign key (emp_id) references engineer
            on delete set null on update cascade);
```

Figure 5.2 UML: one-to-one binary relationship between two entities: (a) one-to-one, both entities mandatory, (b) one-to-one, one entity optional, one mandatory, (c) one-to-one, both entities optional.

The one-to-many relationship can be shown as either mandatory or optional on the "many" side, without affecting the transformation. On the "one" side it may be either mandatory (Figure 5.1d) or optional (Figure 5.1e). In all cases the foreign key must appear on the "many" side,

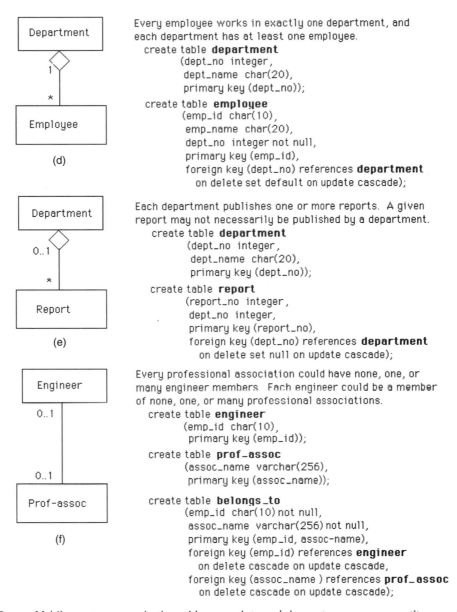

Every employee works in exactly one department, and each department has at least one employee.

```
create table department
        (dept_no integer,
         dept_name char(20),
         primary key (dept_no));
create table employee
        (emp_id char(10),
         emp_name char(20),
         dept_no integer not null,
         primary key (emp_id),
         foreign key (dept_no) references department
            on delete set default on update cascade);
```

Each department publishes one or more reports. A given report may not necessarily be published by a department.

```
create table department
        (dept_no integer,
         dept_name char(20),
         primary key (dept_no));
create table report
        (report_no integer,
         dept_no integer,
         primary key (report_no),
         foreign key (dept_no) references department
            on delete set null on update cascade);
```

Every professional association could have none, one, or many engineer members   Each engineer could be a member of none, one, or many professional associations.

```
create table engineer
        (emp_id char(10),
         primary key (emp_id));
create table prof_assoc
        (assoc_name varchar(256),
         primary key (assoc_name));
create table belongs_to
        (emp_id char(10) not null,
         assoc_name varchar(256) not null,
         primary key (emp_id, assoc-name),
         foreign key (emp_id) references engineer
            on delete cascade on update cascade,
         foreign key (assoc_name ) references prof_assoc
            on delete cascade on update cascade);
```

Figure 5.2, cont'd (d) one-to-many, both entities mandatory, (e) one-to-many, one entity mandatory, one optional, and (f) many-to-many, both entities optional.

which represents the child entity, with nulls allowed for foreign keys only in the optional "one" case. Foreign key constraints are set according to the specific meaning of the relationship and may vary from one relationship to another.

The many-to-many relationship, shown in Figure 5.1(f) as optional for both entities, requires a new table containing the primary keys of both entities. The same transformation applies to either the optional or mandatory case, including the fact that the "not null" clause must appear for the foreign keys in both cases. Note also that an optional entity means that the SQL table derived from it may have zero rows for that particular relationship. This does not affect "null" or "not null" in the table definition.

Binary Recursive Relationships

A single entity with a one-to-one relationship implies some form of entity occurrence pairing, as indicated by the relationship name. This pairing may be completely optional, completely mandatory, or neither. In all of these cases (Figure 5.3a for ER and Figure 5.4a for UML), the pairing entity key appears as a foreign key in the resulting table. The two key attributes are taken from the same domain but are given different names to designate their unique use. The one-to-many relationship requires a foreign key in the resulting table (Figure 5.3b). The foreign key constraints can vary with the particular relationship.

The many-to-many binary recursive relationship is shown as optional (Figure 5.3c) and results in a new table; it could also be defined as mandatory (using the word "must" instead of "may"). Both cases have the foreign keys defined as "not null." In many-to-many relationships, foreign key constraints on delete and update must always be cascaded because each entry in the SQL table depends on the current value or existence of the referenced primary key.

Ternary and *n*-ary Relationships

An *n*-ary relationship has (n + 1) possible variations of connectivity: all *n* sides with connectivity "one"; $(n - 1)$ sides with connectivity "one" and one side with connectivity "many"; $(n - 2)$ sides with connectivity "one" and two sides with "many"; and so on until all sides are "many."

The four possible varieties of a ternary relationship are shown in Figure 5.5 for the ER model and Figure 5.6 for UML. All variations are transformed by creating an

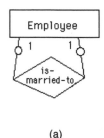

(a)

Any employee is allowed to be married
to another employee in this company.

```
create table employee
        (emp_id  char(10),
         emp_name  char(20),
         spouse_id  char(10),
         primary key (emp_id),
         foreign key (spouse_id) references employee
             on delete set null on update cascade);
```

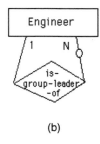

(b)

Engineers are divided into groups for certain
projects. Each group has a leader.

```
create table engineer
        (emp_id  char(10),
         leader_id  char(10) not null,
         primary key (emp_id),
         foreign key (leader_id) references engineer
             on delete set default on update cascade);
```

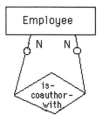

(c)

Each employee has the opportunity to coauthor a
report with one or more other employees, or to
write the report alone.

```
create table employee
        (emp_id  char(10),
         emp_name  char(20),
         primary key (emp_id));
```

```
create table coauthor
        (author_id  char(10) not null,
         coauthor_id  char(10) not null,
         primary key (author_id, coauthor-id),
         foreign key (author_id) references employee
           on delete cascade on update cascade,
         foreign key (coauthor_id) references employee
             on delete cascade on update cascade);
```

Figure 5.3 ER model: binary recursive relationship: (a) one-to-one, both sides optional, (b) one-to-many, "one" side mandatory, "many" side optional, and (c) many-to-many, both sides optional.

SQL table containing the primary keys of all entities; however, in each case the meaning of the keys is different. When all three relationships are "one" (Figure 5.5a), the resulting SQL table consists of three possible distinct keys. This represents the fact that there are three

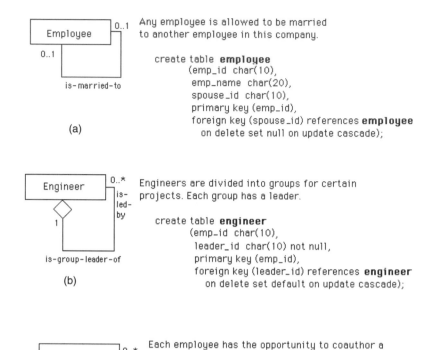

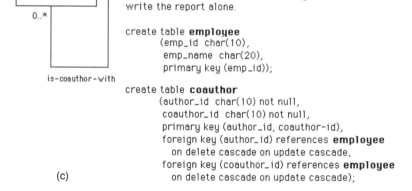

Figure 5.4 UML: binary recursive relationship: (a) one-to-one, both sides optional, (b) one-to-many, "one" side mandatory, "many" side optional, and (c) many-to-many, both sides optional.

functional dependencies (FDs) that are needed to describe this relationship. The optionality constraint is not used here because all n entities must participate in every instance of the relationship to satisfy the FD constraints. (See Chapter 6 for more discussion of functional dependencies.)

In general, the number of entities with connectivity "one" determines the lower bound on the number of FDs. Thus, in Figure 5.5(b), which is one-to-one-to-many, there are two FDs; in Figure 5.5(c), which is one-to-many-to-many, there is only one FD. When all relationships are "many" (Figure 5.5d), the relationship table is all one composite key unless the relationship has its own attributes. In that case, the key is the composite of all three keys from the three associated entities.

Foreign key constraints on delete and update for ternary relationships transformed to SQL tables must always be cascade because each entry in the SQL table depends on the current value of, or existence of, the referenced primary key.

Generalization and Aggregation

The transformation of a generalization abstraction can produce separate SQL tables for the generic or supertype entity and each of the subtypes (Figure 5.7 for the ER model and Figure 5.8 for UML). The table derived from the supertype entity contains the supertype entity key and all common attributes. Each table derived from subtype entities contains the supertype entity key and only the attributes that are specific to that subtype. Update integrity is maintained by requiring all insertions and deletions to occur in both the supertype table and relevant subtype table—that is, the foreign key constraint cascade must be used. If the update is to the primary key of the supertype table, then all subtype tables as well as the supertype table must be updated. An update to a nonkey attribute affects either the supertype or one subtype table, but not both. The transformation rules (and integrity rules) are the same for both the disjoint and overlapping subtype generalizations.

Another approach is to have a single table that includes all attributes from the supertype and subtypes (the whole hierarchy in one table) with nulls used when necessary. A third possibility is one table for each subtype, pushing down the common attributes into the specific subtypes. There are advantages and disadvantages to each of these three approaches. Several software tools are now supporting all three options (Fowler, 2003; Ambler, 2003).

Database practitioners often add a discriminator to the supertype when they implement generalization. The discriminator is an attribute that has a separate value for each

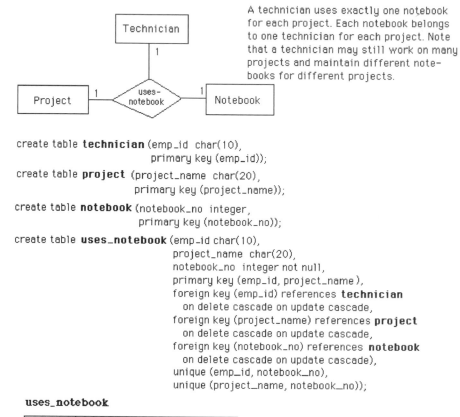

A technician uses exactly one notebook for each project. Each notebook belongs to one technician for each project. Note that a technician may still work on many projects and maintain different notebooks for different projects.

```
create table technician (emp_id char(10),
                    primary key (emp_id));
create table project (project_name char(20),
                    primary key (project_name));
create table notebook (notebook_no integer,
                    primary key (notebook_no));
create table uses_notebook (emp_id char(10),
                    project_name char(20),
                    notebook_no integer not null,
                    primary key (emp_id, project_name),
                    foreign key (emp_id) references technician
                      on delete cascade on update cascade,
                    foreign key (project_name) references project
                      on delete cascade on update cascade,
                    foreign key (notebook_no) references notebook
                      on delete cascade on update cascade),
                    unique (emp_id, notebook_no),
                    unique (project_name, notebook_no));
```

uses_notebook

emp_id	project_name	notebook-no
35	alpha	5001
35	gamma	2008
42	delta	1004
42	epsilon	3005
81	gamma	1007
93	alpha	1009
93	beta	5001

Functional dependencies

emp_id, project_name -> notebook_no
emp_id, notebook_no -> project_name
project_name, notebook_no -> emp_id

(a)

Figure 5.5 ER model: ternary and *n*-ary relationships: (a) one-to-one-to-one,

subtype and indicates which subtype to use to get further information. This approach works up to a point. However, there are situations requiring multiple levels of supertypes and subtypes, where more than one discriminator may be required.

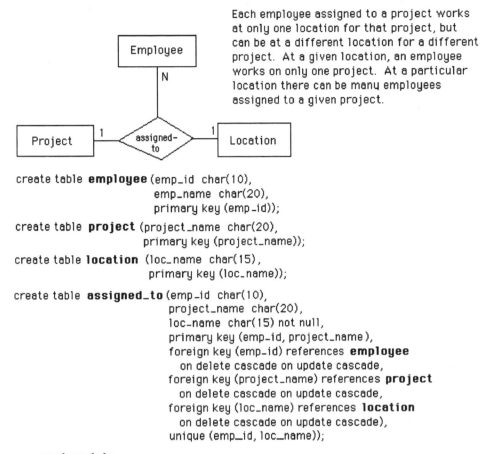

Each employee assigned to a project works at only one location for that project, but can be at a different location for a different project. At a given location, an employee works on only one project. At a particular location there can be many employees assigned to a given project.

```
create table employee (emp_id char(10),
                       emp_name char(20),
                       primary key (emp_id));
create table project (project_name char(20),
                      primary key (project_name));
create table location (loc_name char(15),
                       primary key (loc_name));
create table assigned_to (emp_id char(10),
                       project_name char(20),
                       loc_name char(15) not null,
                       primary key (emp_id, project_name),
                       foreign key (emp_id) references employee
                         on delete cascade on update cascade,
                       foreign key (project_name) references project
                         on delete cascade on update cascade,
                       foreign key (loc_name) references location
                         on delete cascade on update cascade),
                       unique (emp_id, loc_name));
```

assigned_to

emp_id	project_name	loc_name
48101	forest	B66
48101	ocean	E71
20702	ocean	A12
20702	river	D54
51266	river	G14
51266	ocean	A12
76323	hills	B66

Functional dependencies

emp_id, loc_name -> project_name
emp_id, project_name -> loc_name

(b)

Figure 5.5, cont'd (b) one-to-one-to-many,

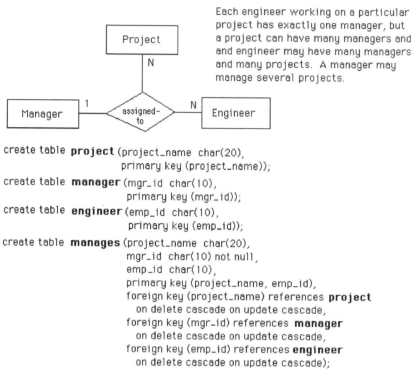

Each engineer working on a particular project has exactly one manager, but a project can have many managers and and engineer may have many managers and many projects. A manager may manage several projects.

```
create table project (project_name char(20),
                       primary key (project_name));
create table manager (mgr_id char(10),
                       primary key (mgr_id));
create table engineer (emp_id char(10),
                        primary key (emp_id));
create table manages (project_name char(20),
                       mgr_id char(10) not null,
                       emp_id char(10),
                       primary key (project_name, emp_id),
                       foreign key (project_name) references project
                         on delete cascade on update cascade,
                       foreign key (mgr_id) references manager
                         on delete cascade on update cascade,
                       foreign key (emp_id) references engineer
                         on delete cascade on update cascade);
```

manages

project_name	emp_id	mgr_id
alpha	4106	27
alpha	4200	27
beta	7033	32
beta	4200	14
gamma	4106	71
delta	7033	55
delta	4106	39
iota	4106	27

Functional dependency

project_name, emp_id -> mgr_id

(c)

Figure 5.5, cont'd (c) one-to-many-to-many, and

The transformation of an aggregation abstraction also produces a separate table for the supertype entity and each subtype entity. However, there are no common attributes and no integrity constraints to maintain. The main function of aggregation is to provide an abstraction to aid the view integration process. In UML, aggregation is a composition relationship, not a type relationship, which corresponds to a weak entity (Muller, 1999).

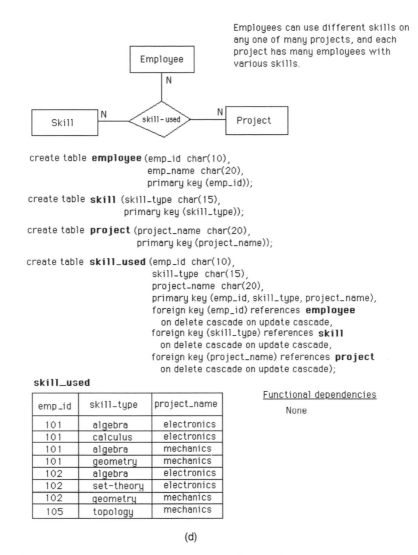

Employees can use different skills on any one of many projects, and each project has many employees with various skills.

```
create table employee (emp_id char(10),
                       emp_name char(20),
                       primary key (emp_id));
create table skill (skill_type char(15),
                    primary key (skill_type));
create table project (project_name char(20),
                      primary key (project_name));
create table skill_used (emp_id char(10),
                         skill_type char(15),
                         project_name char(20),
                         primary key (emp_id, skill_type, project_name),
                         foreign key (emp_id) references employee
                           on delete cascade on update cascade,
                         foreign key (skill_type) references skill
                           on delete cascade on update cascade,
                         foreign key (project_name) references project
                           on delete cascade on update cascade);
```

skill_used

emp_id	skill_type	project_name
101	algebra	electronics
101	calculus	electronics
101	algebra	mechanics
101	geometry	mechanics
102	algebra	electronics
102	set-theory	electronics
102	geometry	mechanics
105	topology	mechanics

Functional dependencies

None

(d)

Figure 5.5, cont'd (d) many-to-many-to-many ternary relationships.

Multiple Relationships

Multiple relationships among *n* entities are always considered to be completely independent. One-to-one, one-to-many binary, or binary recursive relationships resulting in tables that are either equivalent or differ only in the addition of a foreign key can simply be merged into a single table containing all the foreign keys. Many-to-many or ternary relationships that result in SQL tables tend to be unique and cannot be merged.

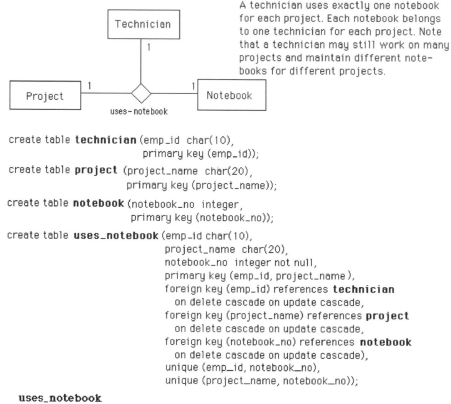

A technician uses exactly one notebook for each project. Each notebook belongs to one technician for each project. Note that a technician may still work on many projects and maintain different notebooks for different projects.

```
create table technician (emp_id char(10),
                    primary key (emp_id));
create table project (project_name char(20),
                    primary key (project_name));
create table notebook (notebook_no integer,
                    primary key (notebook_no));
create table uses_notebook (emp_id char(10),
                    project_name char(20),
                    notebook_no integer not null,
                    primary key (emp_id, project_name),
                    foreign key (emp_id) references technician
                      on delete cascade on update cascade,
                    foreign key (project_name) references project
                      on delete cascade on update cascade,
                    foreign key (notebook_no) references notebook
                      on delete cascade on update cascade),
                    unique (emp_id, notebook_no),
                    unique (project_name, notebook_no));
```

uses_notebook

emp_id	project_name	notebook-no
35	alpha	5001
35	gamma	2008
42	delta	1004
42	epsilon	3005
81	gamma	1007
93	alpha	1009
93	beta	5001

Functional dependencies

emp_id, project_name -> notebook_no
emp_id, notebook_no -> project_name
project_name, notebook_no -> emp_id

(a)

Figure 5.6 UML: ternary and *n*-ary relationships: (a) one-to-one-to-one,

Weak Entities

Weak entities differ from entities only in their need for keys from other entities to establish their uniqueness. Otherwise, they have the same transformation properties as entities, and no special rules are needed. When a weak entity is already derived from two or more entities in the ER diagram, it can be directly transformed into a table without further change.

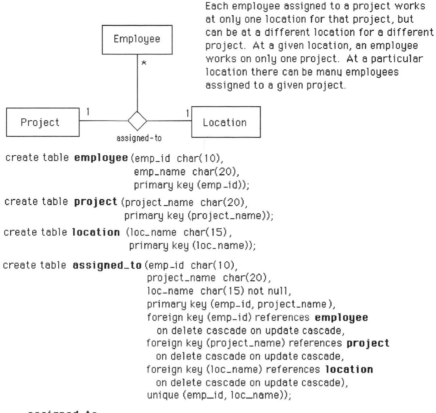

Each employee assigned to a project works at only one location for that project, but can be at a different location for a different project. At a given location, an employee works on only one project. At a particular location there can be many employees assigned to a given project.

```
create table employee (emp_id char(10),
                        emp_name char(20),
                        primary key (emp_id));
create table project (project_name char(20),
                       primary key (project_name));
create table location (loc_name char(15),
                        primary key (loc_name));

create table assigned_to (emp_id char(10),
                          project_name char(20),
                          loc_name char(15) not null,
                          primary key (emp_id, project_name),
                          foreign key (emp_id) references employee
                            on delete cascade on update cascade,
                          foreign key (project_name) references project
                            on delete cascade on update cascade,
                          foreign key (loc_name) references location
                            on delete cascade on update cascade),
                          unique (emp_id, loc_name));
```

assigned_to

emp_id	project_name	loc_name
48101	forest	B66
48101	ocean	E71
20702	ocean	A12
20702	river	D54
51266	river	G14
51266	ocean	A12
76323	hills	B66

Functional dependencies

emp_id, loc_name -> project_name
emp_id, project_name -> loc_name

(b)

Figure 5.6, cont'd (b) one-to-one-to-many,

Continued

Transformation Steps

The following list summarizes the basic transformation steps from an ER diagram to SQL tables:

- Transform each entity into a table containing the key and nonkey attributes of the entity.

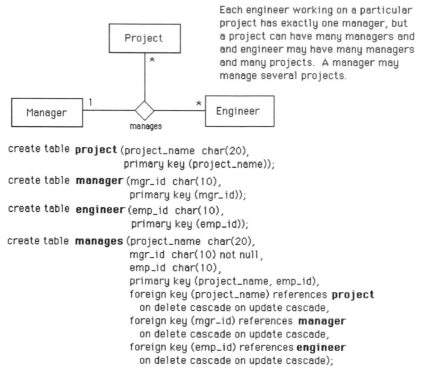

Each engineer working on a particular project has exactly one manager, but a project can have many managers and and engineer may have many managers and many projects. A manager may manage several projects.

```
create table project (project_name char(20),
                      primary key (project_name));
create table manager (mgr_id char(10),
                      primary key (mgr_id));
create table engineer (emp_id char(10),
                       primary key (emp_id));
create table manages (project_name char(20),
                      mgr_id char(10) not null,
                      emp_id char(10),
                      primary key (project_name, emp_id),
                      foreign key (project_name) references project
                        on delete cascade on update cascade,
                      foreign key (mgr_id) references manager
                        on delete cascade on update cascade,
                      foreign key (emp_id) references engineer
                        on delete cascade on update cascade);
```

manages

project_name	emp_id	mgr_id
alpha	4106	27
alpha	4200	27
beta	7033	32
beta	4200	14
gamma	4106	71
delta	7033	55
delta	4106	39
iota	4106	27

Functional dependency

project_name, emp_id -> mgr_id

(c)

Figure 5.6, cont'd (c) one-to-many-to-many, and

- Transform every many-to-many binary or binary recursive relationship into a table with the keys of the entities and the attributes of the relationship.
- Transform every ternary or higher-level *n*-ary relationship into a table.

Now let us study each step in turn.

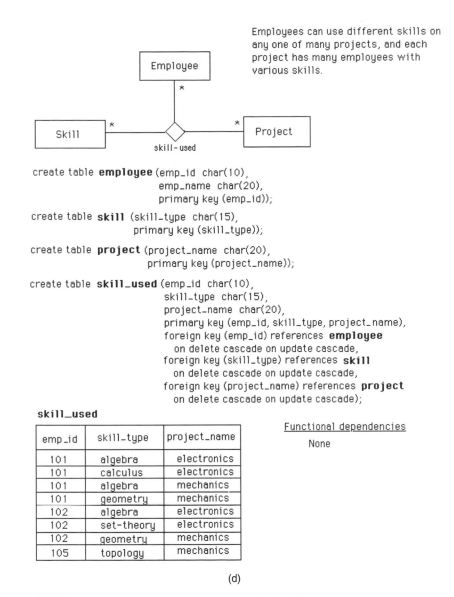

Employees can use different skills on any one of many projects, and each project has many employees with various skills.

```
create table employee (emp_id char(10),
                       emp_name char(20),
                       primary key (emp_id));

create table skill (skill_type char(15),
                    primary key (skill_type));

create table project (project_name char(20),
                      primary key (project_name));

create table skill_used (emp_id char(10),
                         skill_type char(15),
                         project_name char(20),
                         primary key (emp_id, skill_type, project_name),
                         foreign key (emp_id) references employee
                           on delete cascade on update cascade,
                         foreign key (skill_type) references skill
                           on delete cascade on update cascade,
                         foreign key (project_name) references project
                           on delete cascade on update cascade);
```

skill_used

emp_id	skill_type	project_name
101	algebra	electronics
101	calculus	electronics
101	algebra	mechanics
101	geometry	mechanics
102	algebra	electronics
102	set-theory	electronics
102	geometry	mechanics
105	topology	mechanics

Functional dependencies
None

(d)

Figure 5.6, cont'd (d) many-to-many-to-many ternary relationships.

Entity Transformation

If there is a one-to-many relationship between two entities, add the key of the entity on the "one" side (the parent) into the child table as a foreign key. If there is a one-to-one relationship between one entity and another entity, add the key of one of the entities into the table for

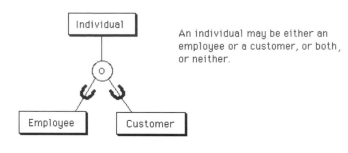

An individual may be either an
employee or a customer, or both,
or neither.

```
create table individual (indiv_id char(10),
                          indiv_name char(20),
                          indiv_addr char(20),
                          primary key (indiv_id));
create table employee (emp_id char(10),
                        job_title char(15),
                        primary key (emp_id),
                        foreign key (emp_id) references individual
                          on delete cascade on update cascade);
create table customer (cust_no char(10),
                        cust_credit char(12),
                        primary key (cust_no),
                        foreign key (cust_no) references individual
                          on delete cascade on update cascade);
```

Figure 5.7 ER model:
generalization and
aggregation.

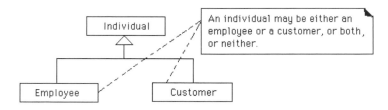

An individual may be either an
employee or a customer, or both,
or neither.

```
create table individual (indiv_id char(10),
                          indiv_name char(20),
                          indiv_addr char(20),
                          primary key (indiv_id));
create table employee (emp_id char(10),
                        job_title char(15),
                        primary key (emp_id),
                        foreign key (emp_id) references individual
                          on delete cascade on update cascade);
create table customer (cust_no char(10),
                        cust_credit char(12),
                        primary key (cust_no),
                        foreign key (cust_no) references individual
                          on delete cascade on update cascade);
```

Figure 5.8 UML:
generalization and
aggregation.

the other entity, thus changing it to a foreign key. The addition of a foreign key due to a one-to-one relationship can be made in either direction. One strategy is to maintain the most natural parent–child relationship by putting the parent key into the child table. Another strategy is based on efficiency: Add the foreign key to the table with fewer rows.

Every entity in a generalization hierarchy is transformed into a table. Each of these tables contains the key of the supertype entity; in reality, the subtype primary keys are foreign keys as well. The supertype table also contains nonkey values that are common to all the relevant entities; the other tables contain nonkey values specific to each subtype entity.

SQL constructs for these transformations may include constraints for not null, unique, and foreign key. A primary key must be specified for each table, either explicitly from among the keys in the ER diagram or by taking the composite of all attributes as the default key. Note that the primary key designation implies that the attribute is not null and unique. It is important to note, however, that not all DBMSs follow the ANSI standard in this regard—it may be possible in some systems to create a primary key that can be null. We recommend that you specify "not null" explicitly for all key attributes.

Many-to-Many Binary Relationship Transformation

In this step, every many-to-many binary relationship is transformed into a table containing the keys of the entities and the attributes of the relationship. The resulting table will show the correspondence between specific instances of one entity and those of another entity. Any attribute of this correspondence, such as the elected office an engineer has in a professional association (Figure 5.1f), is considered intersection data and is added to the table as a nonkey attribute.

SQL constructs for this transformation may include constraints for not null. The unique constraint is not used here because all keys are composites of the participating primary keys of the associated entities in the relationship.

The constraints for primary key and foreign key are required, because a table is defined as containing a composite of the primary keys of the associated entities.

Ternary Relationship Transformation

In this step, every ternary (or higher n-ary) relationship is transformed into a table. Ternary or higher n-ary relationships are defined as a collection of the n primary keys in the associated entities in that relationship, with possibly some nonkey attributes that are dependent on the key formed by the composite of those n primary keys.

SQL constructs for this transformation must include constraints for not null, since optionality is not allowed. The unique constraint is not used for individual attributes, because all keys are composites of the participating primary keys of the associated entities in the relationship. The constraints for primary key and foreign key are required because a table is defined as a composite of the primary keys of the associated entities. The unique clause must also be used to define alternate keys that often occur with ternary relationships. Note that a table derived from an n-ary relationship has n foreign keys.

Example of ER-to-SQL Transformation

ER diagrams for the company personnel and project database (see Chapter 4) can be transformed to SQL tables. A summary of the transformation of entities and relationships to SQL tables is illustrated in the following lists.

SQL tables derived directly from entities (see Figure 4.3d):
division
department
employee
manager
secretary
engineer
technician
skill
project
location
prof_assoc

desktop
SQL tables derived from many-to-many binary or many-to-many binary recursive relationships:
belongs_to
SQL tables transformed from ternary relationships:
skill_used
assigned_to

Summary

Entities, attributes, and relationships in the ER model and classes, attributes, and associations in UML can be transformed directly into SQL table definitions with some simple rules. Entities are transformed into tables, with all attributes mapped one-to-one to table attributes. Tables representing entities that are the child ("many" side) of a parent–child (one-to-many or one-to-one) relationship must also include, as a foreign key, the primary key of the parent entity. A many-to-many relationship is transformed into a table that contains the primary keys of the associated entities as its composite primary key; the components of that key are also designated as foreign keys in SQL. A ternary or higher-level n-ary relationship is transformed into a table that contains the primary keys of the associated entities; these keys are designated as foreign keys in SQL. A subset of those keys can be designated as the primary key, depending on the functional dependencies associated with the relationship. Rules for generalization require the inheritance of the primary key from the supertype to the subtype entities when transformed into SQL tables. Optionality constraints in the ER or UML diagrams translate into nulls allowed in the relational model when applied to the "one" side of a relationship. In SQL, the lack of an optionality constraint determines the not null designation in the *create table* definition.

Tips and Insights for Database Professionals

Tip 1. Use software (CASE) tools when possible (e.g., ERwin). These transformations are fairly mechanical in nature.

Tip 2. Entities become tables.

Tip 3. Simple attributes become data items in tables.

Tip 4. Complex attributes—consider redefining as entities (tables) with foreign keys back to the parent entity (its primary key).

Tip 5. One-to-one or one-to-many relationships must be connected by primary key/foreign key pairs between tables.

Tip 6. Many-to-many relationships become an "interconnect" table that simulates two equivalent one-to-many relationships.

Tip 7. *n*-ary relationships becomes an "interconnect" table with primary key/foreign key pairs to simulate actual relationships among attributes.

Tip 8. Generalization defines a table for the supertype entity and all subtype entities. Analyze carefully before creating extra tables; ask, "Are they really needed?"; if so, then maintain the primary key/foreign key connection.

Tip 9. Analyze the SQL tables you defined to determine which data is redundant, and also where there is insufficient data to answer typical queries stated in the requirements specifications. Make adjustments as needed to avoid these problems.

Literature Summary

Definition of the basic transformations from the ER model to tables is covered in McGee (1974), Wong and Katz (1979), Sakai (1983), Martin (1983), Hawryszkiewyck (1984), Jajodia and Ng (1984), and for UML in Muller (1999).

6

NORMALIZATION

This chapter focuses on the fundamentals of normal forms for relational databases and the database design step that normalizes the candidate tables (Step II.d of the database design life cycle). It also investigates the equivalence between the conceptual data model (e.g., the entity–relationship (ER) model) and normal forms for tables. As we go through the examples in this chapter it should become obvious that good, thoughtful design of a conceptual model will result in databases that are either already normalized or can be easily normalized with minor changes. This illustrates the beauty of the conceptual modeling approach to database design, in that the experienced relational database designer will develop a natural gravitation toward a normalized model from the beginning.

For most database practitioners, the first three sections of this chapter cover the critical normalization needed for everyday use, through Boyce-Codd Normal Form (BCNF). The final section describes an algorithm for finding the minimum set of third normal form (3NF) tables when the initial design of tables becomes large and unwieldy.

Fundamentals of Normalization

Relational database tables, whether they are derived from ER or Unified Modeling Language (UML) models, sometimes suffer from some rather serious problems in terms of performance, integrity, and maintainability. For example, when the entire database is defined as a single large table, it can result in a large amount of redundant data and lengthy searches for just a small number of target rows. It can also result in long and expensive updates, and deletions in particular can result in the elimination of useful data as an unwanted side effect.

Such a situation is shown in Figure 6.1, where products, salespersons, customers, and orders are all stored in a single table called **Sales**. In this table we see that certain product and customer information is stored redundantly, wasting storage space. Certain queries, such as "Which customers ordered vacuum cleaners last month?," would require a search of the entire table. Also, updates, such as changing the address of the customer Dave Bachmann,

Sales

product-name	order-no	cust-name	cust-addr	credit	date	sales-name
vacuum cleaner	1458	Dave Bachmann	Austin	6	1-3-03	Carl Bloch
computer	2730	Qiang Zhu	Plymouth	10	4-15-05	Ted Hanss
refrigerator	2460	Mike Stolarchuck	Ann Arbor	8	9-12-04	Dick Phillips
DVD player	519	Peter Honeyman	Detroit	3	12-5-04	Fred Remley
radio	1986	Charles Antonelli	Chicago	7	5-10-05	R. Metz
CD player	1817	C.V. Ravishankar	Mumbai	8	8-3-02	Paul Basile
vacuum cleaner	1865	Charles Antonelli	Chicago	7	10-1-04	Carl Bloch
vacuum cleaner	1885	Betsy Karmeisool	Detroit	8	4-19-99	Carl Bloch
refrigerator	1943	Dave Bachmann	Austin	6	1-4-04	Dick Phillips
television	2315	Sakti Pramanik	East lansing	6	3-15-04	Fred Remley

Figure 6.1 Single table database.

would require changing many rows. Finally, deleting an order by a valued customer, such as Qiang Zhu (who bought an expensive computer), if that is his only outstanding order, deletes the only copy of his address and credit rating as a side effect. Such information may be difficult (or sometimes impossible) to recover. These problems also occur for situations in which the database has already been set up as a collection of many tables, but some of the tables are still too large.

If we had a method of breaking up such a large table into smaller tables so that these types of problems would be eliminated, the database would be much more efficient and reliable. Classes of relational database schemes or table definitions, called *normal forms*, are commonly used to accomplish this goal. The creation of a normal form database table is called *normalization*. Normalization is accomplished by analyzing the interdependencies among individual attributes associated with those tables and taking projections (subsets of columns) of larger tables to form smaller ones.

Let us first review the basic normal forms that have been well established in the relational database literature and in practice.

First Normal Form

Relational database tables, such as the **Sales** table illustrated in Figure 6.1, have only atomic values for each row for each column. Such tables are considered to be in first normal form, the most basic level of normalized tables.

To better understand the definition for first normal form, it helps to know the difference between a domain, an attribute, and a column. A *domain* is the set of all possible values for a particular type of attribute, but may be used for more than one attribute. For example, the domain of people's names is the underlying set of all possible names that could be used for either customer-name or salesperson-name in the database table in Figure 6.1. Each column in a relational table represents a single attribute, but in some cases more than one column may refer to different attributes from the same domain. When this occurs,

A table is in *first normal form (1NF)* if and only if all columns contain only atomic values—that is, each column can have only one value for each row in the table.

the table is still in 1NF because the values in the table are still atomic. In fact, standard SQL assumes only atomic values and a relational table is by default in 1NF. A nice explanation of this is given in Muller (1999).

Superkeys, Candidate Keys, and Primary Keys

A table in 1NF often suffers from data duplication, update performance degradation, and update integrity problems, as noted above. To understand these issues better, however, we must define the concept of a key in the context of normalized tables. A *superkey* is a set of one or more attributes that, when taken collectively, allows us to identify uniquely an entity or table. Any subset of the attributes of a superkey that is also a superkey and not reducible to another superkey is called a *candidate key*. A *primary key* is selected arbitrarily from the set of candidate keys to be used in an index for that table.

As an example, in Table 6.1 a composite of all the attributes of the table forms a superkey because duplicate rows are not allowed in the relational model. Thus, a trivial superkey is formed from the composite of all attributes in a table. Assuming that each department address (dept_addr) in this table is single valued, we can conclude that the composite of all attributes except dept_addr is also a superkey. Looking at smaller and smaller composites of attributes and making realistic assumptions about which

Table 6.1 Report Table

report_no	editor	dept_no	dept_name	dept_addr	author_id	author_name	author_addr
4216	woolf	15	design	argus1	53	tremaine	rutgers
4216	woolf	15	design	argus1	44	bolton	mathrev
4216	woolf	15	design	argus1	71	koenig	mathrev
5789	koenig	27	analysis	argus2	26	fry	folkstone
5789	koenig	27	analysis	argus2	38	umar	prise
5789	koenig	27	analysis	argus2	71	koenig	mathrev

attributes are single valued, we find that the composite (report_no, author_id) uniquely determines all the other attributes in the table and is therefore a superkey. However, neither report_no nor author_id alone can determine a row uniquely, and the composite of these two attributes cannot be reduced and still be a superkey. Thus, the composite (report_no, author_id) becomes a candidate key. Since it is the only candidate key in this table, it also becomes the primary key.

A table can have more than one candidate key. If, for example, in Table 6.1, we had an additional column for author_ssn, and the composite (report_no, author_ssn) uniquely determined all the other attributes of the table, then both (report_no, author_id) and (report_no, author_ssn) would be candidate keys. The primary key would then be an arbitrary choice between these two candidate keys.

Other examples of multiple candidate keys can be seen in Figure 5.5 (see Chapter 5). In Figure 5.5(a) the table **uses_notebook** has three candidate keys: (emp_id, project_name), (emp_id, notebook_no), and (project_name, notebook_no); and in Figure 5.5(b) the table **assigned_to** has two candidate keys: (emp_id, loc_name) and (emp_id, project_namc). Figures 5.5(c) and (d) each have only a single candidate key.

Second Normal Form

In explaining the concept of second normal form (2NF) and higher, we introduce the concept of functional dependence, which was briefly described in Chapter 2. The property of one or more attributes uniquely determining the value of one or more other attributes is called *functional dependence* (FD). Given a table **R**, a set of attributes B is functionally dependent on another set of attributes A if, at each instant of time, each A value is associated with only one B value. Such a functional dependence is denoted by A -> B. In the preceding example from Table 6.2, let us assume we are given the following functional dependencies for the table **report**:

    report: report_no -> editor, dept_no
       dept_no -> dept_name, dept_addr
       author_id -> author_name, author_addr

A table is in *second normal form (2NF)* if and only if it is in 1NF and every nonkey attribute is fully dependent on the primary key. An attribute is fully dependent on the primary key if it is on the right side of an FD for which the left side is either the primary key itself or something that can be derived from the primary key using the transitivity of FDs.

An example of a transitive FD in the **report** table is the following:

report_no -> dept_no

dept_no -> dept_name

Therefore, we can derive the FD (report_no -> dept_name) since dept_name is transitively dependent on report_no.

Continuing our example, the composite key in Table 6.1, (report_no, author_id), is the only candidate key and is therefore the primary key. However, there exists one FD (dept_no -> dept_name, dept_addr) that has no component of the primary key on the left side, and two FDs (report_no -> editor, dept_no and author_id -> author_name, author_addr) that contain one component of the primary key on the left side, but not both components. As such, the **report** table does not satisfy the condition for 2NF for any of the FDs.

Consider the disadvantages of 1NF in the **report** table. Report_no, editor, and dept_no are duplicated for each author of the report. Therefore, if the editor of the report changes, for example, several rows must be updated. This is known as the *update anomaly*, and it represents a potential degradation of performance due to the redundant updating. If a new editor is to be added to the table, this can only be done if the new editor is editing a report: both the report number and editor number must be known to add a row to the table, because you cannot have a primary key with a null value in most relational databases. This is known as the *insert anomaly*. Finally, if a report is withdrawn, all rows associated with that report must be deleted. This has the side effect of deleting the information that associates an author_id with author_name and author_addr. Deletion side effects of this nature are known as *delete anomalies*. They represent a potential loss of integrity, because the only way the data can be restored is to find the data somewhere outside the database and insert it back into the database. All three of these anomalies represent problems to database designers, but the delete anomaly is by far the most serious because you might lose data that cannot be recovered.

These disadvantages can be overcome by transforming the 1NF table into two or more 2NF tables by using the projection operator on a subset of the attributes of the 1NF table. In this example we project **report** over report_no, editor, dept_no, dept_name, and dept_addr to form **report1**; and project **report** over author_id, author_name, and author_addr to form **report2**; and finally, project **report** over report_no and author_id to form **report3**. The projection of **report** into three smaller tables has preserved the FDs and the association between report_no and author_no that was important in the original table. Data for the three tables is shown in Figure 6.2. The FDs for these 2NF tables are:

report1: report_no -> editor, dept_no
    dept_no -> dept_name, dept_addr
report2: author_id -> author_name,
    author_addr
report3: (report_no, author_id) is a
    candidate key (no FDs)

We now have three tables that satisfy the conditions for 2NF, and we have eliminated the worst problems of 1NF, especially integrity (the delete anomaly). First, editor, dept_no, dept_name, and dept_addr are no longer duplicated for each author of a report. Second, an editor change results in only an update to one row for **report1**. And third, and most important, the deletion of the report does not have the side effect of deleting the author information.

Not all performance degradation is eliminated, however; report_no is still duplicated for each author and deletion of a report requires updates to two tables (**report1** and **report3**) instead of one. However, these are minor problems compared to those in the 1NF **report** table.

Note that these three tables in 2NF could have been generated directly from an ER (or UML) diagram that equivalently modeled this situation with entities Author and Report and a many-to-many relationship between them.

report1

report_no	editor	dept_no	dept_name	dept_addr
4216	woolf	15	design	argus 1
5789	koenig	27	analysis	argus 2

report2

author_id	author_name	author_addr
53	mantei	cs-tor
44	bolton	mathrev
71	koenig	mathrev
26	fry	folkstone
38	umar	prise
71	koenig	mathrev

report3

report_no	author_id
4216	53
4216	44
4216	71
5789	26
5789	38
5789	71

Figure 6.2 2NF tables.

Third Normal Form

The 2NF tables we established in the previous section represent a significant improvement over 1NF tables. However, they still suffer from the same types of anomalies as the 1NF tables, although for different reasons associated with transitive dependencies. If a transitive (functional) dependency exists in a table, it means that two separate facts are represented in that table, one fact for each functional dependency involving a different left side. For example, if we delete a report from the database, which involves deleting the appropriate rows from **report1** and **report3** (see Figure 6.2), we have the side effect of deleting the association between dept_no, dept_name, and dept_addr as well. If we could project **report1** over report_no, editor, and dept_no to form table **report11**, and project **report1** over dept_no, dept_name, and dept_addr to form table **report12**, we could eliminate this problem. Example tables for **report11** and **report12** are shown in Figure 6.3.

In the preceding example, after projecting **report1** into **report11** and **report12** to eliminate the transitive dependency report_no -> dept_no -> dept_name, dept_addr we have the following 3NF tables and their functional dependencies (and example data in Figure 6.3):

> **report11:** report_no -> editor, dept_no
> **report12:** dept_no -> dept_name, dept_addr

> A table is in *third normal form (3NF)* if and only if for every nontrivial functional dependency X -> A, where X and A are either simple or composite attributes, one of two conditions must hold: either attribute X is a superkey, or attribute A is a member of a candidate key. If attribute A is a member of a candidate key, A is called a prime attribute. Note: A trivial FD is of the form YZ -> Z.

report11

report_no	editor	dept_no
4216	woolf	15
5789	koenig	27

report12

dept_no	dept_name	dept_addr
15	design	argus1
27	analysis	argus2

report2

author_id	author_name	author_addr
53	mantei	cs-tor
44	bolton	mathrev
71	koenig	mathrev
26	fry	folkstone
38	umar	prise
71	koeing	mathrev

report3

report_no	author_id
4216	53
4216	44
4216	71
5789	26
5789	38
5789	71

Figure 6.3 3NF tables.

report2: author_id -> author_name, author_addr
report3: (report_no, author_id) is a candidate key (no FDs)

Boyce-Codd Normal Form

Third normal form, which eliminates most of the anomalies known in databases today, is the most common standard for normalization in commercial databases and computer-aided software engineering (CASE) tools. The few remaining anomalies can be eliminated by the Boyce-Codd normal form. Boyce-Codd normal form is considered to be a strong variation of 3NF.

BCNF is a stronger form of normalization than 3NF because it eliminates the second condition for 3NF, which allowed the right side of the FD to be a prime attribute. Thus, every left side of an FD in a table must be a superkey. Every table that is BCNF is also 3NF, 2NF, and 1NF, by the previous definitions.

> A table **R** is in *Boyce-Codd normal form (BCNF)* if for every nontrivial FD X ->A, X is a superkey.

The following example shows a 3NF table that is not BCNF. Such tables have delete anomalies similar to those in the lower normal forms.

Assertion 1: For a given team, each employee is directed by only one leader. A team may be directed by more than one leader.

emp_name, team_name -> leader_name

Assertion 2: Each leader directs only one team.

leader_name -> team_name

The following table is 3NF with a composite candidate key (emp_name, team_name).

team:	emp_name	team_name	leader_name
	Sutton	Hawks	Wei
	Sutton	Condors	Bachmann
	Niven	Hawks	Wei
	Niven	Eagles	Makowski
	Wilson	Eagles	DeSmith

The **team** table has the following delete anomaly: If Sutton drops out of the Condors team, then we have no record of Bachmann leading the Condors team. As shown by Date (2003), this type of anomaly cannot have a lossless decomposition and preserve all FDs. A lossless decomposition requires that when you decompose the table into two smaller tables by projecting the original table over two overlapping subsets of that table, the natural join of those subset tables must result in the original table without any extra unwanted rows. The simplest way to avoid the delete anomaly for this kind of situation is to create a separate table for each of the two assertions. These two tables are partially redundant, enough so to avoid the delete anomaly. This decomposition is lossless (trivially) and preserves functional dependencies, but it also degrades update performance due to redundancy, and necessitates additional storage space. The trade-off is often worth it because the delete anomaly is avoided.

The Design of Normalized Tables: A Simple Example

The example in this section is based on the ER diagram in Figure 6.4 and the following FDs. In general, FDs can be given explicitly, derived from the ER diagram, or derived from intuition—that is, from experience with the problem domain.

1. emp_id, start_date -> job_title, end_date
2. emp_id -> emp_name, phone_no, office_no, proj_no, proj_name, dept_no
3. phone_no -> office_no

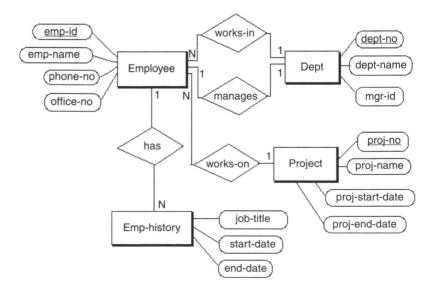

Figure 6.4 ER diagram for employee database.

4. proj_no -> proj_name, proj_start_date, proj_end_date

5. dept_no -> dept_name, mgr_id

6. mgr_id -> dept_no

Our objective is to design a relational database schema that is normalized to at least 3NF and, if possible, minimize the number of tables required. Our approach is to apply the definition of 3NF given previously to the FDs given above, and create tables that satisfy the definition.

If we try to put FDs 1–6 into a single table with the composite candidate key (and primary key) (emp_id, start_date) we violate the 3NF definition, because FDs 2–6 involve left sides of FDs that are not superkeys. Consequently, we need to separate FD 1 from the rest of the FDs. If we then try to combine 2–6 we have many transitivities. Intuitively, we know that 2, 3, 4, and 5 must be separated into different tables because of transitive dependencies. We then must decide whether 5 and 6 can be combined without loss of 3NF; this can be done because mgr_id and dept_no are mutually dependent and both attributes are superkeys in a combined table. Thus, we can define the following tables by appropriate projections from 1–6.

emp_hist: emp_id, start_date -> job_title, end_date

employee: emp_id -> emp_name, phone_no, proj_no, dept_no

phone: phone_no -> office_no

project: proj_no -> proj_name, proj_start_date, proj_end_date

department: dept_no -> dept_name, mgr_id

mgr_id -> dept_no

This solution, which is BCNF as well as 3NF, maintains all the original FDs. It is also a minimum set of normalized tables. In the "Determining the Minimum Set of 3NF Tables" section, we will look at a formal method of determining a minimum set that we can apply to much more complex situations.

Alternative designs may involve splitting tables into partitions for volatile (frequently updated) and passive (rarely updated) data, consolidating tables to get better query performance, or duplicating data in different tables to get better query performance without losing integrity. In summary, the measures we use to assess the trade-offs in our design are:

• Query performance (time).

- Update performance (time).
- Storage performance (space).
- Integrity (avoidance of delete anomalies).

Normalization of Candidate Tables Derived from ER Diagrams

Normalization of candidate tables (Step II.d in the database life cycle) is accomplished by analyzing the FDs associated with those tables: explicit FDs from the database requirements analysis ("The Design of Normalized Tables: A Simple Example" section), FDs derived from the ER diagram, and FDs derived from intuition.

Primary FDs represent the dependencies among the data elements that are keys of entities—that is, the inter-entity dependencies. *Secondary FDs*, on the other hand, represent dependencies among data elements that comprise a single entity—that is, the intraentity dependencies. Typically, primary FDs are derived from the ER diagram, and secondary FDs are obtained explicitly from the requirements analysis. If the ER constructs do not include nonkey attributes used in secondary FDs, the data requirements specification or data dictionary must be consulted. Table 6.2 shows the types of primary FDs derivable from each type of ER construct.

Each candidate table will typically have several primary and secondary FDs uniquely associated with it that determine the current degree of normalization of the table. Any of the well-known techniques for increasing the degree of normalization can be applied to each table, to the desired degree stated in the requirements specification. Integrity is maintained by requiring the normalized table schema to include all data dependencies existing in the candidate table schema.

Any table **B** that is subsumed by another table **A** can potentially be eliminated. Table **B** is subsumed by another table **A** when all the attributes in **B** are also contained in **A**, and all data dependencies in **B** also occur in **A**. As a trivial case, any table containing only a composite key and no nonkey attributes is automatically subsumed by any other table containing the same key attributes because

Table 6.2 Primary FDs Derivable from ER Constructs

Degree	Connectivity	Primary FD
Binary or Binary Recursive	one-to-one	2 ways: key(one side) -> key(one side)
	one-to-many	key(many side) -> key(one side)
	many-to-many	none (composite key from both sides)
Ternary	one-to-one-to-one	3 ways: key(one), key(one) -> key(one)
	one-to-one-to-many	2 ways: key(one), key(many) -> key(one)
	one-to-many-to-many	1 way: key(many), key(many) -> key(one)
	many-to-many-to-many	none (composite key from all three sides)
Generalization	none	none (secondary FD only)

the composite key is the weakest form of data dependency. If, however, tables **A** and **B** represent the supertype and subtype cases, respectively, of entities defined by the generalization abstraction, and **A** subsumes **B** because **B** has no additional specific attributes, the designer must collect and analyze additional information to decide whether or not to eliminate **B**.

A table can also be subsumed by the construction of a join of two other tables (a "join" table). When this occurs, the elimination of a subsumed table may result in the loss of retrieval efficiency, although storage and update costs will tend to be decreased. This trade-off must be further analyzed during physical design with regard to processing requirements to determine whether elimination of the subsumed table is reasonable.

To continue our example company personnel and project database, we want to obtain the primary FDs by applying the rules in Table 6.2 to each relationship in the ER diagram in Figure 4.3 (see Chapter 4). The results are shown in Table 6.3.

Next we want to determine the secondary FDs. Let us assume that the dependencies in Table 6.4 are derived from the requirements specification and intuition.

Table 6.3 Primary FDs Derived from the ER diagram in Figure 4.3

dept_no -> div_no	in Department from relationship "contains"
emp_id -> dept_no	in Employee from relationship "has"
div_no -> emp_id	in Division from relationship "is-headed-by"
dept_no -> emp_id	from binary relationship "is-managed-by"
emp_id -> desktop_no	from binary relationship "is-allocated"
desktop_no -> emp_id	from binary relationship "is-allocated"
emp_id -> workstation_no	from binary relationship "has-allocated"
workstation_no -> emp_id	from binary relationship "has-allocated"
emp_id -> spouse_id	from binary recursive relationship "is-married-to"
spouse_id -> emp_id	from binary recursive relationship "is-married-to"
emp_id, loc_name -> project_name	from ternary relationship "assigned-to"

Table 6.4 Secondary FDs Derived from the Requirements Specification

FD	Entity
div_no -> div_name, div_addr	Division
dept_no -> dept_name, dept_addr, mgr_id	Department
emp_id -> emp_name, emp_addr, office_no, phone_no	Employee
skill_type -> skill_descrip	Skill
project_name -> start_date, end_date, head_id	Project
loc_name -> loc_county, loc_state, zip	Location
mgr_id -> mgr_start_date, beeper_phone_no	Manager
assoc_name -> assoc_addr, phone_no, start_date	Prof-assoc
desktop_no -> computer_type, serial_no	Desktop
workstation_no -> computer_type, serial_no	Workstation

Normalization of the candidate tables is accomplished next. In Table 6.5 we bring together the primary and secondary FDs that apply to each candidate table. We note that for each table except **employee**, all attributes are functionally dependent on the primary key (denoted by the left

Table 6.5 Candidate Tables (and FDs) from ER Diagram Transformation

division	div_no -> div_name, div_addr
	div_no -> emp_id
department	dept_no -> dept_name, dept_addr, mgr_id
	dept_no -> div_no
	dept_no -> emp_id
employee	emp_id -> emp_name, emp_addr, office_no, phone_no
	emp_id -> dept_no
	emp_id -> spouse_id
	spouse_id -> emp_id
manager	mgr_id -> mgr_start_date, beeper_phone_no
secretary	none
engineer	emp_id -> desktop_no
technician	none
skill	skill_type -> skill_descrip
project	project_name -> start_date, end_date, head_id
location	loc_name -> loc_county, loc_state, zip
prof_assoc	assoc_name -> assoc_addr, phone_no, start_date
desktop	desktop_no -> computer_type, serial_no
	desktop_no -> emp_id
workstation	workstation_no -> computer_type, serial_no
	workstation_no -> emp_id
assigned_to	emp_id, loc_name -> project_name
skill_used	none
belongs_to	none

side of the FDs), and are thus BCNF. In the case of the **employee** table we note that spouse_id determines emp_id and emp_id is the primary key; thus, spouse_id can be shown to be a superkey (see Superkey Rule 2 in the "Determining the Minimum Set of 3NF Tables" section). Therefore, **employee** is found to be BCNF.

In general, we observe that candidate tables, like the ones shown in Table 6.5, are fairly good indicators of the final schema and normally require very little refinement to get to 3NF or BCNF. This observation is important—good initial conceptual design usually results in tables that are already normalized or are very close to being normalized, and thus the normalization process is usually a simple task.

Determining the Minimum Set of 3NF Tables

A minimum set of 3NF tables can be obtained from a given set of FDs by using the well-known synthesis algorithm developed by Bernstein (1976). This process is particularly useful when you are confronted with a list of hundreds or thousands of FDs that describe the semantics of a database. In practice, the ER modeling process automatically decomposes this problem into smaller subproblems: The attributes and FDs of interest are restricted to those attributes within an entity (and its equivalent table) and any foreign keys that might be imposed upon that table. Thus, the database designer will rarely have to deal with more than 10 or 20 attributes at a time, and in fact, most entities are initially defined in 3NF already. For those tables that are not yet in 3NF, only minor adjustments will be needed in most cases.

In the following, we briefly describe the synthesis algorithm for those situations where the ER model is not useful for the decomposition. In order to apply the algorithm, we make use of the well-known Armstrong axioms, which define the basic relationships among FDs.

Inference Rules (Armstrong Axioms)

Reflexivity	If Y is a subset of the attributes of X, then X -> Y (i.e., if X is ABCD and Y is ABC, then X -> Y; trivially, X -> X).
Augmentation	If X -> Y and Z is a subset of table **R** (i.e., Z is any attribute in **R**), then XZ -> YZ.
Transitivity	If X -> Y and Y -> Z, then X -> Z.
Pseudotransitivity	If X -> Y and YW -> Z, then XW -> Z. (Transitivity is a special case of pseudotransitivity when W = null.)
Union	If X -> Y and X -> Z, then X -> YZ (or equivalently X -> Y,Z).
Decomposition	If X -> YZ, then X -> Y and X -> Z.

These axioms can be used to derive two practical rules of thumb for deriving superkeys of tables where at least one superkey is already known.

Superkey Rule 1 Any FD involving all attributes of a table defines a superkey as the left side of the FD.

Given: Any FD containing all attributes in the table **R**(W, X,Y,Z), i.e. XY -> WZ.

Proof:

1. XY -> WZ as given.
2. XY -> XY by applying the reflexivity axiom.
3. XY -> XYWZ by applying the union axiom.
4. XY uniquely determines every attribute in table **R**, as shown in 3.
5. XY uniquely defines table **R**, by the definition of a table as having no duplicate rows.
6. XY is therefore a superkey, by definition.

Superkey Rule 2 Any attribute that functionally determines a superkey of a table is also a superkey for that table.

Given: Attribute A is a superkey for table **R**(A,B,C,D,E), and E -> A.

Proof:

1. Attribute A uniquely defines each row in table **R**, by the definition of a superkey.
2. A -> ABCDE by applying the definition of a superkey and a relational table.
3. E -> A as given.
4. E -> ABCDE by applying the transitivity axiom.
5. E is a superkey for table **R**, by definition.

Before we can describe the synthesis algorithm, we must define some important concepts. Let H be a set of FDs that represents at least part of the known semantics of a database. The closure of H, specified by H^+, is the set of all FDs derivable from H using the Armstrong axioms or inference rules. For example, we can apply the transitivity rule to the following FDs in set H:

A-> B, B -> C, A -> C, and C -> D

to derive the FDs A -> D and B -> D. All six FDs constitute the closure H^+. A cover of H, called H', is any set of FDs from which H^+ can be derived. Possible covers for this example are:

1. A -> B, B -> C, C -> D, A -> C, A -> D, B -> D (trivial case where H' and H^+ are equal)

2. A -> B, B -> C, C -> D, A -> C, A -> D
3. A -> B, B -> C, C -> D, A -> C (this is the original set H)
4. A -> B, B -> C, C -> D

A nonredundant cover of H is a cover of H that contains no proper subset of FDs that is also a cover. In this example, cover 4 is nonredundant. The following synthesis algorithm requires nonredundant covers.

3NF Synthesis Algorithm

Given a set of FDs, H, we determine a minimum set of tables in 3NF.

$$
\begin{array}{lll}
\text{H:} & \text{AB -> C} & \text{DM -> NP} \\
& \text{A -> DEFG} & \text{D -> M} \\
& \text{E -> G} & \text{L -> D} \\
& \text{F -> DJ} & \text{PQR -> ST} \\
& \text{G -> DI} & \text{PR -> S} \\
& \text{D -> KL} &
\end{array}
$$

From this point the process of arriving at the minimum set of 3NF tables consists of five steps:
1. Eliminate extraneous attributes in the left sides of the FDs.
2. Search for a nonredundant cover, G of H.
3. Partition G into groups so that all FDs with the same left side are in one group.
4. Merge equivalent keys.
5. Define the minimum set of normalized tables.

Now we discuss each step in turn, in terms of the preceding set of FDs, H.

Step 1: Elimination of Extraneous Attributes

The first task is to get rid of extraneous attributes in the left sides of the FDs. The following two relationships (rules) among attributes on the left side of an FD provide the means to reduce the left side to fewer attributes.

Reduction Rule 1 XY -> Z and X -> Z => Y is extraneous on the left side (applying the reflexivity and transitivity axioms).

Reduction Rule 2 XY -> Z and X -> Y => Y is extraneous; therefore, X -> Z (applying the pseudotransitivity axiom).

Applying these *reduction rules* to the set of FDs in H, we get:

DM -> NP and D -> M => D -> NP

PQR -> ST and PR -> S => PQR -> T

Step 2: Search for a Nonredundant Cover

We must eliminate any FD derivable from others in H using the inference rules. The transitive FDs to be eliminated are:

A-> E and E -> G => eliminate A -> G

A-> F and F -> D => eliminate A -> D

Step 3: Partitioning of the Nonredundant Cover

To partition the nonredundant cover into groups so that all FDs with the same left side are in one group, we must separate the nonfully functional dependencies and transitive dependencies into separate tables. At this point we have a feasible solution for 3NF tables, but it is not necessarily the minimum set.

These nonfully functional dependencies must be put into separate groups (potential tables):

AB -> C

A-> EF

The groups with the same left side are:

G1: AB -> C	G6: D -> KLMNP
G2: A -> EF	G7: L -> D
G3: E -> G	G8: PQR -> T
G4: G -> DI	G9: PR -> S
G5: F -> DJ	

Step 4: Merge of Equivalent Keys (Merge of Tables)

In this step we merge groups with left sides that are equivalent (e.g., X -> Y and Y -> X imply that X and Y are equivalent). This step produces a minimum set of tables.

1. Write out the closure of all left side attributes resulting from Step 3, based on transitivities.
2. Using the closures, find tables that are subsets of other groups and try to merge them. Use Superkey Rule 1 and Superkey Rule 2 to establish if the merge will result in FDs with superkeys on the left side. If not, try using the axioms to modify the FDs to fit the definition of superkeys.

3. After the subsets are exhausted, look for any overlaps among tables and apply Superkey Rules 1 and 2 (and the axioms) again.

In this example, note that G7 (L -> D) has a subset of the attributes of G6 (D -> KLMNP). Therefore, we merge to a single table, **R6**, with FDs D -> KLMNP, L -> D, because it satisfies 3NF: D is a superkey by Superkey Rule 1 and L is a superkey by Superkey Rule 2.

Step 5: Definition of the Minimum Set of Normalized Tables

The minimum set of normalized tables has now been determined. We define these tables below in terms of the table name, the attributes in the table, the FDs in the table, and the candidate keys for that table:

R1: ABC (AB -> C with key AB)
R2: AEF (A -> EF with key A)
R3: EG (E -> G with key E)
R4: DGI (G -> DI with key G)
R5: DFJ (F -> DJ with key F)
R6: DKLMNP (D -> KLMNP, L -> D, with keys D, L)
R7: PQRT (PQR -> T with key PQR)
R8: PRS (PR -> S with key PR)

Note that this result is not only 3NF, but also BCNF, which is very frequently the case. This fact suggests a practical algorithm for a (near) minimum set of BCNF tables: Use Bernstein's algorithm to attain a minimum set of 3NF tables, then inspect each table for further decomposition (or partial replication, as shown in the "Boyce-Codd Normal Form" section above) to BCNF.

Summary

In this chapter we defined the constraints imposed on tables, most commonly the functional dependencies, or FDs. Based on these constraints, practical normal forms for database tables are defined: 1NF, 2NF, 3NF, and BCNF. All are based on the types of FDs present. In this chapter, a practical algorithm for finding the minimum set of 3NF tables is given.

The following statements summarize the functional equivalence between the ER model and normalized tables:
1. *Within an entity.* The level of normalization is totally dependent on the interrelationships among the key

and nonkey attributes. It could be any form from unnormalized to BCNF.

2. *Binary (or binary recursive) one-to-one or one-to-many relationship.* Within the "child" entity, the foreign key (a replication of the primary key of the "parent") is functionally dependent on the child's primary key. This is at least BCNF, assuming that the entity by itself, without the foreign key, is already BCNF.

3. *Binary (or binary recursive) many-to-many relationship.* The intersection table has a composite key and possibly some nonkey attributes functionally dependent on it. This is BCNF.

4. *Ternary relationship:*
   a. one-to-one-to-one => three overlapping composite keys, BCNF
   b. one-to-one-to-many => two overlapping composite keys, BCNF
   c. one-to-many-to-many => one composite key, BCNF
   d. many-to-many-to-many => one composite key with three attributes, BCNF

In summary, we observed that a good, methodical conceptual design procedure often results in database tables that are either normalized (BCNF) already, or can be normalized with very minor changes.

Tips and Insights for Database Professionals

Tip 1. Analyze the potential for performance benefits first before normalizing; you want to see if performance gains can be had.
   a. Potential to reduce storage space by reducing redundancy (potential, but not guaranteed).
   b. Potential to reduce update time (as a result of reducing redundancy).
   c. Potential to reduce query time (as a result of smaller tables).

Tip 2. Boyce-Codd normal form (BCNF), a variant of third normal form (3NF), is the most practical goal for tables in relational databases. It is easy to conceptualize (has the simplest definition) and eliminates almost all delete anomalies, and thus preserves data integrity to a high degree. Most entities in ER models translate directly to BCNF tables. Those entities that don't can usually be split into BCNF tables by simple decomposition applying the BCNF definition.

Tip 3. Consider denormalization if performance is compromised too much by normalization. Sometimes you can trade off the increase in update cost due to redundancy versus lower query cost due to redundancy, and still maintain data integrity.

Literature Summary

Good summaries of normal forms can be found in Date (2003), Kent (1983), Dutka and Hanson (1989), and Smith (1985). Algorithms for normal form decomposition and synthesis techniques are given in Bernstein (1976), Fagin (1977), and Maier (1983). The earliest work done in normal forms was by Codd (1970, 1974) and by Armstrong (1974).

7

AN EXAMPLE OF LOGICAL DATABASE DESIGN

The following example illustrates how to proceed through the requirements analysis and logical design steps of the database life cycle, in a practical way, for a relational database.

Requirements Specification

The management of a large retail store would like a database to keep track of sales activities. The requirements analysis for this database led to the six entities and their unique identifiers shown in Table 7.1.

The following assertions describe the data relationships:

- Each customer has one job title, but different customers may have the same job title.
- Each customer may place many orders, but only one customer may place a particular order.
- Each department has many salespeople, but each salesperson must work in only one department.
- Each department has many items for sale, but each item is sold in only one department ("item" means item type, like IBM PC).
- For each order, items ordered in different departments must involve different salespeople, but all items ordered

Table 7.1 Requirements Analysis Results

Entity	Entity Key	Key Length (max) in characters	Number of Occurrences
Customer	cust-no	6	80,000
Job	job-no	24	80
Order	order-no	9	200,000
Salesperson	sales-id	20	150
Department	dept-no	2	10
Item	item-no	6	5000

within one department must be handled by exactly one salesperson. In other words, for each order, each item has exactly one salesperson; and for each order, each department has exactly one salesperson.

For physical design (access methods, etc.) it is necessary to determine what kind of processing needs to be done on the data—that is, what are the queries and updates needed to satisfy the user requirements, and what are their frequencies? In addition, the requirements analysis should determine if there will be substantial database growth (i.e., volumetrics); what time frame that growth will take place over; and whether the frequency and type of queries and updates will change, as well. Decay as well as growth should be estimated, as each will have a significant effect on the later stages of database design.

Design Problems

1. Using the information given and, in particular, the five assertions, derive a conceptual data model and a set of functional dependencies (FDs) that represent all the known data relationships.
2. Transform the conceptual data model into a set of candidate SQL tables. List the tables, their primary keys, and other attributes.
3. Find the minimum set of normalized (BCNF) tables that are functionally equivalent to the candidate tables.

Logical Design

Our first step is to develop a conceptual data model diagram and a set of FDs to correspond to each of the assertions given. Figure 7.1 presents the diagram for the entity–relationship (ER) model and Figure 7.2 shows the equivalent diagram for the Unified Modeling Language (UML). Normally, the conceptual data model is developed without knowing all the FDs, but in this example the non-key attributes are omitted so that the entire database can be represented with only a few statements and FDs. The results of this analysis, relative to each of the assertions given, are shown in Table 7.2.

The candidate tables needed to represent the semantics of this problem can be derived easily from the constructs for entities and relationships. Primary keys and foreign keys are explicitly defined.

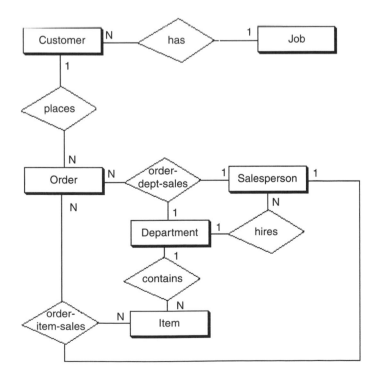

Figure 7.1 Conceptual data model diagram for the ER model.

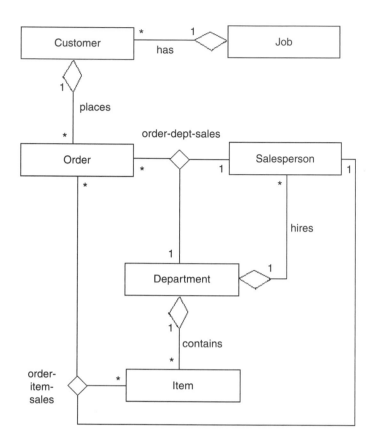

Figure 7.2 Conceptual data
model diagram for UML.

Table 7.2 Results of the Analysis of the Conceptual Data Model

ER Construct	FDs
Customer(many): Job(one)	cust-no -> job-title
Order(many): Customer(one)	order-no -> cust-no
Salesperson(many): Department(one)	sales-id -> dept-no
Item(many): Department(one)	item-no -> dept-no
Order(many): Item(many): Salesperson(one)	order-no, item-no -> sales-id
Order(many): Department(many): Salesperson(one)	order-no, dept-no -> sales-id

```
create table customer
   (cust_no char(6),
   job_title varchar(256),
   primary key (cust_no),
   foreign key (job_title) references job
      on delete set null on update cascade);
create table job
   (job_no char(6),
   job_title varchar(256),
   primary key (job_no));
create table order
   (order_no char(9),
   cust_no char(6) not null,
   primary key (order_no),
   foreign key (cust_no) references customer
      on delete set null on update cascade);
create table salesperson
   (sales_id char(10)
   sales_name varchar(256),
   dept_no char(2),
   primary key (sales_id),
   foreign key (dept_no) references department
      on delete set null on update cascade);
create table department
   (dept_no char(2),
   dept_name varchar(256),
   manager_name varchar(256),
   primary key (dept_no));
create table item
   (item_no char(6),
   dept_no char(2),
   primary key (item_no),
   foreign key (dept_no) references department
      on delete set null on update cascade);
create table order_item_sales
   (order_no char(9),
   item_no char(6),
   sales_id varchar(256) not null,
```

```
        primary key (order_no, item_no),
        foreign key (order_no) references order
           on delete cascade on update cascade,
        foreign key (item_no) references item
           on delete cascade on update cascade,
        foreign key (sales_id) references salesperson
           on delete cascade on update cascade);

create table order_dept_sales
    (order_no char(9),
    dept_no char(2),
    sales_id varchar(256) not null,
    primary key (order_no, dept_no),
    foreign key (order_no) references order
       on delete cascade on update cascade,
    foreign key (dept_no) references department
       on delete cascade on update cascade,
    foreign key (sales_id) references salesperson
       on delete cascade on update cascade);
```

Note that it is often better to put foreign key definitions in separate (alter) statements. This prevents the possibility of getting circular definitions with very large schemas.

This process of decomposition and reduction of tables moves us closer to a minimum set of normalized (BCNF) tables, as shown in Table 7.3.

The reductions shown in this section have decreased storage space and update costs and have maintained the normalization of BCNF (and thus 3NF). On the other hand,

Table 7.3 Decomposition and Reduction of Tables

Table	Primary Key	Likely Nonkeys
customer	cust_no	job_title, cust_name, cust_address
order	order_no	cust_no, item_no, date_of_purchase, price
salesperson	sales_id	dept_no, sales_name, phone_no
item	item_no	dept_no, color, model_no
order_item_sales	order_no, item_no	sales_id
order_dept_sales	order_no, dept_no	sales_id

however, we have potentially higher retrieval cost—for example, given the transaction "list all job_titles"—and have increased the potential for loss of integrity because we have eliminated simple tables with only key attributes. Resolution of these trade-offs depends on your priorities for your database.

The details of indexing are covered in the companion book *Physical Database Design* (Lightstone et al., 2007). However, during the logical design phase of defining SQL tables, it makes sense to start considering where to create indexes. At a minimum, all primary keys and all foreign keys should be indexed. Indexes are relatively easy to implement and store, and make a significant difference in reducing the access time to stored data.

Summary

In this chapter we developed a global conceptual schema and a set of SQL tables for a relational database, given the requirements specification for a retail store database. The example illustrates the database life cycle steps of conceptual data modeling, global schema design, transformation to SQL tables, and normalization of those tables. It summarizes the techniques presented in Chapters 1–6.

Tips and Insights for Database Professionals

Tip 1. Separate the logical and physical design steps to satisfy different objectives.

Tip 2. Tune a database periodically after initial implementation is completed.

8

OBJECT-RELATIONAL DESIGN

CHAPTER OUTLINE

Object orientation is a standard feature of many modern programming languages and software systems. This notion has also been incorporated into data management systems. In this chapter we will study the interplay of object orientation and databases. Programming languages in which application software is written play a large role in this interplay, and will be discussed. This will also lead naturally into a discussion of how to store XML data in a relational database (see Chapter 9).

This chapter begins with an overview describing object orientation. The following two sections continue with a discussion of object-oriented and object-relational databases.

Object Orientation

The world is modeled as a collection of objects that interact with one another. Correspondingly, software is also designed as a collection of interacting objects. A software object is a logical unit: a bundle of data and procedures that belong together. Frequently, a software object represents a real-world object.

Figure 8.1 shows a real-world object and its representation as a collection of software objects. Observe that many components of the real-world object have been pulled out and represented as objects themselves, which indeed they are. All edges in this figure represent inclusion links. What unit of information comprises a software object is a design decision. In this example, the designer has chosen to

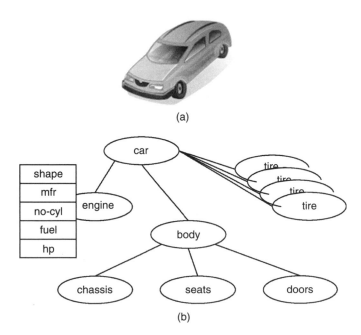

Figure 8.1 (a) A real-world object and (b) its representation as a collection of software objects.

represent each tire as a separate object, but grouped all four doors together as a single object. Objects have attributes, which are shown only for the engine object in the figure.

There are several notions central to most object-oriented systems. Note that there is no single agreed upon hard definition of an object-oriented system or database; rather, there is a list of properties, most of which one would expect an object-oriented system to have. We briefly describe some central notions below.

Classes and Instances

Many objects are similar. Similar objects are grouped together into a *class*. Individual objects in the class are called *instances* of the class. From a programming perspective, data structures and methods are associated with the class, and are part of the class definition. From a database perspective, one can think of each relation as a class, and each tuple (or record) in the relation as an instance of the relation class.

Inheritance

Often, there are related classes that share some properties but not all. For example, a vehicle may be a car, truck, or motorcycle, each of which has some unique properties (for example, the number of axles is a variable that matters for trucks, is unnecessary for cars (which always have two), and is meaningless for motorcycles). Yet, all vehicles share many common properties, such as owner, model year, brand name, registration number, etc. In such situations, inheritance is useful, as we have already seen with the generalization hierarchy in the context of entity-relationship (ER) design in Chapter 2. Inheritance is a central concept in object-oriented systems.

Identity

A crucial property of object-oriented systems is the notion of object *identity*. Over time, attributes of an object may change value; however, its identity remains the same. Think of a person—over their lifetime there are likely to be several changes of address, phone number, and so on; there may even be changes in name; however, we know that it is still the same person even with the new name and new address—their identity has not changed. In an object-oriented system, the identity of an object is a hidden, system-managed attribute. Programs cannot directly access or manipulate the value of this attribute. However, one can compare the identities of two object instance variables to see if they indeed refer to the same object instance. Two object instances are distinct if their identities are different, even if they are identical on every other attribute.

Encapsulation

Typically, to interact with an object, it suffices to know its behavior. There is no need to know how this behavior is implemented. The notion of encapsulation is that an object makes only its interface public. Following this discipline permits changes to the internal implementation of an object with no impact on the correctness of other code. In contrast, if we did not use encapsulation, whenever any change is made anywhere, we would have to worry about all the places in our code that could possibly be impacted. Note that both the behavior and the interface of an object are determined by the class the object belongs to. When we talk about encapsulation, we are considering object classes. (In contrast, when we talk about object identities, we are considering object instances—it makes no sense to talk about the identity of an object class.)

Abstraction

Abstraction is a central concept in all of computer science, but is particularly important in the context of object orientation. The basic idea is to strip away the details and retain exactly as much of real-life complexity as is required for the task at hand. In other words, given the complexity of the world around us, do not try to reflect all of this complexity. Rather, choose only what is required. When real-world objects are placed into classes, there is usually a process of abstraction—we make choices about the properties of the objects we really care about, and ignore differences between objects in other respects.

There is no formal definition of object orientation. There is no complete list of properties for objects. As such,

we have focused here on the most important characteristics of object orientation. Object orientation is a
core part of the computer science curriculum at most
universities today. Most programmers learn at least the
basic concepts of object orientation, and its use in
programming languages such as C++ and Java.

Object-Oriented Databases

Given the importance of object orientation to much of
computer science, a natural question to consider is what
this means in the context of databases. In the late 1980s
and early 1990s, object-oriented databases were developed
as an attempt to address this question. In this section,
we will describe the main features of object-oriented
databases. However, before doing so, it is worthwhile to
consider key differences between programming language
models of data and database models of data: a difference
popularly known as the *impedance mismatch*.

The Impedance Mismatch

When you run a computer program, it explicitly reads
any input it requires, performs the computations it is sup-
posed to perform, and then explicitly writes its output.
While the program is running, it has many variables that
it is manipulating. These variables have values, and the
state of the program is recorded in the computer system
memory (or virtual memory). However, once the program
stops running, it has no data saved. The program releases
all of the system memory it had acquired. The typical
source of program input and destination of program output is a file. Multiple programs can run simultaneously
on a computer, but each works with its own private data
in its part of the system memory. Even if multiple programs
read inputs from the same system files, any manipulations
they performed on that data are their own, unless explicitly communicated to others through a heavyweight
mechanism.

In contrast, a database system is designed for sharing
persistent data. The data in a database does not go away
when some program stops running. Furthermore, it is

expected that multiple applications will access the database concurrently, and database systems build extensive transaction management support for this purpose.

For these reasons, data does not pass easily between the database world and the programming language world. The database wants to see queries and updates in a language such as SQL, whereas the program wants to read to and write from a sequential file. Furthermore, the unit of access for a relational database is a set of records—when an SQL query is run, the result is itself a relation (or table) with a schema determined by the query, and this relation, in general, may have any number of records in it. In contrast, the unit of access for the program is at most one record at a time. Usually, the program has to execute code on a per-record basis. For example, reading a record into a program involves the steps of obtaining the record in database format, parsing it, using its content to populate elements of a suitable data structure in the program (or an instance of an appropriate object class), and then manipulating it as required. If the database provides a set of records, these have to be "held" in a temporary space while the program loops through and processes the set one record at a time.

In short, transferring data between a database and an application program is an onerous process, because of both difficulty of programming and performance overhead. This difficulty is attributed to an *impedance mismatch* between databases and programming systems. Note that the impedance mismatch is not on account of object orientation; it is equally present if the programming system is not object-oriented.

Object-Relational Mapping

Beyond the impedance mismatch just described, there is also a mismatch of "schema." Typically, a program is written in an object-oriented programming language, such as Java or C++. The unit of input and output is an object, which often has a complex structure, including potentially repeated subelements and references to other objects. In contrast, relational databases have normalized schema, designed according to the principles discussed in the preceding chapters. Typically, the information contained in an object does not fit into a single tuple (or record). Rather, it is "shredded" across multiple records in multiple tables.

Figure 8.2 shows the car object from Figure 8.1 as a collection of tables. Included objects (such as engine) have been placed in their own tables. If we do not do this, the **car** table would have hundreds of attributes. Observe also that we have no choice, if we want a normalized design, with respect to the ownership data—some cars, such as C2, may have had only one owner, while others, such as C1, may have had many. There is no way to include all this ownership history within a single car record as a collection of software objects. Observe that many components of the real-world object have been pulled out and represented as objects themselves, which indeed they are. All edges in this figure represent inclusion links. What unit of information comprises a software object is a design decision. In this example, the designer has chosen to represent each tire as a separate object, but grouped all four doors together as a single object. Objects have attributes, which are shown only for the engine object in the figure.

If you use object-relational mapping software, it will take care of the mapping and at least paper over the impedance mismatch. There are dozens of software systems with object-relational mapping capability, such as

car	engine	body	tire1	tire2	tire3	tire4
C1	E23	B35	T2417	T2418	T2419	T2420
C2	E99	B77	T2819	T2820	T3219	T3220

engine	shape	num-cylinders	fuel	manufacturer	horsepower
E23	V	8	Gasoline	Ford	150
E99	Straight	4	Diesel	Chrysler	120

body	chassis	seats	doors
B35	H5	S3	D4
B77	H7	S7	D7

car	owner	purchase date
C1	Arnold	Jan. 2010
C1	Betty	Jan. 2011
C1	Charlie	May 2011
C2	Diane	April 2011

Figure 8.2 The car object of Figure 8.1 represented as a collection of tables.

Hibernate, ADO.NET Entity Framework, Django, Toplink, and ActiveRecord. In the less likely scenario that you have to manage the mapping yourself, there is a need to first define the database schema and then the mapping. Since the object classes in the programming language have already been defined, this is a very different schema design problem than the green fields design discussed in the rest of this book. The choices are limited greatly by the object classes already defined. Yet, there remains considerable choice, and the factors in evaluating these choices are similar to the general case. We discuss the major differences below.

The space of design choices is limited by two extremes. At one extreme, each object is mapped to a table. Sometimes this may not be possible. For example, there is no way to capture in one table an object that includes other objects in a nested structure. There is also no way to represent set-valued attributes. In such cases, one has to create additional tables through the standard normalization process.

At the other extreme, each attribute can be shredded into its own table, with a two-column schema: an object ID column and an attribute column. The object can then be reconstructed by joining together all records from multiple tables with the same object ID. There are no normalization issues at this extreme.

The trade-off between the two extremes, and design choices in between, is primarily driven by performance. Since the database is expected to be accessed through the program, and since the program object class design is already fixed, there is less of a concern regarding the matching of schema to real-world objects, ease of expressing SQL queries, etc.

Persistent Programming Languages

A simple way to address the impedance mismatch is to permit programming languages to make selected objects persistent and then take care of the consequences "under the hood." If the programming language is object-oriented, we get the beginnings of an object-oriented database.

There are many issues to consider regarding persistent objects. First, a persistent object must have a referenceable location on disk, similar to a file locator. The identifier of the persistent object must be sufficient to find this location. Usually, this is implemented by having the identifier be the location address. But now an object identifier for a persistent object is a disk address, and therefore much bigger than an identifier for a regular (transient, in-memory) program object, for which the identifier is a location in memory.

This immediately leads to the second issue, having to do with object references. Object-oriented systems frequently include references to other objects. Traditional object systems use object identifiers for this purpose. Now that identifiers for persistent and in-memory objects are different, this difference impacts not only the object being identified, but also objects that reference them.

Figure 8.3 shows how pointers must be manipulated, as objects are moved in and out of the memory buffer. In Figure 8.3(a), there are four objects on the disk, with persistent pointers between them. In Figure 8.3(b), a copy of object B is brought into memory. Pointers from B both point to objects not in memory, so they remain unchanged. Pointers to B from objects on disk (such as A) do not need

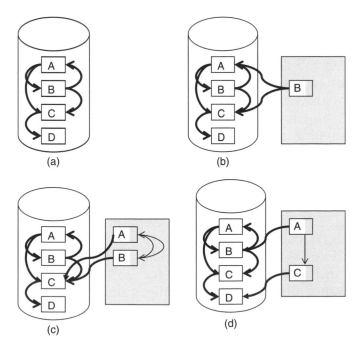

(a)

(b)

(c)

(d)

Figure 8.3 Persistent and in-memory pointers are different: (a) four objects on disk, with persistent pointers between them, (b) a copy of object B is brought into memory, (c) object A is brought into memory, and (d) object B is now placed back into disk and object C is brought into memory instead.

to be changed, because A cannot have its pointers dereferenced while being on disk. In Figure 8.3(c), Object A is also brought into memory. Now, any pointers between A and B become in-memory pointers rather than persistent pointers. But pointers to and from disk objects remain unchanged. Finally, in Figure 8.3(d) Object B is now placed back into disk, and object C brought into memory instead. All pointers to B from in-memory objects, such as A, have to be converted back to persistent pointers. However, pointers between C and in-memory objects, such as A, now become in-memory pointers.

One way to address these challenges with persistent objects is to have two distinct "flavors" of objects: those that are persistent, and those that are in-memory. Thus, for example, we could have an object class Queue and another object class Persistent_queue. Object instances of the former type would have ordinary object identifiers, whereas those of the latter would have the large persistent object identifiers.

However, this proposed solution introduces more problems of its own. When an object is referenced, the referencing object must know whether the object it references is persistent or not. Furthermore, it makes no sense for a persistent object to reference an in-memory object, because the latter may not be there the next time someone looks at the persistent object. These choices are not easy to make, and could lead to a combinatorial explosion of object types, one for each different type of reference. Furthermore, we require that objects be in memory to operate on them. Therefore, access to persistent objects will involve copying them into temporary in-memory objects, of a different object class, before manipulating them. That is to say, to be able to add an entry to a persistent queue, we have to copy it into an in-memory queue, add the entry, and then copy it back to the persistent queue. This is a great deal of computational effort and complexity for a simple task.

To avoid these difficulties, object-oriented database systems introduce a requirement for *orthogonality between persistence and type*. By this we mean that types in the persistent program language, or object classes in our terms, should not specify whether they are persistent. It should be possible to take an object of any class and make it persistent, without requiring transfer to a different persistent class.

Meeting this requirement is no easy feat, and is usually performed using some form of *pointer swizzling*. All object references in a persistent object are, obviously, persistent, disk-based pointers. When the object is read into memory, these references can be converted (swizzled) into in-memory pointers if the objects referred to are in memory, or are proactively also brought into memory. There are engineering decisions with regard to how proactive to be, and implementation complexity in maintaining a table of persistent objects currently read in. The exact choices made differ between implementations, and are beyond the scope of this book.

Features of Object-Oriented Database Systems

Once we have achieved the ability to move objects easily between in-memory application programs and persistent storage, the impedance mismatch is largely resolved. However, there remain many database features that are missing from the persistent programming language idea expressed above. Foremost among these is a declarative query facility, allowing a programmer to specify objects of interest from a potentially large collection.

While there is no formal definition of an object-oriented database system, there is broad consensus on a set of expected features. These were captured in an *Object-Oriented Database System Manifesto* (see Atkinson et al., 1989). The manifesto has two lists of features: a first list that is mandatory and a second list that is optional. In effect, the second list has features that many object-oriented database systems have, but have been deemed not required in every object-oriented database system. We will walk through these lists of features below.

Mandatory features of object-oriented database systems can be divided in three main categories:

Mandatory: basic programming features.
- Computational completeness. Relational databases are not computationally complete. For example, SQL was not able to express recursion until recently. In contrast,

most programming languages are computationally complete in that any computable function can be expressed in the language. We require that this also be true for the data manipulation language of an object-oriented database system.

- Extensibility. Users should be able to define new types in addition to system-defined types that come with the database. Objects of the two types should be manipulated in the same manner—there should be no visible difference in the way they are referenced in the data manipulation language, even if there are significant differences in the implementation.

Mandatory: features that have to do with object orientation.

- Complex objects
- Object identity
- Encapsulation
- Types and classes
- Class or type Hierarchies.

We have previously discussed inheritance in the context of ER diagrams. Object-oriented systems typically deal with inheritance in a much more serious way. To this end, we identify a sequence of progressively more restrictive inheritance policies. We say that a type *t substitution inherits* from a type *t'*, if any place where we can have an object of type *t'*, we can substitute for it an object of type *t*. *Inclusion inheritance* states that *t* is a subtype of *t'*, if every object of type *t* is also an object of type *t'*. Clearly, if inclusion holds, then substitution is possible. So inclusion inheritance is a special case of substitution inheritance. *Constraint inheritance* is next and is a special case of inclusion inheritance. Here, *t* is a subtype of a type *t'*, if it consists of all objects of type *t* that satisfy a given constraint. If the constraint is that objects of type *t'* contain additional, more specific information, then we have *specialization inheritance*. Figure 8.4 illustrates the four types of inheritance.

- Overriding, overloading, and late binding. If a single function name applies to multiple functions it is called *overloading*. Thus, for numbers 2 and 3, we may have $2 + 3 = 5$, but for strings 2 and 3, we may have $2 + 3 = 23$. The operator $+$ has been overloaded to mean addition in the former case and concatenation in the latter case.

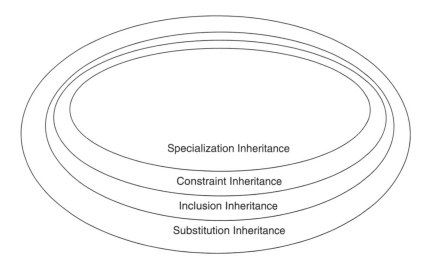

Figure 8.4 A Venn diagram showing the four types of inheritance, and how each completely includes the next.

Overriding of an inherited method occurs when the inheriting class defines its own implementation in preference to the one inherited. For example, a class Parallelogram may define a method area as a*b*sinθ. A class Rectangle may inherit from the Parallelogram class but redefine the method area more simply as just a*b, since θ is 90 degrees in this case. A class Square may inherit from the Rectangle class, and further redefine the method area as a^2. Which of these function implementations to use may not be evident at compile time if we simply write x.area(). If at runtime the system can determine the type of x and choose the correct method implementation, that is called *late-binding*.

Mandatory: features that are central to a database system. These features set an object-oriented database system apart from a persistent programming language.

- Persistence. Ordinary programming languages do not have persistence: All program data is lost when the program terminates, except what has explicitly been written to a file. The persistence facility allows data elements to remain forever, until explicitly deleted.
- Secondary storage management. Databases usually are too large to fit in main memory, and their implementation is cognizant of this.
- Concurrency.
- Recovery.

- Ad hoc query facility. In SQL, simple queries are very simple to express. In typical programming languages, there is so much bookkeeping stuff to do that a simple selection could take many lines of code. Object-oriented databases must somehow make it easier than this for users.

Optional features. These are features found in many object-oriented database system implementations, and in the minds of some people somehow associated with object-oriented databases, but not accepted, at least by the manifesto writers, as necessary for a system to call itself an object-oriented database.

- Multiple inheritance. The type Square inherits from both the type Rhombus and the type Rectangle. There are many difficult issues that arise, not the least of which is what precisely is inherited, particularly when there are differences between the parent types (Rhombus and Rectangle, respectively) in their attributes and methods.

- Type checking and type inferencing. *Type checking* is where the system uses its knowledge of the functionality of declared types to catch programming errors. For example, multiplication is meaningless for strings, so there is a type error if we write a=b*c, where b and c are strings. (Of course, this would have been a fine thing to say if b and c were integers.) *Type inferencing* is when the programmer does not declare the type in advance, and the system determines this by seeing what operations are invoked. For example, seeing the characters 23, the system may not know whether to interpret these as the string 23 or the number twenty-three. If it sees a statement such as a=23*2, then it knows 23 couldn't have been a string—it must be an integer.

- Distribution. Whether a database is centralized or distributed has nothing to do with object orientation. That this property is even mentioned is a historical artifact.

- Design transactions. Another historical artifact on account of the fact that at the time object-oriented systems were being developed, researchers were also studying systems that effectively supported long-lived transactions, such as those executed by human designers. (Traditional database transactions are optimized for short transactions.)

- Versions. This is yet another historical artifact. When human design is involved, it is often useful to keep multiple versions of objects around.

  Open features. Finally, with a view to being inclusive, the manifesto explicitly left completely open the choice of:
- Programming paradigm—for example, imperative, logical, or functional.
- Representation system. What the atomic types are, from which more complex object types are built.
- Type system. Many different techniques have been proposed for the definition of new types.
- Uniformity. The question is whether metadata is uniformly treated as a first-class object in the same way as data. Is a type an object? Is a method itself an object?

Object-Relational Databases

Relational databases had the lion's share of the market at the time object-oriented databases were created. In a very successful defensive move, relational database vendors scrambled to add object-oriented concepts to relational databases, thereby undercutting the market potential for object-oriented databases even before they had a chance to mature and become a market threat. The resulting products were not fully object-oriented. In fact, retaining the basic relational look and feel, as well as full compatibility with the pure relational databases in wide use, was a priority. In consequence, these databases were called *object-relational*.

User-Defined Functions and Abstract Data Types

A central feature that object-relational systems add to relational databases is the notion of an abstract data type. Traditional databases have a small set of predefined types (such as integer, date, double precision, etc.). An abstract data type (ADT) permits a complex object class to be defined as a database type. Instances of this data type can then be stored as attribute values in a table column of which the type has been defined as this ADT.

Storing a complex object as an attribute value limits the database to treating the object as an uninterpreted set of bits. But we may want the database to access components of the object. For example, we may wish to perform a selection based on the value of an attribute of the object. Or perhaps we want to define a sort order on the objects. For the database to be able to accomplish these tasks, *user-defined functions* are introduced. These are functions defined by the user, as the name suggests, rather than by the database system, and may be invoked during query processing. User-defined functions are invaluable in the manipulation of abstract data types, but they may be of use even otherwise. For example, we may wish to represent a yearly revenue attribute as the summation of four quarterly revenue attributes for every product class. The yearly revenue is clearly a redundant attribute. Nonetheless, one can imagine scenarios where we would want to store this explicitly, whether in the same table as the quarterly revenue or in a separate yearly revenue table (one row per product class in either case). A user-defined function could be used to compute the yearly revenue from the quarterly revenues, even though all fields involved are of type integer.

Support for user-defined functions in database systems introduces several challenges. The first involves security— poorly written code could corrupt the database. Database system builders have to take precautions to protect against this. Most systems perform a careful balancing act between giving users unfettered ability to do what they need to and preventing them from doing harm. The second challenge is performance—the database system may not know how long any user-defined function will run. This makes it difficult to perform the usual query optimization that is so important for database performance. Most database systems request hints from users regarding the expected runtimes of user-defined functions, and make conservative assumptions where this information is not available.

An Evaluation of Object-Relational Systems

A relational database with user-defined functions and abstract data types is called object-relational. Note that such a database does not provide true object orientation. In particular, the type system for abstract data types could be limited with respect to what a full-fledged programming language provides. Certainly, we do not have notions such as late binding. Furthermore, there is no notion of object identity.

In spite of these limitations, object-relational systems are in wide use today, and most experts generally agree that the relational database vendors have successfully fended off competition from object-oriented database systems by providing enough object-oriented functionality to satisfy most users. Some functionality not provided can be simulated. For example, object-relational systems do not have a notion of object identity, as mentioned above. However, relational database systems do have a notion of identifier key in many relational tables—for example, a **Student** table will have a student_id field as the primary key, an **Employee** table will have employee_id as the primary key, and so forth. These ID fields are visible to the user, but in effect serve the role of "object identifiers" for the object represented by the record. While the user could manipulate these fields, we do not expect the user to manipulate them, and in this way we weakly achieve the desired identifier behavior.

Design Considerations

When objects are stored in a relational database, there are many choices with regard to how this is done, as discussed above. With abstract data types, we have even more options. At one extreme, we could encapsulate the entire object and store it as a single attribute of a suitable abstract data type. At the other extreme, each part of the object can be its own attribute, and each object will then correspond to a record (or even multiple records, if there are nested objects or repeated attributes). The advantage of the former is that all of the member functions (or methods) associated with the object class can still be used. Some or all of them can even be registered as user-defined functions and made available to be called within the database. However, what these functions do, and what the values are for individual component attributes in the object, are all not visible to the database, and hence can only be used in limited ways when processing queries. In contrast, the latter design exposes all components of the object to the database, making it possible to query on, and return, parts of objects. The disadvantage is that there is no longer an integral object on which the original object member functions (or methods) can be run. Rather, new user-defined functions must be created to mimic the object methods that we wish to retain.

Sometimes, objects can be very large. This is particularly true when they contain multimedia content. One facility relational databases provide is that of "large objects." The idea is simply to have a database type for a large collection of bits that the database system does not attempt to interpret. This interpretation is left to some external application. Such objects are often called binary large objects (or BLOBs).

Figure 8.5 shows an example of a "mixed object size" table that may be created by the radiology department in a hospital. Each record has several small attributes, such as patient ID, date of X-ray, etc. In addition, there are two unusual fields: one, with radiologist's notes, is large, perhaps a few kilobytes; the second is very large, several megabytes, and contains the radiological image. A typical design in such cases is to place the text report and the image into a separate storage area. This figure shows two ways of accomplishing this partitioning. In Figure 8.5(a), an image ID and a note ID are used (as foreign keys) in the table at hand. A separate image table (not shown in the figure) is created, with the image ID as the key. Similarly, a separate notes table is also created. In Figure 8.5(b), notes and images are stored in files outside

Patient	Body Part	Date	Time	Radiologist	Notes	Image
P2345	Knee	Feb 2, 2011	3.45 p.m.	R2	N5	I5
P1278	Wrist	Aug 11, 2010	9.20 a.m.	R2	N7	I7

(a)

Patient	Body Part	Date	Time	Radiologist	Notes	Image
P2345	Knee	Feb 2, 2011	3.45 p.m.	R2	a.txt	a.bmp
P1278	Wrist	Aug 11, 2010	9.20 a.m.	R2	b.txt	b.bmp

(b)

Figure 8.5 An example of a "mixed object size" table: (a) an image ID and note ID are used as foreign keys, and (b) notes and images are stored in files outside the database system.

the database system. File names are recorded in the database to match images and notes with patient, date, etc.

Large object attributes have special design considerations. Usually, in a relational database, the unit of manipulation is the record. When a selection is performed, the entire record is retrieved, even if only some attributes of the record are actually required for display or downstream processing. If the discarded attributes are small, the additional cost of retrieving the entire record is not large. However, when there is a large attribute, it is extremely wasteful to retrieve it only to discard it. Furthermore, standard relational database backend processing is designed on the assumption that many records fit on a page. Some operations, such as a relational scan, can become extremely expensive if the record is very large.

To address this challenge we can separate the large object from the database record and store it separately. One way to do this is to have a file for each large object, and store the file name in the record. In this way, the size of the record is greatly reduced, and the large object is fetched only when it is required. The disadvantage is that the large object is no longer managed in the database. In consequence, for example, transactional consistency guarantees no longer apply to data in the large object.

In summary, there is a choice of placing large objects in the table or putting them in a separate file. The larger the object, the greater the cost of having it be part of the record. At some size, it becomes preferable to store it separately, even though such separation introduces its own issues.

Recognizing this trade-off, modern database systems often provide facilities to store each BLOB-valued attribute separately from the rest of the record it is part of. This is a form of vertical partitioning of the table. Note that the BLOB partition only has a single attribute, and even the table key is not replicated. This is really a second-class partition, linked from the main partition that has the rest of the table. Since the BLOB is not interpreted by the database, there is no possibility of an index.

Thus far we have considered two extremes: full-fledged objects that are managed by the database system, and BLOBs that are left completely uninterpreted. Some systems also provide facilities at an intermediate point, in the form of character large objects (or CLOBs). Here, the database system knows that the large object is a string of characters. As such, functions can be provided to process these character strings. However, any additional structure within the CLOB is not visible to the database system. For example, if a long book (or an XML document) is stored as a CLOB, the database system will know about the character strings in the document, but nothing about its paragraphs or sections.

Summary

Object orientation is a popular programming paradigm, and is widely used in modern programs. Central features of object-oriented systems include inheritance, identity, encapsulation, and abstraction. Objects bear some resemblance to entities in an ER model. For example, both objects and entities have attributes. Entities participate in relationships while objects have links to other objects.

The notion of types (or classes) is central in object-oriented systems. Each object has a type, and is considered an instance of its type.

Typical database systems are relational and not object-oriented. This results in an "impedance mismatch" as data is moved between tables in a relational database and objects in the application program. Considerable effort can be spent in marshalling arguments and moving data between the two.

Object-oriented database systems have been proposed as a means for addressing this mismatch by having the database system explicitly designed to support objects with links. There are many technical challenges in this regard, not the least of which is how to translate between in-memory pointers and disk pointers transparently when the respective address spaces are different, as are the space requirements for a pointer. One common solution to this particular problem is known as pointer swizzling.

There are many flavors of systems that try to marry concepts from object orientation and databases. These run the gamut from persistent programming languages to object-relational systems. There is no formal definition of what precisely is an object-oriented database system. However, there is a widely accepted manifesto jointly written by several leaders in the field that lays out the defining characteristics of an object-oriented database system.

Rather than build an object-oriented database, one could also attempt to manage better the mismatch between object-oriented systems and relational databases. Toward this end, relational database systems have added some object management capabilities, including support for large objects, user-defined functions, and abstract data types. In parallel with these efforts, there are also many tools that simplify and automate the task of storing object data in a relational database.

Tips and Insights for Database Professionals

Tip 1. Understand the respective strengths and weaknesses of object-oriented programming systems and of relational databases. The former are computationally complete, have sophisticated type management, and often better match the user view of the world; the latter are easier to manipulate in bulk, are easier to scale efficiently, and provide superior support for concurrency.

Tip 2. Recognize that most commercially available database systems today are object-relational in that they are not only relational databases, but also have at least some support for objects.

Tip 3. Exploit the complementary strengths of relational and object-oriented technology in designing your application flow. Since there remains an impedance mismatch, you will need to pay attention to make sure you are not crossing the boundary between the two more often than you need to.

Tip 4. Use commercial object-relational mapping software to simplify your life and better manage the impedance mismatch.

Literature Summary

Object-oriented programming as a concept was first described in the context of the Smalltalk language by Goldberg (1983), though earlier uses of the object concept in programming can be found, for example, in Simula 67 (see Kirkerud, 1989). Today, the Object Management Group (*www.omg.org*) serves as a central clearinghouse for information related to object orientation. Among other things, they also specify the standard for UML (*www.uml.org*).

There were many independent efforts at introducing some features of object orientation to databases and some features of persistence to programming languages. The *Object-Oriented Database System Manifesto* (see Atkinson et al., 1989) brought the community together to define the key characteristics of an object-oriented database. Over the next several years, a group called the Object Data Management Group carefully defined the standard, and published a book by Cattell (2000). A current portal for information on object-oriented databases is *www.odbms.org*.

9

XML AND WEB DATABASES

The eXtensible Markup Language (XML) has become a very popular way to represent data and transfer it between systems. XML also underlies many important Web technologies, and therefore is important when we consider the use of databases in the context of the Web. We begin this chapter with a quick overview of XML in the first section. We then discuss XML database design in the second section. We conclude, in the third section, with a discussion of Web-based database applications.

XML

Background

Whenever two parties have to share information, they have to agree on how this information is to be represented.

This agreement can come at several levels. Consider two humans trying to share some written information. A first step is to agree on the alphabet to be used. But that is not enough—if I write in German and you only know French, it is the same alphabet, but there can be no sharing. A second step is to agree on the language. Let us say we have settled on English. Even that is not quite enough—if I give you a document written in "legalese," or a scientific paper replete with medical terms, you are likely to have difficulty with many of the terms and language constructs I use. Finally, even having the same vocabulary may not be enough—think of how many times you have had misunderstandings because some meaning was misconstrued by the reader.

In the same vein, there is a hierarchy of levels at which standards can be established for the interchange of information. Each step up in the hierarchy makes sharing that much easier. To begin with, all modern computation is performed using a binary system with ones and zeroes. That much has been standard. Initially, each computer manufacturer had their own way of representing characters as zeroes and ones. Moving data from one brand of machine to another would involve painstaking recoding of individual characters. ASCII (and its successor universal character representations) came along and established a standard at the level of characters. But data was still shared as "streams" of characters. XML provides a standard syntax for representing arbitrary data structures. Now, computers and programs can share data structures instead of sharing character strings. Think of how you write programs in your favorite programming language. Chances are that you spend considerable effort reading in a stream of input characters, parsing this stream, and populating data structures before you get to doing anything useful in the program. In turn, the output is written out as a stream of characters. With XML, you can directly read in relevant data structures, perform the manipulations desired, and then write out data structures into XML.

Having a shared syntax for data structures still does not mean that there is perfect sharing of information. The next level up is the sharing of terminology and structural constructs. This turns out to be hard to do in a global way. However, the extensibility of XML has permitted shared-interest communities to define their own tag sets and schemas in XML to create their own markup language. Thus, we have ChemML, BioML, StatML, MathML, etc.— hundreds of languages that are easy to create and modify on top of XML, and serve as effective local standards. We can think of XML as comparable to English, and each of the specialized languages like the professional jargon used by various disciplines.

Definitions in XML

A *markup language* is a way of indicating, in a document, any items of interest, including items such as headings, paragraph boundaries, and highlighted concepts. Popular markup languages include LaTex for document processing and HTML for Web page construction. Most markup languages define a set of tags with associated meanings. For example, the tag <P> in HTML indicates the beginning of a new paragraph.

As noted, XML stands for eXtensible Markup Language, and was explicitly designed from the ground up with extensibility in mind. There are no predefined tags in XML. A tag <P> can refer to a paragraph boundary as in HTML, or to something entirely different, such as a price attribute. Obviously, markup is not very useful if it does not have meaning. The expectation is that groups of users will define sets of tags for which they agree on a shared meaning. This has facilitated the proliferation of XML-based markup languages, one for each application niche and user community, as described above.

An XML document is said to be *well formed* if (1) it has a matching end tag for every start tag, and if this start–end pair is properly nested either completely included in, completely including, or completely nonoverlapping with every other start–end tag pair, and (2) it has a "root" tag pair enclosing the entire document. Note that well-formedness is a purely syntactic property—it says nothing about what the tags are or what they mean. See Figure 9.1.

To be able to understand an XML document, one needs to know what the structure of the document is and what tags it contains. Such information about the structure of each document type is stated in a *Document Type Definition* (DTD). The notion of a DTD was first introduced in an influential

```
<document>
        <title> Not Well-Formed Example </title>
        <P>
                This document would look better in many colors.
                <font color="red">
                So we have made this text red,
        </P>
        <P>
                It is good to continue the same color across paragraphs.
                </font>
                But not forever.
        </P>
</document>
(a)


<item>
        <name> socks </name>
        <color> blue </color>
        <price>$5.00</price>
</item>
<item>
        <name> shoes </name>
        <color> black </color>
</item>
(b)
```

Figure 9.1 Two XML documents that are not well formed: (a) the <P> and <font> tags do not nest properly and (b) there is no root tag.

markup language called SGML, of which XML can be considered a lightweight version. Thus, each XML document has a type specified in a DTD. This description could be included directly with the document itself, in a preamble; or it could merely be a reference to (the URL of) a DTD defined elsewhere. Think of this the way you treat variable declarations in software. Most of the time, you declare variables in separate header files that are then included into your source files. But occasionally you may have additional declarations to make in your file itself (e.g., for some local variables). Also, for small projects, you may choose to do everything in one file without pulling out the declarations into a separate include file. In a similar vein, one expects that in most situations, documents will use known DTDs from some agreed on (within some community of interest) standard source. But occasionally, the creators of an XML document may wish to define their own DTD.

An XML document is said to be *valid* if it follows the rules specified in its DTD. Note that an XML document must be well formed before we can even begin to check its validity. Note also, that there can be well-formed XML documents that either do not specify a DTD at all, or are invalid with respect to a specified DTD.

Much of XML's heritage derives from document markup, and indeed the definitions given so far all clearly show this heritage. However, once you have the ability to specify tags of your choice, it becomes straightforward to encode databases in XML. For example, Figure 9.2 shows a relational table, of which the encoding in XML is in Figure 9.3. The resulting encoded relation is still called an XML *document*, even though it is really an XML representation of a database table. Multiple tables can also be encoded in a single XML document, merely by surrounding the set of individual table encodings with a `<database>` tag, as shown in Figure 9.4.

As databases began to be encoded in XML, the expressiveness of DTDs was found to be rather limiting. The notion of document type was "upgraded" to the notion of schema and a formal *XML Schema Definition* (XSD) language was developed. With this, we now require a valid XML document to follow the schema specified in its XSD (Figure 9.5).

XML elements may have attributes in addition to subelements. An *attribute* is used to record a property of, or some information about, the element. In contrast, a *subelement* is an element in its own right that just happens to be included as part of its parent element. For example, the paragraphs that are part of a document should be its subelements, while the date of creation should be an attribute. However, there are also limitations to attributes, which sometimes force things that are really attributes to be recorded as subelements. Attributes cannot have

id	name	address
123	Acme	3 Canyon Drive, Hell, MI, 48169
248	Perfection	5 Cloudy Way, Paradise, MI 49768
345	Foobar	88 Forever Loop, Purgatory, MI 49042
689	Far Out	55 Nowhere Road, Lost River, MN 56756

Figure 9.2 A relational table, shown encoded in the document of Figure 9.3.

```
<?xml version="1.0" ?>

<!DOCTYPE SUPPLIER-TABLE [
<!ELEMENT SUPPLIER-TABLE (SUPPLIER-TUPLE+)>
<!ELEMENT SUPPLIER-TUPLE(ID, NAME, ADDRESS)>
<!ELEMENT ID(#PCDATA)>
<!ELEMENT NAME(#PCDATA)>
<!ELEMENT ADDRESS(#PCDATA)>
]>

<SUPPLIER-TABLE>
   <SUPPLIER-TUPLE>
      <ID> 123 </ID>
      <NAME> Acme </NAME>
      <ADDRESS> 3 Canyon Drive, Hell, MI 48169</ADDRESS>
   </SUPPLIER-TUPLE>
   <SUPPLIER-TUPLE>
      <ID> 248 </ID>
      <NAME> Perfection </NAME>
      <ADDRESS> 5 Cloudy Way, Paradise, MI 49768</ADDRESS>
   </SUPPLIER-TUPLE>
   <SUPPLIER-TUPLE>
      <ID> 345 </ID>
      <NAME> Foobar </NAME>
      <ADDRESS> 88 Forever Loop, Purgatory, MI 49042</ADDRESS>
   </SUPPLIER-TUPLE>
   <SUPPLIER-TUPLE>
      <ID> 689 </ID>
      <NAME>Far Out </NAME>
      <ADDRESS> 55 Nowhere Road, Lost River, MN 56756 </ADDRESS>
   </SUPPLIER-TUPLE>
</SUPPLIER-TABLE>
```

Figure 9.3 A valid XML document. The preamble is the DTD.

structure—if we wish to record the first and last names of a document author separately, there is no way to have these as part of a single author attribute. One could (very inelegantly) have two separate attributes for author-firstname and author-lastname, or accept placing author as a subelement of the document. Furthermore, attributes cannot be repeated: They must have unique values. If the document has multiple authors, these cannot all be recorded as separate author attributes. We either have to include all author names into a single attribute, or make author a subelement.

```
<DATABASE>
<SUPPLIER-TABLE>
  <SUPPLIER-TUPLE>
    <ID> 123 </ID>
    <NAME> Acme </NAME>
    <ADDRESS> 3 Canyon Drive, Hell, MI 48169</ADDRESS>
  </SUPPLIER-TUPLE>
  <SUPPLIER-TUPLE>
    <ID> 248 </ID>
    <NAME> Perfection </NAME>
    <ADDRESS> 5 Cloudy Way, Paradise, MI 49768</ADDRESS>
  </SUPPLIER-TUPLE>
  <SUPPLIER-TUPLE>
    <ID> 345 </ID>
    <NAME> Foobar </NAME>
    <ADDRESS> 88 Forever Loop, Purgatory, MI 49042</ADDRESS>
  </SUPPLIER-TUPLE>
  <SUPPLIER-TUPLE>
    <ID> 689 </ID>
    <NAME>Far Out </NAME>
    <ADDRESS> 55 Nowhere Road, Lost River, MN 56756 </ADDRESS>
  </SUPPLIER-TUPLE>
</SUPPLIER-TABLE>
<OTHER-TABLE>
  <OTHER-TUPLE>
    <PART>widget </PART>
    <PRICE> 2 </PRICE>
    <QUANTITY> 4 </QUANTITY>
  </OTHER-TUPLE>
</OTHER-TABLE>
</DATABASE>
```

Figure 9.4 An XML encoding of multiple relational tables.

```
<?xml version="1.0" encoding="ISO-8859-1" ?>
<xs:schema xmlns:xs="http://www.w3.org/2001/XMLSchema">



<xs:element name="SUPPLIER-TABLE">
  <xs:complexType>
    <xs:element name="SUPPLIER-TUPLE" minOccurs=1
        maxOccurs="unbounded">
      <xs:complexType>
        <xs:sequence>
          <xs:element name="ID" type="xs:positiveInteger "/>
          <xs:element name="NAME" type="xs:string"/>
          <xs:element name="ADDRESS" type="xs:string"/>
        </xs:sequence>
      </xs:complexType>
    </xs:element>
  </xs:complexType>
</xs:element>
</xs:schema>
```

Figure 9.5 The schema corresponding to the document of Figure 9.3.

XML Design

XML provides great flexibility in structuring information—the syntax itself imposes few restrictions and permits the complete individualization of each element occurrence. However, if anyone is to use XML data, it is important to use this flexibility in a responsible way—there should be some sense to the structure, some pattern in which the information is represented. These structural patterns are captured in an XML DTD or schema definition. In the next section, we consider some of the issues to keep in mind while creating such patterns.

As should be evident from the history of XML, it is a format suitable for representing text documents as well as databases. This flexibility permits XML databases to manage text fields in a much richer way than is possible with relational databases. The interplay between text and structured data is discussed in the "Text" section.

Schema Design

In a relational table, each row represents a relationship, which could be rendered in an English sentence. Consider a table **Orders** with columns partnum, supplierID, price, and quantity as shown in Figure 9.6. A row in it, with the tuple of values 123, ABC, 5, and 10 can be read as "10 units of part 123 are ordered from supplier ABC at a price of 5 dollars each." The astute reader will notice that the English sentence includes a great deal of semantics not present in the column names: the price is in dollars, it applies per unit and not to the whole order, and so on.

Now consider the same data in XML (Figure 9.7). We may have a supplier element with a part element below it, and price and quantity as subelements of part. There isn't a single unique tuple that is pulled out. However,

partnum	supplierID	price	quantity
123	ABC	5	10
258	DEF	9	3
389	GH	2	22

Figure 9.6 An **Orders** table, used as a running example.

```
<Supplier supplierID="ABC">
     <Part partnum="123">
          <Price> 5 </Price>
          <Quantity> 10 </Quantity>
     </Part>
</Supplier>
<Supplier supplierID="DEF">
     <Part partnum="258">
          <Price> 9 </Price>
          <Quantity> 3</Quantity>
     </Part>
</Supplier>
<Supplier supplierID="GH">
     <Part partnum="389">
          <Price> 2 </Price>
          <Quantity> 22 </Quantity>
     </Part>
</Supplier>
```

(a)

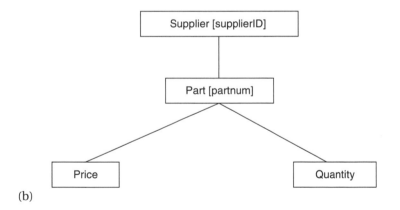

(b)

Figure 9.7 One XML design representing the table in Figure 9.6: (a) XML document and (b) an intuitive graphical representation.

any ancestor–descendant path in the graph should "make sense" in that it should be interpretable as an English sentence. Begin with single-element "sentences" such as "There is a part." These obviously are okay. The ID of the part has to be made an attribute of the element. Our one-element sentence then reads, "There is a part with ID 123." The maximum path length is now 3, and we can form a sentence that reads "10 units of part 123 are ordered from supplier ABC," and another sentence that reads "Part 123 is ordered from supplier ABC at a price of 5." Notice that the price is determined by part and supplier, and not by the order or order quantity. If we expect the price to be different for different orders, even from the same supplier, we may need to introduce an additional node order below supplier, and then make part, price, and quantity all children of order, as shown in Figure 9.8.

The main point of the above example is to show that there is an issue with database design in the XML context. There are many different types of errors possible. A few common ones are:

Incorrectly promoting an element to an attribute. An attribute at any level in the XML tree should apply to the entire subtree below it. If an attribute of an element X is irrelevant with respect to an element Y, descendant of X, then it is likely that the attribute really should have been rendered as an element, child of X. See Figure 9.9. In most XML implementations, attributes are dereferenced much more quickly than child subelements. So there is an efficiency reason to use attributes rather than subelements.

Incorrect use of an attribute as an element. Essential information about an element, of possible concern to its descendants, should be included in the element itself, as an attribute, rather than being pulled out in a subelement. For example, the ID of a supplier should

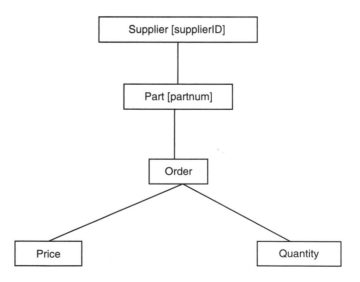

Figure 9.8 Another XML design representing the table of Figure 9.6.

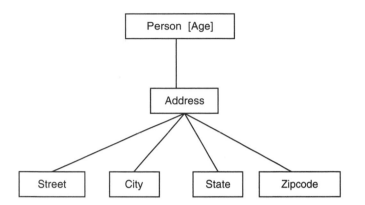

Figure 9.9 Age is related to person in the same manner as Address, so it should not be an attribute while Address is a subelement.

be part of the supplier element, and not in a separate suppID subelement. Note that attributes must be single valued and cannot have structure. These restrictions are significant, and can require that certain attributes be treated as subelements, even though they are logically attributes based on the argument above.

Inadequately grouped data. Information that forms a single logical unit should be grouped together under a common parent element. For example, if a supplier's address has a street, city, state, and zip, recorded as four different elements, these should be grouped together as children of an address element. In the relational world, such grouping is often not performed. For example, in a single table, we would have these four fields and also supplier name, telephone number, year established, etc. Looking at the table structure, all these fields are coequal without any additional structure among them. See Figure 9.10.

Promoting data to metadata. Since XML permits the schema to change from one part of the database to another, it is easy to fall into the trap of making everything into an element tag. Things that are data should remain data. For example, it would be bad design to have 50 different tags, one for each state, rather than record the state name as data. See Figure 9.11.

Demoting metadata into data. This is an error that is less likely in XML databases. However, it is very common in relational databases that have to represent semi-structured data. For example, one could create a table with three columns: objectID, attributeName, and

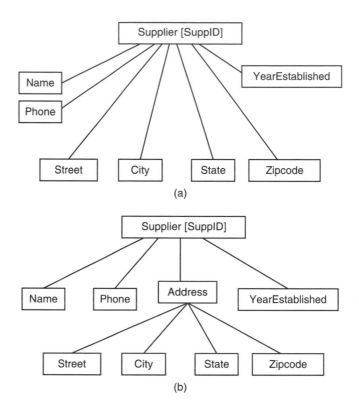

Figure 9.10 Two schema designs: (a) a design with inadequate grouping, and (b) a better design.

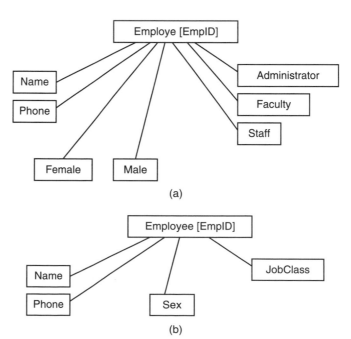

Figure 9.11 Two schema designs: (a) a design with improperly promoted data, and (b) a better design.

attributeValue. With such a table you can represent anything you wish! But note that attributeName is a column that stores as values information that is better represented as real names of attributes. See Figure 9.12.

Text

XML is very similar to HTML and therefore is great for representing text. XML tags provide a means for structuring text documents. A very simple, completely unstructured document could have just a start and an end tag, with thousands of words of text in between. Of course, the typical XML document has much more structure than this. However, there still could be large amounts of text between any pair of tags.

In short, a pure text document is represented in XML as a set of nested tags, just as a database is. In the case of a document, the tags may represent document constructs, such as chapter, section, paragraph, etc., whereas in a database, the tags represent schema elements as we saw above. Thus, there is an opportunity to merge text documents and structured databases. It is straightforward to have an arbitrarily complex document be a schema element anywhere in an XML database. In fact, it is just as straightforward to have an arbitrarily complex database be a component of an XML document that otherwise contains text. XML even permits the two types of elements to be intermixed, leading to arbitrarily deep nestings of documents in databases in documents. See Figure 9.13.

Let us consider how this works in practice, by looking at a couple of examples at different points in the spectrum of

objectID	attributeName	attributeValue
123	Title	Iliad
123	Author	Homer
123	Price	22
135	Title	Macbeth
135	Author	Shakespeare
135	Price	17
135	Year	1605

Figure 9.12 A triple store showing demoted metadata.

```
<SALES-REPORT Date="Jan 11, 2011">
<To> Bertha the Boss </To>
<From> Wally Worker </From>
<Report>
```
There was a healthy uptick in our sales last quarter, across all product categories, as you will see from the table below.

```
<Table Caption="Fourth Quarter Sales by Category">
    <Product-Category>
        <Name> Twist Ties </Name>
        <Sales> 260 </Sales>
        <Previous-Quarter-Sales> 220 </Previous-Quarter Sales>
    </Product-Category>
    <Product-Category>
        <Name> Shoestrings </Name>
        <Sales> 480 </Sales>
        <Previous-Quarter-Sales>200 </Previous-Quarter Sales>
        <Footnote> Previous quarter sales do not include sales of Cowlick Corp., which we have since
            acquired, and whose sales are included in the fourth quarter numbers. </Footnote>
    </Product-Category>
    <Product-Category>
        <Name> Bungee Cords </Name>
        <Sales> 770 </Sales>
        <Previous-Quarter-Sales> 740 </Previous-Quarter Sales>
    </Product-Category>
<Table>
```

Whereas we expect continued growth in the shoestring category this quarter, on account of our recent acquisition of Cowlick Corp., whether we see growth in other product categories will depend primarily on the state of the overall economy.
```
</Report>
</SALES-REPORT>
```

Figure 9.13 An XML document with nested data.

balancing text and structure. For our first example, consider a structured database with an address field. In a typical relational database design, this address field may be a single variable-length character string. With XML, there is an opportunity to break down the address into its components, each as a separate XML element. Note that the flexibility of XML, where some elements may be absent, is important here—one address may have an apartment number, for example, and another may not. Because of these differences in the expected structure of addresses, it is painful to pull out individual components of a street address for a relational database. Indeed, this decomposition is rarely done beyond city, state, ZIP code, and country—street addresses are almost always stored as a single string. With this decomposition in place in XML, we are able to ask queries about street addresses that would be very difficult otherwise. For example, with an address represented as in Figure 9.14, one can issue queries such as "Find persons who live in apartment number 23 (of their building or housing complex)."

For a second example, consider a bibliographic database that includes abstracts of articles. The abstract is a text "field" that may have additional document structure internal to it, such as multiple paragraphs, a keyword list, and so on. The primary way in which this case differs from the previous one (the example about street addresses) is that the quantity of text is much greater. In consequence,

```
<InternationalFriendsAddresses>
    <Address>
        <Name> Maria Eder </Name>
        <Street> Gartenweg </Street>
        <Number> 8 </Number>
        <Locality> Rafing </Locality>
        <PostCode> 3741 </PostCode>
        <City> Pulkau </City>
        <Country> Austria </Austria>
    </Address>
    <Address>
        <Name> LIM Chee-Seung </Name>
        <Apt> Flat 23 </Apt>
        <Floor> 12/F </Floor>
        <Building> Acacia Building</Building>
        <Number> 120 </Number>
        <Street> Kennedy Road </Street>
        <Locality> Wan Chai </Locality>
        <City> Hong Kong </City>
        <Country> China </Country>
    </Address>
    <Address>
        <Name> John Smith </Name>
        <Number> 15 </Number>
        <Street> Downing Street </Street>
        <Apt> 3C </Apt>
        <City> London </City>
        <PostCode> EC1Y 8SY </PostCode>
        <Country> United Kingdom </Country>
    </Address>
</InternationalFriendsAddresses>
```

Figure 9.14
A heterogeneous list of addresses, each decomposed into multiple XML elements, all within a single XML document.

selection queries are unlikely to specify the whole text field or even large parts of it. Rather, we may specify a few query terms and want "relevant" text snippets to be found. This is how information retrieval works, and this query paradigm is very different from that of a database, where a query is defined as the satisfaction of a logic predicate with a very well-defined answer set. Putting these two query paradigms together is hard, and is the subject of continuing research.

XML Data in an RDBMS

Relational database management systems (RDBMSs) are ubiquitous, and XML data is often stored in an RDBMS. The simplest way to do this is to treat the entire XML document as a single BLOB: a large data object of which the inner details are not interpreted by the relational database. The drawback of this setup is that the entire XML object has to be retrieved from the database and into an XML data management system before any data from it can be accessed. This can be expensive, particularly when the size of the XML stored is large. One attempt to manage size could be to divide the XML database to be stored into multiple XML documents, each stored in a separate BLOB. But then, we would still need to extract labels or indexing attributes to be able to determine which BLOBs to access in response to any query.

With object-relational capabilities, one can define a user-defined XML "type" and build suitable user-defined functions (UDFs) with it. This way, some of the difficulties mentioned above can be ameliorated. Nonetheless, since UDFs remain second-class citizens in a relational database, this sort of implementation usually still leaves a lot to be desired.

The typical way to store XML data in an RDBMS is to "shred" it into records that can be stored in relational tables. Each data element and each attribute in the XML becomes an attribute value in the relational representation. Each relational record represents a set of related elements and attributes. Our challenge is to create sets of relational records with identical structures, which can be represented as a table, given the heterogeneity and repetition so common in XML. The design considerations we face are similar to those for object-relational mapping, as discussed in Chapter 8. See the example shown in Figure 9.15.

```
<Library>
   <Book>
      <ISBN> 123 </ISBN>
      <Title> A Fun Book </Title>
      <Publisher>
         <Name> Crown </Name>
         <Address>
            <Street> 3 Canyon Drive </Street>
            <City> Hell, MI </City>
            <Zip> 48169 </Zip>
         </Address>
      </Publisher>
      <Author>
         <Name> Bonzo </Name>
         <Institution> Ringling Brothers </Institution>
      </Author>
   </Book>
   <Book>
      <ISBN> 258 </ISBN>
      <Title> Database Design </Title>
      <Publisher>
         <Name> Elsevier </Name>
         <Address>
            <Street> 5 Cloudy Way </Street>
            <City> Paradise, MI </City>
            <Zip> 49768 </Zip>
         </Address>
      </Publisher>
      <Author>
         <Name> Teorey </Name>
         <Institution> University of Michigan </Institution>
      </Author>
      <Author>
         <Name> Lightstone </Name>
         <Institution> IBM </Institution>
      </Author>
   </Book>
</Library>
```

ISBN	Title	PubName	PubAddrStreet	PubAddrCity	PubAddrZip
123	A Fun Book	Crown	3 Canyon Drive	Hell, MI	48169
258	Database Design	Elsevier	5 Cloudy Way	Paradise, MI	49768

ISBN	authorName	authorInstitution
123	Bonzo	Ringling Bros.
258	Teorey	U. Michigan
258	Lightstone	IBM

Figure 9.15 An XML document and its relational representation.

Web-Based Applications

Databases often power websites today. The Web is the medium through which many databases are accessed. In this section, we will first present an overview of how data is organized on the Web, and then discuss some of the design considerations when databases are placed on the Web.

An Overview of HTTP

The Internet makes it possible for computers around the world to communicate with one another. Using these facilities, the first services constructed included email and file transfer. In 1994, Tim Berners-Lee built a system connecting files on the Internet in a new way—this is what has grown into "the Web" today.

The central notion of the Web is that there is asymmetry between servers and clients. There are Web servers that have information resources (files, Web pages, database query results) that they can provide to remotely located Web clients. How precisely this transfer is orchestrated is specified in the *HyperText Transfer Protocol* (HTTP).

HTTP is a *request/response* protocol (Figure 9.16). The protocol begins with a request from the client to the server, followed by a response from the server to the client. A typical request from the client is to ask the server for a resource, to which a typical response is for the server to provide the resource. There is no way for the server to initiate communication using HTTP.

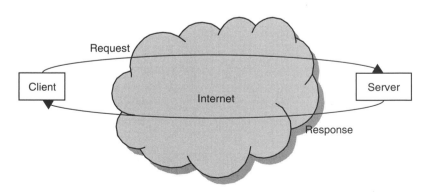

Figure 9.16 An overview of HTTP: A request from the client gets a response from the server.

Communication in each direction includes a header, with all sorts of useful fields, and an optional body, with the actual payload. HTTP specifies the fields that may be included in the header, and the exact format in which to specify each field. The body is just treated as a bucket of bits by HTTP: It is not manipulated in any way. The client and server each implement HTTP, by which we mean that they write out headers in the manner specified by HTTP and also read and interpret HTTP headers.

HTTP defines eight *methods*, or types of requests that can be made. The GET method is by far the one used most often. The client specifies the resource of interest to it, in a request that looks something like this:

```
GET /foo.html HTTP/1.1
Referer: http://www.google.com/search?q=web+databases
```

The server, in response, will send the file foo.html back, if indeed such a file exists at the server. The response also includes, among other things, a status code field in its header—for example, "200 OK" or "404 Not found."

Thus, the response may have a header that looks as follows, along with a body that comprises the requested resource (foo.html):

```
HTTP/1.1 200 OK
Server: Apache/2.2.11 (Unix)
Content-Type: text/html
```

GET has some limitations—for example, no more than 1024 bytes may be used. The POST method is similar to GET, except that it has a body in addition to the request header. Whenever copious or complex information is to be sent as part of the request, POST is the method used. The flexibility afforded by having a separate body part comes at a cost: Storing POST requests is problematic, since just the header does not suffice. Similarly, POST requests are difficult to link to or bookmark. Note that the POST method is also a request that receives a response, similar to the response for GET. In other words, even though the name of the method is POST, it also can be used to "get" a remote resource.

Since the HTTP protocol is asymmetric, different pieces of software implement the client and the server. The HTTP client protocol is implemented by Web browsers, such as Internet Explorer, Firefox, and Chrome. Web browser software usually has a great deal of additional functionality: HTTP itself is a simple protocol, and a basic client implementation is only a very small part of the code in these browsers.

Web server software implements the HTTP server protocol. The Apache Web server is the leading Web server today, and is perhaps the best-known example of open-source software. Internet Information Services, by Microsoft, is another popular Web server.

Web server software runs on machines that are also called Web servers. In consequence, there is some ambiguity when people speak of Web servers. When "a server is unreachable," it could be the machine or the software that is meant; in many cases, the difference may not be material. Since we are primarily concerned with software in this book, whenever we say "Web server" we mean the Web server software.

Resources

The unit of access in HTTP is a *resource*, which is most often just an HTML file. However, in general, a resource can be any unit of transfer. Indeed, HTTP requests often are for resources that are images, remotely invoked Web services, outputs of dynamically executed programs, and so on. Of course, for a resource to be requested and transferred, it must first be identified. This leads to the following, somewhat circular, definition for a resource: A resource is any object on the Web that has a Uniform Resource Identifier (URI).

Resources on the Web are typically identified by means of a Uniform Resource Locator (URL). (We will say more about URI versus URL in a moment.) A URL is of the form *http://server:port/path#fragment?search*.

The server part of the URL may be specified as a human-understandable host name or as a network-understandable IP address. An Internetwide *domain name service* (DNS) is used to translate a server machine name, such as *www.umich.edu*, to a numeric IP address, which may look something like 135.22.87.1. A Web browser can take a URL, find the server specification part of it, and have that converted to an IP address using DNS.

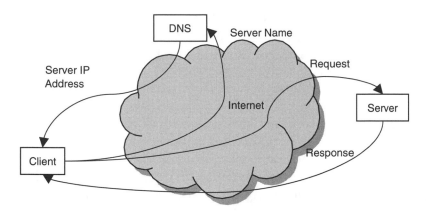

Figure 9.17 Address lookup in HTTP. The DNS query loop happens before the client can send its request to the server.

The IP address identifies the computer to connect to, just as a street address identifies a house in the real world (Figure 9.17). A single computer will usually support dozens of *port*s. Think of each port as a separate door leading to a separate apartment in the building identified by the IP address. By convention, particular ports are used for particular applications. Thus, port 25 is for email (SMTP), port 53 is for DNS, and so on. By convention, port 80 is for HTTP, and port 443 for HTTPS (a secure variant of HTTP that is beyond the scope of discussion in this book). However, a computer can be configured to have additional ports that can accept HTTP requests. Numbers frequently chosen for these additional ports are 8000 and 8080.

Typically, the path specifies a file name, and this is the file to be retrieved and returned. What if the URL specifies a directory? The server may have a convention in this case. Typically, it will look for a file called index.htm or index .html, and return this file if it exists. If not, perhaps the server should provide a directory listing. Exactly which file to look for, and what else to do, is completely up to the way the Web server has been configured: Neither the HTTP protocol nor the definition of a URL will specify this.

The fragment specification merely points to a portion of the resource being retrieved. In a typical implementation, with HTML, the entire resource is still obtained, while the fragment of focus is just identified. In other words, the server does nothing differently with this specification. Due to this, browsers may frequently not send the fragment specification to the server. Rather, they may keep this local, and once the file has been retrieved, use the fragment specification to scroll down when displaying the file and position the cursor at the desired location.

The search specification provides a general-purpose mechanism to send parameters to the Web server that could be used to modify the request. We will have much more to say about this in the next section.

In the manner described above, a URL explicitly describes exactly where a resource of interest is located in the Internet. Sometimes we may be interested in specifying a resource without tying it down to a particular file location on a particular host machine. In such cases, we use a Uniform Resource Name (URN). The syntax for a URN is rather simple. It is just: urn:nid:nss.

Here, nid is a namespace identifier and nss is a namespace-specific string. In other words, the resource has nss as its name, but since we'd like names to be unique, we make sure to obtain a name for the resource from some authority that manages names in some conceptual space. This is the namespace identified by the nss. For example, many countries have national identification numbers or social security numbers for their citizens. If you want to identify a person uniquely, you can "name" them by their national identification number (the nss), but you also have to say which country you got this from (the nid). This notion of namespace is widely used in XML, where it is commonplace to have tags such as abc:form, which means we are specifying a form as defined in the abc namespace. There may be other forms defined in other namespaces, but those are completely irrelevant: We have explicitly stated the specific form we are interested in.

A URI is a way of identifying a resource of interest unambiguously. We could do so by name, using a URN, or by location, using a URL. In the context of HTTP requests, most resources are identified by URL.

Dynamic Pages

In the simplest case, the resources managed by a Web server comprise a set of files that have been created in the past. The Web server simply determines the file name (including directory path) from the HTTP request and sends the file back to the requester (provided the file exists, and is readable). As a website grows, and there is more information that it would like to be able to provide, it quickly becomes cumbersome to create a separate HTML page for each possible information request and store it as a separate file.

It is commonplace for the requested resource not to be a simple static HTML page, but rather a "dynamic page," where the entire page, or a chunk of it, is obtained by executing a program. Of course, if any deterministic program is executed repeatedly, without changing inputs, it will produce the same results every time. This is not very interesting. The benefit of dynamic pages is obtained when programs are run with different input parameters, specified in the resource request. The definition of a URL provides for this in the form of the search string that comes at the end of the URL. This string is typically not interpreted by the Web server. Rather it is passed on to the program identified by the path part of the URL. This program then executes with the search string as the input parameter. The output produced is sent back by the server as the response to the request.

Let us make this a bit more concrete. If the requested resource is to be displayed as a Web page, then the output of the program must be an HTML file. Furthermore, the program need not accept only a single input parameter—logically, it could have as many parameters as appropriate: We merely have the entire set of parameters all encoded into a single search string. (In fact, for security reasons, many websites encrypt search strings so that the client does not learn what the structure of the program on the server side is and what sorts of parameters it accepts.) Finally, there is nothing that prevents the program from calling other programs and passing along some or all of the invocation parameters obtained from the search string.

What would these programs compute? In theory, it could be anything at all. In practice, the purpose is to populate the information of interest on the result Web page. Frequently, this information is obtained by performing a database lookup. In other words, the server-side program uses the information in the search string to generate a query that it issues to a local database. It then uses the database result to populate a Web page that it sends back to the client. Of course, there is no reason to restrict the program to issuing a single database query—there could be a string of queries and arbitrary additional computation involved in generating the final result desired.

For example, consider the ABC Company that maintains an electronic parts catalog. When a user browses this catalog and clicks on a particular widget of interest, which happens to have a part number of 12345, an HTTP request is sent to ABC's Web server, to run the program show_detail with a search string of 12345. The show_detail program issues a database query to pull up a nice image for the part, another query to pull up the technical specifications, yet another query for the price, and so on. It combines the results of all these queries to generate a nice-looking Web page, which it returns as the result to the client. A great deal of work happened behind the scenes to respond to a simple click. See Figure 9.18.

Website Structure

Now that we understand how Web servers operate, let us look at the logical structure of a website. As shown in Figure 9.19, there are three tiers. At the user-facing end is the Web server, and the software that stitches the final result together. This is often called the *presentation tier*. Next is the *application tier* with the bulk of the business logic and computation. Finally, at the back end is the *database tier*. Here, we have the databases that store the information required by the other tiers (and typically also for business operations beyond the website).

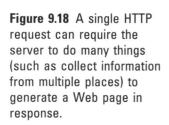

Figure 9.18 A single HTTP request can require the server to do many things (such as collect information from multiple places) to generate a Web page in response.

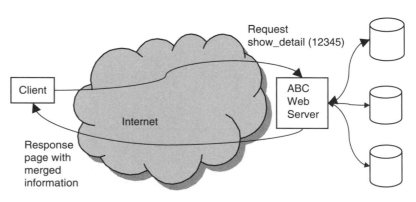

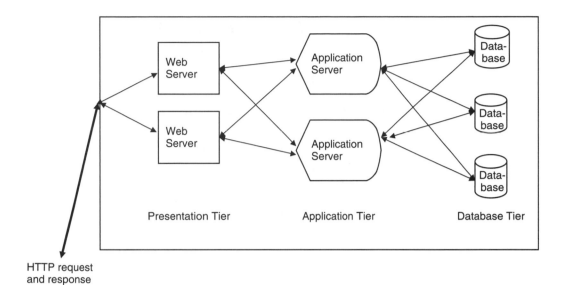

HTTP request
and response

Figure 9.19 Multiple tiers in a website.

As websites become popular, load management becomes an issue. The usual solution is to replicate servers and have a simple dispatcher manage the flow of requests. With a three-tier architecture, such replication decisions can be made independently at each layer. For example, if the application logic is the most compute-intensive piece, we could replicate servers at the middle tier without having to replicate the presentation layer server or the database.

Summary

In this chapter, we took a look at Web technologies and how they impact databases. XML is perhaps one of the best known of these, and definitely the one that has had the greatest impact on databases today. In the first section we presented an overview of XML, and in the second section we explored some database design issues that are specific to XML, beyond the more general design issues considered in the bulk of this book. Most databases today are accessed across the Web, so it is important to understand the impact of this context. We got an overview of Web technologies in the third section, followed by a description of the architecture of databases in websites.

Tips and Insights for Database Professionals

Tip 1. XML is a universal way of packaging and communicating structured information. It has become a standard just like ASCII has become a standard. Even if you never actually manipulate information in XML directly, expect to use it as a "wire format" to transfer data between systems.

Tip 2. When data is represented in XML, good design is just as important as for relational databases. Even though the bulk of this book is about relational database design, and even though most people mean relational design when they speak of database design, the same sorts of design considerations apply to all types of data representations, including XML.

Tip 3. While XML provides a convenient way to integrate text with structured data, the query paradigms for the two are very different. Text is often accessed through keyword queries and through approximate specification. Databases are queried in a controlled, structured way. If one of these types of information predominates in a mixed document, which query paradigm to use is obvious. If there is a more even mix, it is likely that one or the other type of data will not be handled as well by the query system as we would like.

Tip 4. Database-backed websites with a three-tier architecture require careful partitioning of work between tiers. Data-intensive work goes in the database server, while presentation-intensive work goes in the front-end HTTP server. The remainder, which is the core application logic, runs on the application servers in the middle.

Literature Summary

The XML standard is defined by the World Wide Web Consortium (W3C), an international society devoted to the development of Web standards and the long-term growth of the Web. The latest standards for the XML language itself, and also for a range of XML-related technologies, can be found at *http://www.w3.org/standards/xml/*. There are many excellent tutorials on XML and related technologies available on the Web, such as *http://www.w3schools.com/xml/default.asp*. A good listing of common XML design patterns is at *http://www.xmlpatterns.com/patterns.shtml*. XML mapping to relational databases is in many commercial and noncommercial products. A listing is maintained at *http://www.rpbourret.com/xml/XMLDatabaseProds.htm*. This site also has academic work in this area. Web technologies are explained at various levels of detail in numerous books and even more websites. An interested reader should have no difficulty finding as much additional information as desired.

10

BUSINESS INTELLIGENCE

Business intelligence has become a buzzword in recent years. The database tools found under the heading of *business intelligence* include data warehousing, online analytical processing (OLAP), and data mining. The functionalities of these tools are complementary and interrelated. *Data warehousing* provides for the efficient storage, maintenance, and retrieval of historical data. *OLAP* is a service that provides quick answers to ad hoc queries against the data warehouse. *Data mining* algorithms find patterns in the data and report models back to the user. All three tools are related to the way data in a data warehouse is logically organized, and performance is highly sensitive to the database design techniques used in

Barquin and Edelstein (1997). The encompassing goal for business intelligence technologies is to provide useful information for decision support.

Each of the major DBMS vendors is marketing the tools for data warehousing, OLAP, and data mining as business intelligence. This chapter covers each of these technologies in turn. We take a close look at the requirements for a data warehouse, its basic components and principles of operation, the critical issues in the design of a data warehouse, and the important logical database design elements in a data warehouse environment. We then investigate the basic elements of OLAP and data mining as special query techniques applied to data warehousing.

Data Warehousing

A data warehouse is a large repository of historical data that can be integrated for decision support. The use of a data warehouse is markedly different from the use of operational systems. Operational systems contain the data required for the day-to-day operations of an organization. This operational data tends to change quickly and constantly. The table sizes in operational systems are kept manageably small by periodically purging old data. The data warehouse, by contrast, periodically receives historical data in batches, and grows over time. The vast size of data warehouses can run to hundreds of gigabytes, or even terabytes. The problem that drives data warehouse design is the need for quick results to queries posed against huge amounts of data. The contrasting aspects of data warehouses and operational systems result in a distinctive design approach for data warehousing.

Overview of Data Warehousing

A data warehouse contains a collection of tools for decision support associated with very large historical databases, which enables the end user to make quick and sound decisions. Data warehousing grew out of the technology for decision support systems (DSSs) and executive information systems (EISs). DSSs are used to analyze data from commonly available databases with multiple sources, and to create reports. The report data is not time critical in the sense that a real-time system is, but must be timely for decision making. EISs are like DSSs, but more powerful, easier to use, and more business specific. EISs were designed to provide an alternative to the classic online transaction processing (OLTP) systems common to most commercially available database systems. OLTP systems are often used to create common applications, including those with mission-critical deadlines or response times. Table 10.1 summarizes the basic differences between OLTP and data warehouse systems.

The basic architecture for a data warehouse environment is shown in Figure 10.1. The diagram shows that the data warehouse is stocked by a variety of source databases from possibly different geographical locations. Each source database serves its own applications, and the data warehouse serves a DSS/EIS with its informational requests. Each feeder system database must be reconciled with the data warehouse data model; this is accomplished during the process of extracting the required data from the feeder database system, transforming the data from the feeder system to the data warehouse, and loading the data into the data warehouse (see Cataldo, 1997).

Table 10.1 Comparison between OLTP and Data Warehouse Systems

OLTP	Data Warehouse
Transaction oriented	Business process oriented
Thousands of users	Few users (typically under 100)
Generally small (MB up to several GB)	Large (from hundreds of GB up to several TB)
Current data	Historical data
Normalized data (many tables, few columns per table)	Denormalized data (few tables, many columns per table)
Continuous updates	Batch updates*
Simple to complex queries	Usually very complex queries

*There is currently a push in the industry toward "active warehousing," in which the warehouse receives data in continuous updates. See the "View Maintenance" section later in the chapter for further discussion.

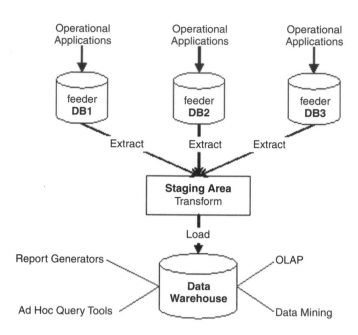

Figure 10.1 Basic data warehouse architecture.

Core Requirements for Data Warehousing

Let us now take a look at the core requirements and principles that guide the design of data warehouses (DWs). See Simon (1995), Barquin and Edelstein (1997), Chaudhuri and Dayal (1997), and Gray and Watson (1998).

1. DWs are organized around subject areas. Subject areas are analogous to the concept of functional areas, such as sales, project management, or employees, as discussed in the context of ER diagram clustering in the "Entity Clustering for ER Models" section. Each subject area has its own conceptual schema and can be represented using one or more entities in the ER data model or by one or more object classes in the object-oriented data model. Subject areas are typically independent of individual transactions involving data creation or manipulation. Metadata repositories are needed to describe source databases, DW objects, and ways of transforming data from the sources to the DW.

2. DWs should have some integration capability. A common data representation should be designed so that all the different individual representations can be mapped to it. This is particularly useful if the warehouse is implemented as a multidatabase or federated database.

3. The data is considered to be nonvolatile and should be mass loaded. Data extraction from current databases to the DW requires that a decision should be made whether to extract the data using standard relational database (RDB) techniques at the row or column level or specialized techniques for mass extraction. Data cleaning tools are required to maintain data quality—for example, to detect missing data, inconsistent data, homonyms, synonyms, and data with different units. Data migration, data scrubbing, and data auditing tools handle specialized problems in data cleaning and transformation. Such tools are similar to those used for conventional relational database schema (view) integration. Load utilities take cleaned data and load it into the DW, using batch-processing techniques. Refresh techniques propagate updates on the source data to base data and derived data in the DW. The decision of when and how to refresh is made by the DW administrator and depends on user needs (e.g., OLAP needs) and existing traffic to the DW.

4. Data tends to exist at multiple levels of granularity. Most important, the data tends to be of a historical nature, with potentially high time variance. In general, however, granularity can vary according to many different dimensions, not only by timeframe but also by geographic region, type of product manufactured or sold, type of store, and so on. The sheer size of the databases is a major problem in the design and implementation of DWs, especially for certain queries, updates, and sequential backups. This necessitates a critical decision between using an RDB or a multidimensional database (MDD) for the implementation of a DW.

5. The DW should be flexible enough to meet changing requirements rapidly. Data definitions (schemas) must be broad enough to anticipate the addition of new types of data. For rapidly changing data retrieval requirements, the types of data and levels of granularity actually implemented must be chosen carefully.

6. The DW should have a capability for rewriting history—that is, allowing for "what-if" analysis. The DW should allow the administrator to update historical data temporarily for the purpose of "what-if" analysis. Once the analysis is completed, the data must be correctly rolled

back. This condition assumes that the data is at the proper level of granularity in the first place.

7. A usable DW user interface should be selected. The leading choices today are SQL, multidimensional views of relational data, or a special-purpose user interface. The user interface language must have tools for retrieving, formatting, and analyzing data.

8. Data should be either centralized or distributed physically. The DW should have the capability to handle distributed data over a network. This requirement will become more critical as the use of DWs grows and the sources of data expand.

The Life Cycle for Data Warehouses

Entire books have been written about select portions of the data warehouse life cycle. Our purpose in this section is to present some of the basics and give the flavor of data warehousing. We strongly encourage those who wish to pursue data warehousing to continue learning through other books dedicated to data warehousing. Kimball and Ross (1998, 2002) have a series of excellent books covering the details of data warehousing activities.

Figure 10.2 outlines the activities of the data warehouse life cycle. The life cycle begins with a dialog to determine the project plan and the business requirements. When the plan and the requirements are aligned, design and implementation can proceed. The process forks into three threads that follow independent time lines, meeting up before deployment (see Figure 10.2). Platform issues are covered in one thread, including technical architectural design, followed by product selection and installation. Data issues are covered in a second thread, including dimensional modeling and then physical design, followed by data staging design and development. The special analytical needs of the users are pursued in the third thread, including analytic application specification followed by analytic application development. These three threads join before deployment. Deployment is followed by maintenance and growth, and changes in the requirements must be detected. If adjustments are needed, the cycle repeats. If the system becomes defunct, then the life cycle terminates.

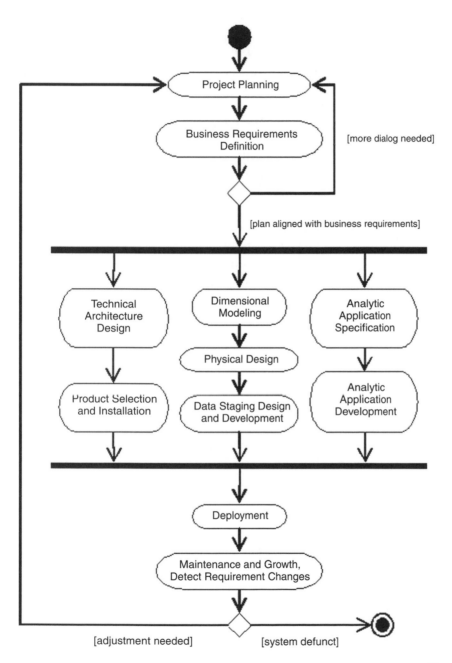

Figure 10.2 Data warehouse life cycle (based heavily on Kimball and Ross, 2002, Figure 16.1).

The remainder of our data warehouse section focuses on the dimensional modeling activity. More comprehensive material can be found in Kimball and Ross (1998, 2002) and Kimball and Caserta (2004).

Logical Design

We discuss the logical design of data warehouses in this section; physical design issues are covered in Lightstone et al. (2007). The logical design of data warehouses is defined by the dimensional data modeling approach. We cover the schema types typically encountered in dimensional modeling, including the star schema and the snowflake schema. We outline the dimensional design process, adhering to the methodology described by Kimball and Ross (2002). Then we walk through an example, covering some of the crucial concepts of dimensional data modeling.

Dimensional Data Modeling

The dimensional modeling approach is quite different from the normalization approach typically followed when designing a database for daily operations. The context of data warehousing compels a different approach to meeting the needs of the user. The need for dimensional modeling will be discussed further as we proceed. If you haven't been exposed to data warehousing before, be prepared for some new paradigms.

The Star Schema

Data warehouses are commonly organized with one large central *fact table*, and many smaller *dimension tables*. This configuration is termed a *star schema*; an example is shown in Figure 10.3. The fact table is composed of two types of attributes: *dimension attributes* and *measures*. The dimension attributes in Figure 10.3 are CustID, ShipDateID, BindID, and JobId. Most dimension attributes have foreign key/primary key relationships with dimension tables. The dimension tables in Figure 10.3 are **Customer**, **Ship Calendar**, and **Bind Style**. Occasionally, a dimension attribute exists without a related dimension table. Kimball and Ross refer to these as *degenerate dimensions*. The JobId attribute in Figure 10.3 is a degenerate dimension (more on this shortly). We indicate the dimension attributes that act as foreign keys using the stereotype «fk». The primary keys of the dimension tables are indicated with the stereotype «pk». Any degenerate dimensions in the fact table are indicated with the stereotype «dd». The fact table also

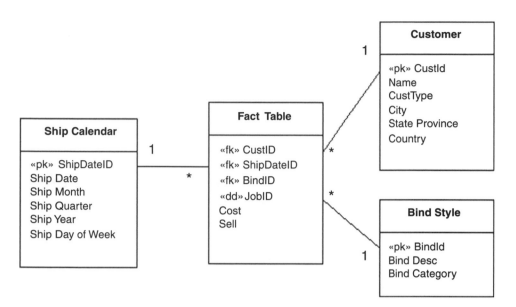

Figure 10.3 Example star schema for a data warehouse.

contains measures, which contain values to be aggregated when queries group rows together. The measures in Figure 10.3 are Cost and Sell.

Queries against the star schema typically use attributes in the dimension tables to select the pertinent rows from the fact table. For example, the user may want to see cost and sell for all jobs where the Ship Month is January 2005. The dimension table attributes are also typically used to group the rows in useful ways when exploring summary information. For example, the user may wish to see the total cost and sell for each Ship Month in the Ship Year 2005. Notice that dimension tables can allow different *levels* of detail the user can examine. For example, the Figure 10.3 schema allows the fact table rows to be grouped by Ship Date, Month, Quarter, or Year. These dimension levels form a *hierarchy*. There is also a second hierarchy in the Ship Calendar dimension that allows the user to group fact table rows by the day of the week. The user can move up or down a hierarchy when exploring the data. Moving down a hierarchy to examine more detailed data is a *drill-down* operation. Moving up a hierarchy to summarize details is a *roll-up* operation.

Together, the dimension attributes compose a candidate key of the fact table. The level of detail defined by the dimension attributes is the *granularity* of the fact table. When designing a fact table, the granularity should be the most detailed level available that any user will wish to examine. This requirement sometimes means that a degenerate dimension, such as JobId in Figure 10.3, must be included. The JobId in this star schema is not used to select or group rows, so there is no related dimension table. The purpose of the JobId attribute is to distinguish rows at the correct level of granularity. Without the JobId attribute, the fact table would group together similar jobs, prohibiting the user from examining the cost and sell values of individual jobs.

Normalization is not the guiding principle in data warehouse design. The purpose of data warehousing is to provide quick answers to queries against a large set of historical data. Star schema organization facilitates quick response to queries in the context of the data warehouse. The core detailed data is centralized in the fact table. Dimensional information and hierarchies are kept in dimension tables, a single join away from the fact table. The hierarchical levels of data contained in the dimension tables of Figure 10.3 violate 3NF, but these violations to the principles of normalization are justified. The normalization process would break each dimension table in Figure 10.3 into multiple tables. The resulting normalized schema would require more join processing for most queries. The dimension tables are small in comparison to the fact table, and typically slow changing. The bulk of operations in the data warehouse are read operations. The benefits of normalization are low when most operations are read only. The benefits of minimizing join operations overwhelm the benefits of normalization in the context of data warehousing. The marked differences between the data warehouse environment and the operational system environment lead to distinct design approaches. Dimensional modeling is the guiding principle in data warehouse design.

Snowflake Schema

The data warehouse literature often refers to a variation of the star schema known as the *snowflake schema*. Normalizing the dimension tables in a star schema leads to a snowflake schema. Figure 10.4 shows the snowflake schema analogous to the star schema of Figure 10.3. Notice that each hierarchical level becomes its own table. The snowflake schema is generally losing favor. Kimball and Ross strongly prefer the

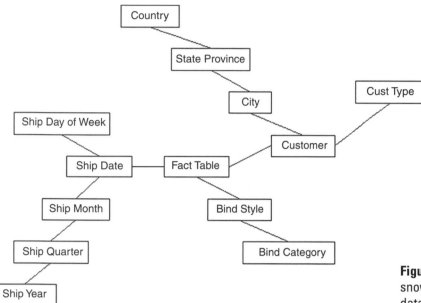

Figure 10.4 Example snowflake schema for a data warehouse.

star schema due to the speed and simplicity. Not only does the star schema yield quicker query response, it is also easier for the user to understand when building queries. We include the snowflake schema here for completeness.

Dimensional Design Process

We adhere to the four-step dimensional design process promoted by Kimball and Ross. Figure 10.5 outlines the activities in the four-step process.

Dimensional Modeling Example

Congratulations, you are now the owner of the ACME Data Mart Company! Your company builds data warehouses. You consult with other companies, design and deploy data warehouses to meet their needs, and support them in their efforts.

Your first customer is XYZ Widget, Inc. XYZ Widget is a manufacturing company with information systems in place. These are operational systems that track the current and recent state of the various business

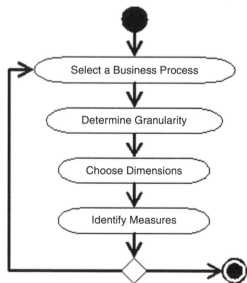

Figure 10.5 Four-step dimensional design process in Kimball and Ross (2002).

processes. Older records that are no longer needed for operating the plant are purged. This keeps the operational systems running efficiently.

XYZ Widget is now ten years old, and growing fast. The management realizes that information is valuable. The CIO has been saving data before it is purged from the operational system. There are tens of millions of historical records, but there is no easy way to access the data in a meaningful way. ACME Data Mart has been called in to design and build a DSS to access the historical data.

Discussions with XYZ Widget commence. There are many questions they want answered by analyzing the historical data. You begin by making a list of what XYZ wants to know.

XYZ Widget Company Wish List

1. What are the trends of our various products in terms of sales dollars, unit volume, and profit margin?
2. For those products that are not profitable, can we drill down and determine why the product is not profitable?
3. How accurately do our estimated costs match our actual costs?
4. When we change our estimating calculations, how are sales and profitability affected?
5. What are the trends in the percentage of jobs that ship on time?
6. What are the trends in productivity by department, for each machine, and for each employee?
7. What are the trends in meeting the scheduled dates for each department, and for each machine?
8. How effective was the upgrade on machine 123?
9. Which customers bring the most profitable jobs?
10. How do our promotional bulk discounts affect sales and profitability?

Looking over the wish list, you begin picking out the business processes involved. The following business processes list is sufficient to satisfy the items on the wish list.

Business Processes

1. Estimating
2. Scheduling

3. Productivity tracking
4. Job costing

These four business processes are interlinked in the XYZ Widget company. Let's briefly walk through the business processes and the organization of information in the operational systems, so we have an idea of what information is available for analysis. For each business process, we'll design a star schema for storing the data.

Estimating Process

The estimating process begins by entering widget specifications. The type of widget determines which machines are used to manufacture the widget. The estimating software then calculates estimated time on each machine used to produce that particular type of widget. Each machine is modeled with a standard setup time and running speed. If a particular type of widget is difficult to process on a particular machine, the times are adjusted accordingly. Each machine has an hourly rate. The estimated time is multiplied by the rate to give labor cost. Each estimate stores widget specifications, a breakdown of the manufacturing costs, the markup and discount applied (if any), and the price. The quote is sent to the customer. If the customer accepts the quote, then the quote is associated with a job number, the specifications are printed as a job ticket, and the job ticket moves to scheduling.

We need to determine the granularity before designing a schema for the estimating data warehouse. The granularity should be at the most detailed level, giving the greatest flexibility for drill-down operations when users are exploring the data. The most granular level in the estimating process is the estimating detail. Each estimating detail record specifies information for an individual cost center for a given estimate. This is the finest granularity of estimating data in the operational system, and this level of detail is also potentially valuable for the data warehouse users.

The next design step is to determine the dimensions. Looking at the estimating detail, we see that the associated attributes are the job specifications, the estimate number and date, the job number and win date if the estimate becomes a job, the customer, the promotion, the cost center, the widget quantity, estimated hours, hourly rate, estimated cost, markup, discount, and price. Dimensions are those attributes that the users want to group by when exploring the data. The users are interested in grouping by the various job specifications and by the cost center. The users also need to be able to group by date ranges. The estimate date and the win date are both of interest. Grouping by customer and promotion are also of interest to the users. These become the dimensions of the star schema for the estimating process.

Next, we identify the measures. Measures are the columns that contain values to be aggregated when rows are grouped together. The measures in the estimating process are estimated hours, hourly rate, estimated cost, markup, discount, and price.

The star schema resulting from the analysis of the estimating process is shown in Figure 10.6. There are five widget qualities of interest: shape, color, texture, density, and size. For example, a given widget might be a medium, round, red, fuzzy, fluffy widget. The estimate and job numbers are included as degenerate dimensions. The rest of the dimensions and measures are as outlined in the previous two paragraphs.

Dimension values are categorical in nature. For example, a given widget might have a density of fluffy or heavy. The

Figure 10.6 Star schema for estimating process.

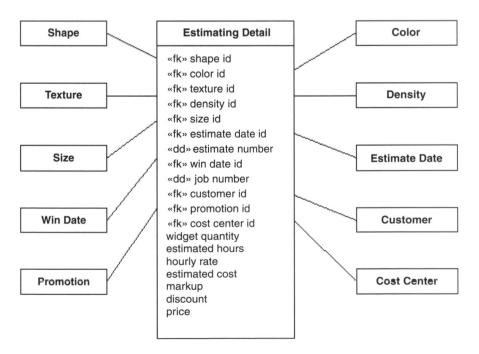

values for the size dimension include small, medium, and large. Measures tend to be numeric, since they are typically aggregated using functions such as sum or average.

The dimension tables should include any hierarchies that may be useful for analysis. For example, widgets are offered in many colors. The colors fall into categories by hue (e.g., pink, blue) and intensity (e.g., pastel, hot). Some even glow in the dark! The user may wish to examine all the pastel widgets as a group, or compare pink versus blue widgets. Including these attributes in the dimension table as shown in Figure 10.7 can accommodate this need.

Dates can also form hierarchies. For example, the user may wish to group by month, quarter, year, or the day of the week. Date dimensions are very common. The estimating process has two date dimensions: the estimate date and the win date. Typically, the date dimensions have analogous attributes. There is an advantage in standardizing the date dimensions across the company. Kimball and Ross (2002) recommend establishing a single standard date dimension, and then creating views of the date dimension for use in multiple dimensions. The use of views provides for standardization, while at the same time allowing the attributes to be named with aliases for intuitive use when multiple date dimensions are present. Figure 10.8 illustrates this concept with a date dimension and two views named Estimate Date and Win Date.

Color
«pk» color id
color description
hue
intensity
glows in dark

Figure 10.7 Color dimension showing attributes.

Scheduling Process

Let's move on to the scheduling process. Scheduling uses the times calculated by the estimating process to plan the workload on each required machine. Target dates are assigned to each manufacturing step. The job ticket moves into production after the scheduling process completes.

Date
«pk» date id
date description
month
quarter
year
day of week

Estimate Date
«pk» estimate date id
estimate date description
estimate month
estimate quarter
estimate year
estimate day of week

Win Date
«pk» win date id
win date description
win month
win quarter
win year
win day of week

Figure 10.8 Date dimensions showing attributes.

XYZ Widget, Inc. has a shop floor automatic data collection (ADC) system. Each job ticket has a bar code for the assigned job number. Each machine has a sheet with bar codes representing the various operations of that machine. Each employee has a badge with a bar code representing that employee. When an employee starts an operation, the job bar code is scanned, the operation bar code is scanned, and the employee bar code is scanned. The computer pulls in the current system time as the start time. When one operation starts, the previous operation for that employee is automatically stopped (an employee is unable do more than one operation at once). When the work on the widget job is complete on that machine, the employee marks the job complete via the ADC system. The information gathered through the ADC system is used to update scheduling, track the employee's work hours and productivity, and also track the machine's productivity.

The design of a star schema for the scheduling process begins by determining the granularity. The most detailed scheduling table in the operational system has a record for each cost center applicable to manufacturing each job. The users in the scheduling department are interested in drilling down to this level of detail in the data warehouse. The proper level of granularity in the star schema for scheduling is determined by the job number and the cost center.

Next we determine the dimensions in the star schema for the scheduling process. The operational scheduling system tracks the scheduled start and finish dates and times, as well as the actual start and finish dates and times. The estimated and actual hours are also stored in the operational scheduling details table, along with a flag indicating whether the operation completed on time. The scheduling team must have the ability to group records by the scheduled and actual start and finish times. Also critical is the ability to group by cost center. The dimensions of the star schema for scheduling are the scheduled and actual start and finish dates and times, and the cost center. The job number must also be included as a degenerate dimension to maintain the proper granularity in the fact table. Figure 10.9 reflects the decisions on the dimensions appropriate for the scheduling process.

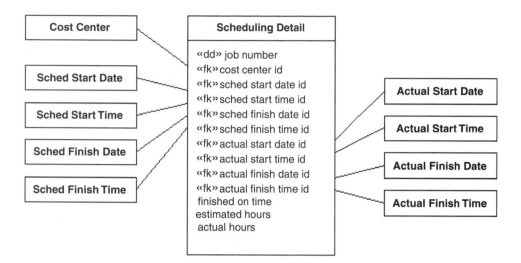

The scheduling team is interested in aggregating the estimated hours and, also, the actual hours. They are also very interested in examining trends in on-time performance. The appropriate measures for the scheduling star schema include the estimated and actual hours and a flag indicating whether the operation was finished on time. The appropriate measures for scheduling are reflected in Figure 10.9.

There are several standardization principles in play in Figure 10.9. Note that there are multiple time dimensions. These should be standardized with a single time dimension, along with views filling the different roles, similar to the approach used for the date dimensions. Also, notice the Cost Center dimension is present both in the estimating and the scheduling processes. These are actually the same, and should be designed as a single dimension. Dimensions can be shared between multiple star schemas. One last point: The estimated hours are carried from estimating into scheduling in the operational systems. These numbers feed into the star schemas for both the estimating and the scheduling processes. The meaning is the same between the two attributes; therefore, they are both named "estimated hours." The rule of thumb is that if two attributes carry the same meaning, they should be named the same, and if two attributes are named the same, they carry the same meaning. This consistency allows discussion and comparison of information between business processes across the company.

Figure 10.9 Star schema for the scheduling process.

Productivity Tracking

The next process we examine is productivity tracking. The granularity is determined by the level of detail available in the ADC system. The detail includes the job number, cost center, employee number, and the start and finish dates and times. The department managers need to be able to group rows by cost center, employee, and start and finish dates and times. These attributes therefore become the dimensions of the star schema for the productivity process, shown in Figure 10.10. The managers are interested in aggregating productivity numbers, including the widget quantity produced, the percentage finished on time, and the estimated and actual hours. Since these attributes are to be aggregated, they become the measures shown in Figure 10.10.

There are often dimensions in common between star schemas in a data warehouse, because business processes are usually interlinked. A useful tool for tracking the commonality and differences of dimensions across multiple business processes is the data warehouse bus (Kimball and Ross, 2002). Table 10.2 shows a data warehouse bus for the four business processes in our dimensional design example. Each row represents a business process. Each column represents a dimension. Each x in the body of the table represents the use of the given dimension in the given business process. The data warehouse bus is a handy means of presenting the organization of a data warehouse at a high level. The dimensions common between multiple business processes need to be standardized or "conformed" in Kimball and Ross' terminology. A dimension is

Figure 10.10 Star schema for the productivity tracking process.

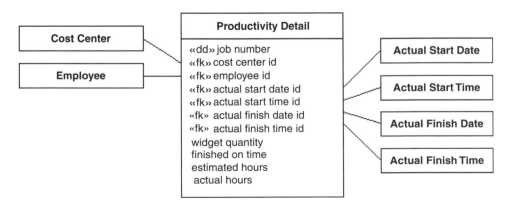

Table 10.2 Data Warehouse Bus for Widget Example

	Shape	Color	Texture	Density	Size	Estimate Date	Win Date	Customer	Promotion	Cost Center	Scheduled Start Date	Scheduled Start Time	Sched Finish Date	Scheduled Finish Time	Actual Start Date	Actual Start Time	Actual Finish Date	Actual Finish Time	Employee	Invoice Date
Estimating	x	x	x	x	x	x	x	x	x	x										
Scheduling										x	x	x	x	x	x	x	x	x		
Productivity tracking										x					x	x	x	x	x	
Job costing	x	x	x	x	x			x	x	x										x

conformed if there exists a most detailed version of that dimension, and all other uses of that dimension utilize a subset of the attributes and a subset of the rows from that most detailed version. Conforming dimensions ensures that whenever data is related or compared across business processes, the result is meaningful.

Job Costing

The data warehouse bus also makes some design decisions more obvious. We have taken the liberty of choosing the dimensions for the job costing process. Table 10.2 includes a row for the job costing process. When you compare the rows for estimating and job costing, it quickly becomes clear that the two processes share most of the same dimensions. It probably makes sense to combine these two processes into one star schema. This is especially true since job costing analysis requires comparing estimated and actual values. Figure 10.11 is the result of combining the estimating and job costing processes into one star schema.

Summarizing Data

The star schemas we have covered so far are excellent for capturing the pertinent details. Having fine granularity available in the fact table allows the users to examine data down to that level of granularity. However, the users will often want summaries. For example, the managers may often query for a daily snapshot of the job costing data. Every query the user may wish to pose against a given star schema can be answered from the detailed fact table. The summary could be aggregated on-the-fly from the fact table. There is an obvious drawback to this strategy. The fact table contains many millions of rows, due to the detailed nature of the data. Producing a summary on-the-fly can be expensive in terms of computer resources, resulting in a very slow response. If a summary table were available to answer the queries for the job costing daily snapshot, then the answer could be presented to the user blazingly fast. The schema for the job costing daily snapshot is shown in Figure 10.12.

Figure 10.11 Star schema for the job costing process.

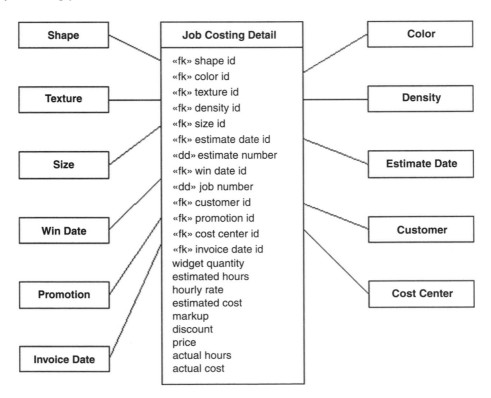

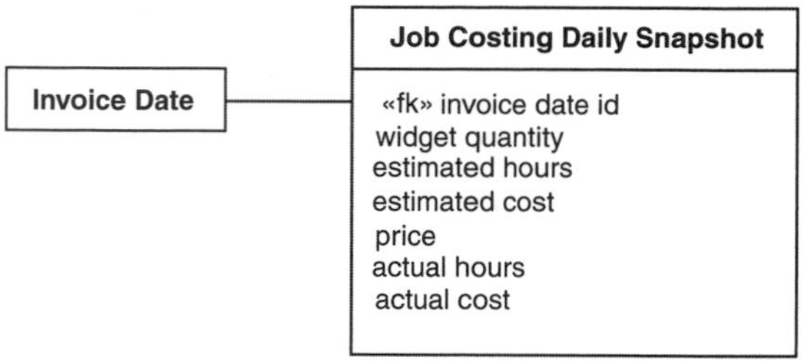

Notice that most of the dimensions used in the job costing detail are not used in the snapshot. Summarizing the data has eliminated the need for most dimensions in this context. The daily snapshot contains one row for each day that jobs have been invoiced. The number of rows in the snapshot would be in the thousands. The small size of the snapshot allows for a very quick response when a user requests the job costing daily snapshot. When there are a small number of summary queries that occur frequently, it is a good strategy to materialize the summary data needed to answer the queries quickly.

The daily snapshot schema in Figure 10.12 also allows the user to group by month, quarter, or year. Materializing summary data is useful for quick response to any query that can be answered by aggregating the data further.

Invoice Date

Job Costing Daily Snapshot
«fk» invoice date id
widget quantity
estimated hours
estimated cost
price
actual hours
actual cost

Figure 10.12 Schema for the job costing daily snapshot.

Online Analytical Processing

Designing and implementing strategic summary tables is a good approach when there is a small set of frequent queries for summary data. However, there may be a need for some users to explore the data in an ad hoc fashion. For example, a user who is looking for types of jobs that have not been profitable needs to be able to roll up and drill down various dimensions of the data. The ad hoc nature of the process makes predicting the queries impossible. Designing a strategic set of summary tables to answer these ad hoc explorations of the data is a daunting task. OLAP provides an alternative.

OLAP is a service that overlays the data warehouse. The OLAP system automatically selects a strategic set of summary views, and saves the automatic summary tables (ASTs) to disk as materialized views. The OLAP system also maintains these views, keeping them in step with the fact tables as new data arrives. When a user requests summary data, the OLAP system figures out which AST can be used for a quick response to the given query. OLAP systems are a good solution when there is a need for ad hoc exploration of summary information based on large amounts of data residing in a data warehouse.

OLAP systems automatically select, maintain, and use the ASTs. Thus, an OLAP system effectively does some of the design work automatically. This section covers some of the issues that arise in building an OLAP engine, and some of the possible solutions. If you use an OLAP system, the vendor delivers the OLAP engine to you. The issues and solutions discussed here are not items that you need to resolve. Our goal here is to remove some of the mystery about what an OLAP system is and how it works.

The Exponential Explosion of Views

Materialized views aggregated from a fact table can be uniquely identified by the aggregation level for each dimension. Given a hierarchy along a dimension, let 0 represent no aggregation, 1 represent the first level of aggregation, and so on. For example, if the Invoice Date dimension has a hierarchy consisting of date id, month, quarter, year, and "all" (i.e., complete aggregation), then date id is level 0, month is level 1, quarter is level 2, year is level 3, and "all" is level 4. If a dimension does not explicitly have a hierarchy, then level 0 is no aggregation, and level 1 is "all."

The scales so defined along each dimension define a coordinate system for uniquely identifying each view in a product graph. Figure 10.13 illustrates a product graph in two dimensions. Product graphs are a generalization of the hypercube lattice structure introduced by Harinarayan et al. (1996), where dimensions may have associated hierarchies. The top node, labeled (0, 0) in Figure 10.13, represents the fact table. Each node represents a view with aggregation levels as indicated by the coordinate. The relationships descending the product graph indicate aggregation relationships. The five shaded nodes indicate that these views have been materialized. A view can be aggregated from any materialized ancestor view. For example, if a user issues a query for rows grouped by year and state, that query would naturally be answered by the view labeled (3, 2). View (3, 2) is not materialized, but the query can be answered from the materialized view (2, 1) since

(2, 1) is an ancestor of (3, 2). Quarters can be aggregated into years, and cities can be aggregated into states.

The central issue challenging the design of OLAP systems is the exponential explosion of possible views as the number of dimensions increases. The Calendar dimension in Figure 10.13 has five levels of hierarchy, and the Customer dimension has four levels of hierarchy. The user may choose any level of aggregation along each dimension. The number of possible views is the product of the number of hierarchical levels along each dimension. The number of possible views for the example in Figure 10.13 is $5 \times 4 = 20$. Let d be the number of dimensions in a data warehouse. Let h_i be the number of hierarchical levels in dimension i. The general equation for calculating the number of possible views is given by Eq. 10.1:

$$\text{Possible views} = \prod_{i=1}^{d} h_i \qquad (10.1)$$

If we express Eq. 10.1 in different terms, the problem of exponential explosion becomes more apparent. Let g be the geometric mean of the number of hierarchical levels in the dimensions. Then Eq. 10.1 becomes Eq. 10.2:

$$\text{Possible views} = g^d \qquad (10.2)$$

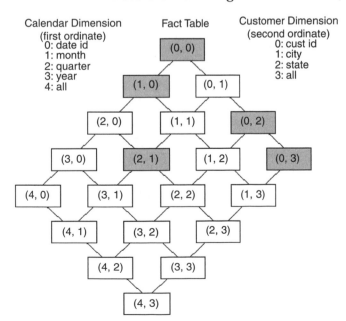

Figure 10.13 Product graph labeled with aggregation level coordinates.

As dimensionality increases linearly, the number of possible views explodes exponentially. If $g = 5$ and $d = 5$, there are $5^5 = 3125$ possible views. Thus, if $d = 10$, then there are $5^{10} = 9,765,625$ possible views. OLAP administrators need the freedom to scale up the dimensionality of their data warehouses. Clearly, the OLAP system cannot create and maintain all possible views as dimensionality increases. The design of OLAP systems must deliver quick response while maintaining a system within the resource limitations. Typically, a strategic subset of views must be selected for materialization.

Overview of OLAP

There are many approaches to implementing OLAP systems presented in the literature. Figure 10.14 maps out one possible approach, which will serve for discussion. The larger problem of OLAP optimization is broken into four subproblems: view size estimation, materialized view selection, materialized view maintenance, and query optimization with materialized views. This division is generally true of the OLAP literature, and is reflected in the OLAP system plan shown in Figure 10.14.

Figure 10.14 A plan for OLAP optimization.

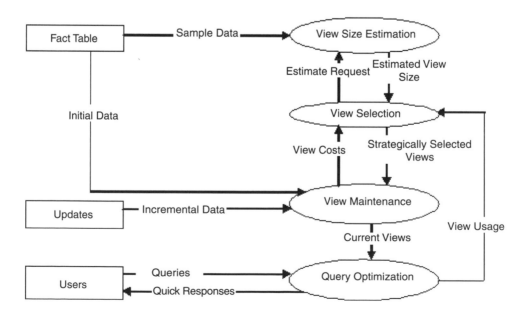

We describe how the OLAP processes interact in Figure 10.14, and then explore each process in greater detail. The plan for OLAP optimization shows *Sample Data* moving from the *Fact Table* into *View Size Estimation*. *View Selection* makes an *Estimate Request* for the view size of each view it considers for materialization. *View Size Estimation* queries the *Sample Data*, examines it, and models the distribution. The distribution observed in the sample is used to estimate the expected number of rows in the view for the full dataset. The *Estimated View Size* is passed to *View Selection*, which uses the estimates to evaluate the relative benefits of materializing the various views under consideration. *View Selection* picks *Strategically Selected Views* for materialization with the goal of minimizing total query costs. *View Maintenance* builds the original views from the *Initial Data* from the *Fact Table*, and maintains the views as *Incremental Data* arrives from *Updates*. *View Maintenance* sends statistics on *View Costs* back to *View Selection*, allowing costly views to be discarded dynamically. *View Maintenance* offers *Current Views* for use by *Query Optimization*. *Query Optimization* must consider which of the *Current Views* can be utilized to most efficiently answer *Queries* from *Users*, giving *Quick Responses* to the *Users*. *View Usage* feeds back into *View Selection*, allowing the system to dynamically adapt to changes in query workloads.

View Size Estimation

OLAP systems selectively materialize strategic views with high benefits in order to achieve quick response to queries, while remaining within the resource limits of the computer system. The size of a view affects how much disk space is required to store the view. More importantly, the size of the view determines in part how much disk input/output will be consumed when querying and maintaining the view. Calculating the exact size of a given view requires calculating the view from the base data. Reading the base data and calculating the view is the majority of the work necessary to materialize the view. Since the objective of view materialization is to conserve resources, it becomes necessary to estimate the size of the views under consideration for materialization.

Cardenas' formula (1975) is a simple equation (Eq. 10.3) that is applicable to estimating the number of rows in a view:

$$\text{Expected distinct values} = v\left(1 - (1 - 1/v)^n\right) \quad (10.3)$$

where n is the number of rows in the fact table, and v is the number of possible keys in the data space of the view.

Cardenas' formula assumes a uniform data distribution. However, many data distributions exist. The data distribution in the fact table affects the number of rows in a view. Cardenas' formula is very quick, but the assumption of a uniform data distribution leads to gross overestimates of the view size when the data is actually clustered. Other methods have been developed to model the effect of data distribution on the number of rows in a view.

Faloutsos et al. (1996) present a sampling approach based on the binomial multifractal distribution. Parameters of the distribution are estimated from a sample. The number of rows in the aggregated view for the full dataset is then estimated using the parameter values determined from the sample. Eqs. 10.4 and 10.5 are presented from their paper for this purpose:

$$\text{Expected distinct values} = \sum_{a=0}^{k} C^k_a \left(1 - (1 - P_a)^n\right) \quad (10.4)$$

$$P_a = P^{k-a}(1 - P)^a \quad (10.5)$$

Figure 10.15 illustrates an example. Order k is the decision tree depth. C^k_a is the number of bins in the set reachable by taking some combination of a left edges and $k - a$ right edges in the decision tree. P_a is the probability of reaching a given bin of which the path contains a left edges, and n is the number of rows in the dataset. Bias P is the probability of selecting the right edge at a choice point in the tree.

The calculations of Eq. 10.4 are illustrated with a small example. An actual database would yield much larger numbers, but the concepts and the equations are the same. These calculations can be done with logarithms, resulting

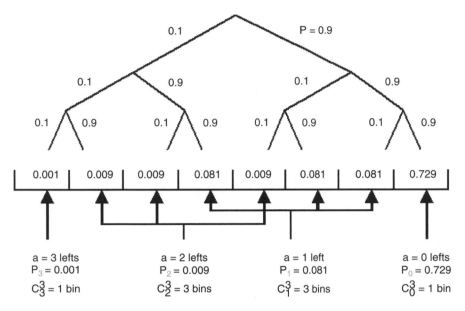

Figure 10.15 Example of a binomial multifractal distribution tree.

in very good scalability. Based on Figure 10.15, given five rows, calculate the expected distinct values using Eq. 10.4:

$$\text{Expected distinct values} =$$
$$1 \times \left(1 - (1 - 0.729)^5\right) + 3 \times \left(1 - (1 - 0.081)^5\right)$$
$$+3 \times \left(1 - (1 - 0.009)^5\right) + 1 \times \left(1 - (1 - 0.0001)^5\right) \approx 1.965$$

$$(10.6)$$

The values of P and k can be estimated based on sample data. The algorithm used in Faloutsos et al. (1996) has three inputs: the number of rows in the sample, the frequency of the most commonly occurring value, and the number of distinct aggregate rows in the sample. The value of P is calculated based on the frequency of the most commonly occurring value. They begin with

$$k = \lceil \log_2(\text{distinct rows in sample}) \rceil \qquad (10.7)$$

and then adjust k upwards, recalculating P until a good fit to the number of distinct rows in the sample is found.

Other distribution models can be utilized to predict the size of a view based on sample data. For example, the use of the Pareto distribution model has been explored in Nadeau and Teorey (2003). Another possibility is to find the best fit to the sample data for multiple distribution models, calculate which model is most likely to produce the given sample data, and then use that model to predict the number of rows for the full dataset. This would require calculation for each distribution model considered, but should generally result in more accurate estimates.

Selection of Materialized Views

Most of the published works in the problem of materialized view selection are based on the hypercube lattice structure of Harinarayan et al. (1996). The hypercube lattice structure is a special case of the product graph structure, where the number of hierarchical levels for each dimension is two. Each dimension can either be included or excluded from a given view. Thus, the nodes in a hypercube lattice structure represent the power set of the dimensions.

Figure 10.16 illustrates the hypercube lattice structure with an example from Harinarayan et al. (1996). Each node of the lattice structure represents a possible view. Each node is labeled with the set of dimensions in the "group by" list for that view. The numbers associated with the nodes represent the number of rows in the view. These numbers are normally derived from a view size estimation algorithm, as discussed previously. However, the numbers in Figure 10.16 follow this same example. The relationships between nodes indicate which views can be aggregated from other views. A given view can be calculated from any materialized ancestor view.

We refer to the algorithm for selecting materialized views introduced by Harinarayan et al. (1996) as HRU. The initial state for HRU has only the fact table materialized. HRU calculates the benefit of each possible view during each iteration, and selects the most beneficial view for materialization. Processing continues until a predetermined number of materialized views is reached.

Table 10.3 shows the calculations for the first two iterations of HRU. Materializing

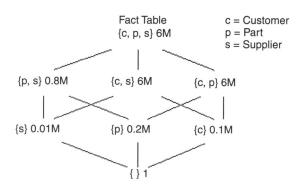

Figure 10.16 Example hypercube lattice structure. From Harinarayan et al. (1996).

Table 10.3 Two Iterations of HRU, Based on Figure 10.16

	Iteration 1 Benefit	Iteration 2 Benefit
{p, s}	$5.2M \times 4 = 20.8M$	
{c, s}	$0 \times 4 = 0$	$0 \times 2 = 0$
{c, p}	$0 \times 4 = 0$	$0 \times 2 = 0$
{s}	$5.99M \times 2 = 11.98M$	$0.79M \times 2 = 1.58M$
{p}	$5.8M \times 2 = 11.6M$	$0.6M \times 2 = 1.2M$
{c}	$5.9M \times 2 = 11.8M$	$5.9M \times 2 = 11.8M$
{}	$6M - 1$	$0.8M - 1$

$\{p, s\}$ saves $6M - 0.8M = 5.2M$ rows for each of four views: $\{p, s\}$ and its three descendants: $\{p\}$, $\{s\}$, and $\{\}$. The view $\{c, s\}$ yields no benefit if materialized, since any query that can be answered by reading 6M rows from $\{c, s\}$ can also be answered by reading 6M rows from the fact table $\{c, p, s\}$. HRU calculates the benefits of each possible view materialization. The view $\{p, s\}$ is selected for materialization in the first iteration. The view $\{c\}$ is selected in the second iteration.

HRU is a greedy algorithm that does not guarantee an optimal solution, although testing has shown that it usually produces a good solution. Further research has built upon HRU, accounting for the presence of index structures, update costs, and query frequencies.

HRU evaluates every unselected node during each iteration, and each evaluation considers the effect on every descendant. The algorithm consumes $O(kn^2)$ time where $k = |$views to select$|$ and $n = |$nodes$|$. This order of complexity looks very good; it is polynomial time. However, the result is misleading. The nodes of the hypercube lattice structure constitute a power set. The number of possible views is therefore 2^d where $d = |$dimensions$|$. Thus, $n = 2^d$, and the time complexity of HRU is $O(k2^{2d})$. HRU runs in time exponentially relative to the number of dimensions in the database.

The Polynomial Greedy Algorithm (PGA) of Nadeau and Teorey (2002) offers a more scalable alternative to HRU. PGA, like HRU, also selects one view for materialization with each iteration. However, PGA divides each iteration into a nomination phase and a selection phase. The first phase nominates promising views into a candidate set. The second phase estimates the benefits of materializing each candidate, and selects the view with the highest evaluation for materialization.

The nomination phase begins at the top of the lattice; in Figure 10.16, this is the node {c, p, s}. PGA nominates the smallest node from among the children. The candidate set is now {{p, s}}. PGA then examines the children of {p, s} and nominates the smallest child, {s}. The process repeats until the bottom of the lattice is reached. The candidate set is then {{p, s}, {s}, {}}. Once a path of candidate views has been nominated, the algorithm enters the selection phase. The resulting calculations are shown in Tables 10.4 and 10.5.

Table 10.4 First Iteration of PGA, Based on Figure 10.16

Candidates	Iteration 1 Benefit
{p, s}	5.2M × 4 = 20.8M
{s}	5.99M × 2 = 11.98M
{}	6M − 1

Table 10.5 Second Iteration of PGA, Based on Figure 10.16

Candidates	Iteration 2 Benefit
{c, s}	0 × 2 = 0
{s}	0.79M × 2 = 1.58M
{c}	5.9M × 2 = 11.8M
{}	6M − 1

Compare Tables 10.4 and 10.5 with Table 10.3. Notice PGA does fewer calculations than HRU, and yet in this example reaches the same decisions as HRU. PGA usually picks a set of views nearly as beneficial as those chosen by HRU, and yet PGA is able to function when HRU fails due to the exponential complexity. PGA is polynomial relative to the number of dimensions. When HRU fails, PGA extends the usefulness of the OLAP system.

The materialized view selection algorithms discussed so far are static; that is, the views are picked once and then materialized. An entirely different approach to the selection of materialized views is to treat the problem similar to memory management as shown in Kotidis and Roussopoulos (1999). The materialized views constitute a view pool. Metadata is tracked on usage of the views. The system monitors both space and update window constraints. The contents of the view pool are adjusted dynamically. As queries are posed, views are added appropriately. Whenever a constraint is violated, the system selects a view for eviction. Thus, the view pool can improve as more usage statistics are gathered. This is a self-tuning system that adjusts to changing query patterns.

The static and dynamic approaches complement each other and should be integrated. Static approaches run fast from the beginning, but do not adapt. Dynamic view selection begins with an empty view pool, and therefore yields slow response times when a data warehouse is first loaded; however, it is adaptable and improves over time. The complementary nature of these two approaches has influenced our design plan in Figure 10.14, as indicated by *Queries* feeding back into *View Selection*.

View Maintenance

Once a view is selected for materialization, it must be computed and stored. When the base data is updated, the aggregated view must also be updated to maintain consistency between views. The original view materialization and the incremental updates are both considered as view maintenance in Figure 10.14. The efficiency of view maintenance is greatly affected by the data structures implementing the view. OLAP systems are multidimensional, and fact tables contain large numbers of rows. The access methods implementing the OLAP system must meet the challenges of high dimensionality in combination with large row counts. The physical structures used are deferred to the companion book *Physical Database Design* by Lightstone et al. (2007).

Most of the research papers in the area of view maintenance assume that new data is periodically loaded with incremental data during designated update windows. Typically, the OLAP system is made unavailable to the users while the incremental data is loaded in bulk, taking advantage of the efficiencies of bulk operations. There is a downside to deferring the loading of incremental data until the next update window. If the data warehouse receives incremental data once a day, then there is a one-day latency period.

There is currently a push in the industry to accommodate data updates close to real time, keeping the data warehouse in step with the operational systems. This is sometimes referred to as *active warehousing* and *real-time analytics*. The need for data latency of only a few minutes presents new problems. How can very large data structures be maintained efficiently with a trickle feed? One solution is to have a second set of data structures with the same schema as the data warehouse. This second set of data structures acts as a holding tank for incremental data, and is referred to as a delta cube in OLAP terminology. The operational systems feed into the delta cube, which is small and efficient for quick incremental changes. The data cube is updated periodically from the delta cube, taking advantage of bulk operation efficiencies. When the user queries the OLAP system, the query can be issued against both the data cube and the delta cube to obtain an up-to-date result. The delta cube is hidden from the user. What the user sees is an OLAP system that is nearly current with the operational systems.

Query Optimization

When a query is posed to an OLAP system, there may be multiple materialized views available that could be used to compute the result. For example, if we have the situation represented in Figure 10.13, and a user issues a query to group rows by month and state, that query is naturally answered from the view labeled (1, 2). However, since (1, 2) is not materialized, we need to find a materialized ancestor to obtain the data. There are three such nodes in the product graph of Figure 10.13. The query can be answered from either node (0, 0), (1, 0), or (0, 2). With the possibility of answering queries from alternative sources, the optimization issue arises as to which source is the most efficient for the given query. Most existing research focuses on syntactic approaches. The possible query translations are carried out, alternative query costs are estimated, and what appears to be the best plan is executed. Another approach is to query a metadata table containing information on the materialized views to determine the best view to query against, and then translate the original SQL query to use the best view.

Database systems contain metadata tables that hold data about the tables and other structures used by the system. The metadata tables facilitate the system in its operations. Here is an example where a metadata table can facilitate the process of finding the best view to answer a query in an OLAP system. The coordinate system defined by the aggregation levels forms the basis for organizing the metadata for tracking the materialized views. Table 10.6 displays the metadata for the materialized views shaded in Figure 10.13. The two dimensions labeled *Calendar* and *Customer* form the composite key. The *Blocks* column tracks the actual

Table 10.6 Example of Materialized View Metadata

Dimensions		Blocks	ViewID
Calendar	*Customer*		
0	0	10,000,000	1
0	2	50,000	3
0	3	1000	5
1	0	300,000	2
2	1	10,000	4

number of blocks in each materialized view. The *ViewID* column is used to identify the associated materialized view. The implementation stores materialized views as tables where the ViewID forms part of the table name. For example, the row with ViewID = 3 contains information on the aggregated view that is materialized as table **AST3** (short for automatic summary table 3).

Observe the general pattern in the coordinates of the views in the product graph with regard to ancestor relationships. Let Value(V, d) represent a function that returns the aggregation level for view V along dimension d. For any two views V_i and V_j, $V_i \neq V_j$, V_i is an ancestor of V_j if and only if for every dimension d of the composite key, Value(V_i, d) $\leq$ Value(V_j, d). This pattern in the keys can be utilized to identify ancestors of a given view by querying the metadata. The semantics of the product graph are captured by the metadata, permitting the OLAP system to search semantically for the best materialized ancestor view by querying the metadata table. After the best materialized view is determined, the OLAP system can rewrite the original query to utilize the best materialized view, and proceed.

Data Mining

Two general approaches are used to extract knowledge from a database. First, a user may have a hypothesis to verify or disprove. This type of analysis is done with standard database queries and statistical analysis. The second approach to extracting knowledge is to have the computer search for correlations in the data, and present promising hypotheses to the user for consideration. The methods included here are data mining techniques developed in the fields of Machine Learning and Knowledge Discovery.

Data mining algorithms attempt to solve a number of common problems. One general problem is categorization: Given a set of cases with known values for some parameters, classify the cases. For example, given observations of patients, suggest a diagnosis. Another general problem type is clustering: Given a set of cases, find natural groupings of the cases. Clustering is useful, for example, in identifying market segments. Association rules, also known as market basket analysis, are another common problem. Businesses sometimes want to know what items are frequently purchased together. This knowledge is useful, for example, when decisions are made about how to lay out a grocery store. There are many types of data mining available. Han and Kamber (2001) cover data mining in the context of data warehouses and OLAP systems. Mitchell (1997) is a rich resource, written from the machine learning perspective. Witten and Frank (2000) give a survey of data mining, along with freeware written in Java available from the Weka website (*www.cs.waikato.ac.nz/ml/weka*). The Weka website is a good option for those who wish to experiment with and modify existing algorithms. The major database vendors also offer data mining packages that function with their databases.

Due to the large scope of data mining, we focus on two forms of data mining: forecasting and text mining.

Forecasting

Forecasting is a form of data mining in which trends are modeled over time using known data, and future trends are predicted based on the model. There are many different prediction models with varying levels of sophistication. Perhaps the simplest model is the least squares line model. The best-fit line is calculated from known data points using the method of least squares. The line is projected into the future to determine predictions. Figure 10.17 shows a least squares line for an actual dataset. The crossed (jagged) points represent actual known data. The circular (dots) points represent the least squares line. When the least squares line projects beyond the known points, this region represents predictions. The intervals associated with the predictions in our figures represent a 90% prediction interval. That is, given an interval, there is a 90% probability that the actual value, when known, will lie in that interval.

The least squares line approach weights each known data point equally when building the model. The predicted upward trend in Figure 10.17 does not give any special consideration to the recent downturn.

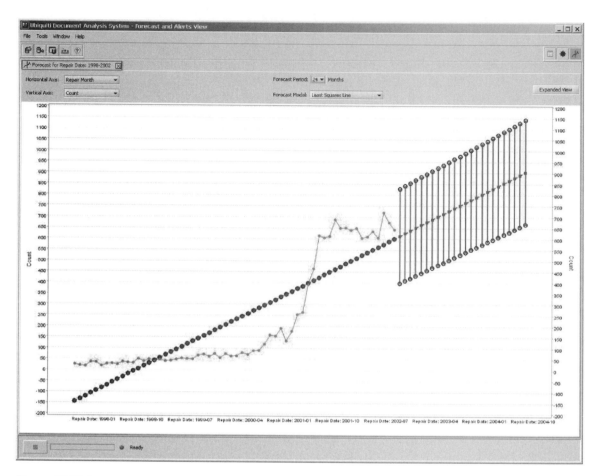

Figure 10.17 Least squares line. Courtesy of Ubiquiti Inc.

Exponential smoothing is an approach that weights recent history more heavily than distant history. Double exponential smoothing models two components: level and trend (hence, "double" exponential smoothing). As the known values change in level and trend, the model adapts. Figure 10.18 shows the predictions made using double exponential smoothing, based on the same dataset used to compute Figure 10.17. Notice the prediction is now more tightly bound to recent history.

Triple exponential smoothing models three components: level, trend, and seasonality. This is more sophisticated than double exponential smoothing, and gives better predictions when the data does indeed exhibit seasonal behavior. Figure 10.19 shows the predictions made by triple

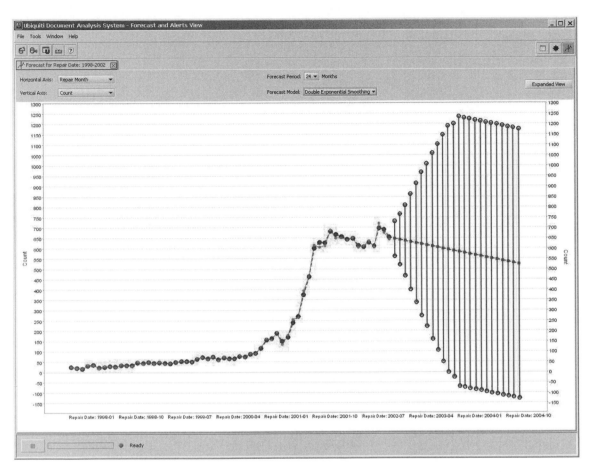

Figure 10.18 Double exponential smoothing. Courtesy of Ubiquiti Inc.

exponential smoothing, based on the same data used to compute Figures 10.17 and 10.18. Notice the prediction intervals are tighter than in Figures 10.17 and 10.18. This is a sign that the data varies seasonally; triple exponential smoothing is a good model for the given type of data.

Exactly how reliable are these predictions? If we revisit the predictions after time has passed and compare the predictions with the actual values, are they accurate? Figure 10.20 shows the actual data overlaid with the predictions made in Figure 10.19. Most of the actual data points do indeed lie within the prediction intervals. The prediction intervals look very reasonable. Why don't we use these forecast models to make our millions on Wall Street? Take a look at Figure 10.21, a cautionary tale. Figure 10.21 is also based on the triple

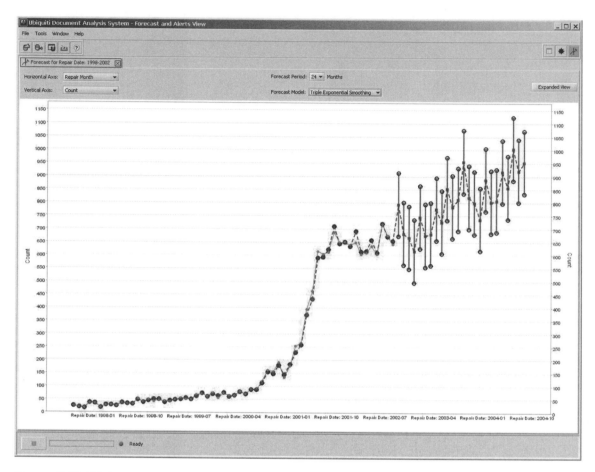

Figure 10.19 Triple exponential smoothing.
Courtesy of Ubiquiti Inc.

exponential smoothing model, using four years of known data for training, compared with five years of data used in constructing the model for Figure 10.20. The resulting predictions match for four months, and then diverge greatly from reality. The problem is that forecast models are built on known data, with the assumption that known data forms a good basis for predicting the future. This may be true most of the time; however, forecast models can be unreliable when the market is changing or about to change drastically. Forecasting can be a useful tool, but the predictions must be taken only as indicators.

The details of the forecast models discussed here, as well as many others, can be found in Makridakis et al. (1998).

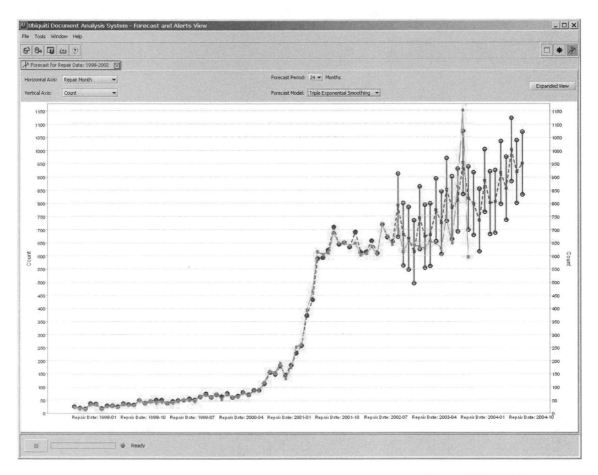

Text Mining

Most of the work on data processing over the past few decades has utilized structured data. The vast majority of systems in use today read and store data in relational databases. The schemas are organized neatly in rows and columns. However, there are large amounts of data that reside in free-form text. Descriptions of warranty claims are written in text. Medical records are written in text. Text is everywhere. Only recently has the work in text analysis made significant headway. Companies are now marketing products that focus on text analysis.

Let's look at a few of the possibilities for analyzing text and their potential impact. We'll take the area of automotive warranty claims as an example. When something goes

Figure 10.20 Triple exponential smoothing with actual values overlaying forecast values, based on five years of training data. Courtesy of Ubiquiti Inc.

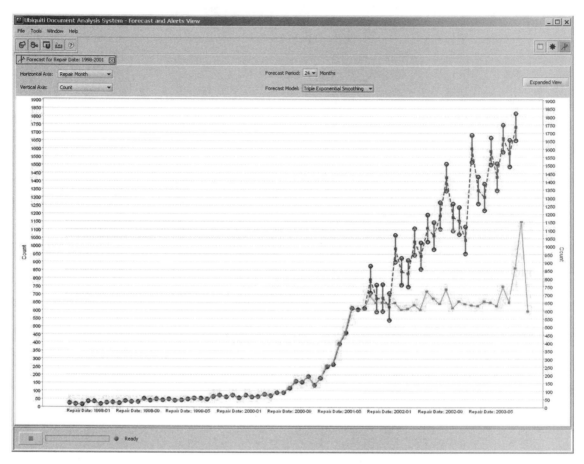

Figure 10.21 Triple exponential smoothing with actual values overlaying forecast values, based on four years of training data. Courtesy of Ubiquiti Inc.

wrong with your car, you bring it to an automotive shop for repairs. You describe to a shop representative what you've observed going wrong with your car. Your description is typed into a computer. A mechanic works on your car, and then types in observations about your car and the actions taken to remedy the problem. This is valuable information for the automotive companies and the parts manufacturers. If the information can be analyzed, they can catch problems early and build better cars. They can reduce breakdowns, saving themselves money, and saving their customers frustration.

The data typed into the computer is often entered in a hurry. The language includes abbreviations, jargon, mis-spelled words, and incorrect grammar. Figure 10.22 shows an example entry from an actual warranty claim database.

As you can see, the raw information entered on the shop floor is barely English. Figure 10.23 shows a cleaned-up version of the same text.

Even the cleaned-up version is difficult to read. The companies paying out warranty claims want each claim categorized in various ways, to track what problems are occurring. One option is to hire many people to read the claims and determine how each claim should be categorized. Categorizing the claims manually is tedious work. A more viable option, developed in the last few years, is to apply a software solution. Figure 10.24 shows some of the information that can be gleaned automatically from the text in Figure 10.22.

The software processes the text, determining the concepts likely represented in the text. This is not a simple word search. Synonyms map to the same concept. Some words map to different concepts depending on the context. The software uses an ontology that relates words and concepts to each other. After each warranty is categorized in various ways, it becomes possible to obtain useful aggregate information, as shown in Figure 10.25.

7 DD40 BASC 54566 CK OUT AC INOP PREFORM PID CK CK PCM PID ACC CK OK OPERATING ON AND OFF PREFORM POWER AND GRONED CK AT COMPRESOR FONED NO GRONED PREFORM PINPONT DIAG AND TRACE GRONED FONED BAD CO NECTION AT S778 REPAIR AND RETEST OK CK AC OPERATION

Figure 10.22 Example verbatim description in warranty claim. Courtesy of Ubiquiti Inc.

7 DD40 Basic 54566 Check Out Air Conditioning Inoperable Perform PID Check Check Power Control Module PID Accessory Check OK Operating On And Off Perform Power And Ground Check At Compressor Found No Ground Perform Pinpoint Diagnosis And Trace Ground Found Bad Connection At Splice 778 Repair And Retest OK Check Air Conditioning Operation

Figure 10.23 Cleaned-up version of description in warranty claim. Courtesy of Ubiquiti Inc.

Automated Coding	Confidence
Primary Group: Electrical	90%
Subgroup: Climate Control	85%
Part: Connector 1008	93%
Problem: Bad Connection	72%
Repair: Reconnect	75%
Location: Engin. Cmprt.	90%

Figure 10.24 Useful information extracted from verbatim description in warranty claim. Courtesy of Ubiquiti Inc.

Summary

Data warehousing, OLAP, and data mining are three areas of computer science that are tightly interlinked and marketed under the heading of business intelligence. The functionalities of these three areas complement each other. Data warehousing provides an infrastructure for storing and accessing large amounts of data in an efficient and user-friendly manner. Dimensional data modeling is the

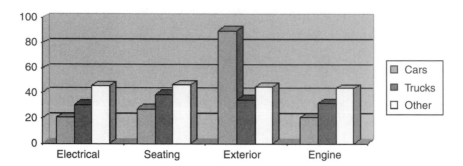

Figure 10.25 Aggregate data from warranty claims. Courtesy of Ubiquiti Inc.

approach best suited for designing data warehouses. OLAP is a service that overlays the data warehouse. The purpose of OLAP is to provide quick response to ad hoc queries, typically involving grouping rows and aggregating values. Roll-up and drill-down operations are typical. OLAP systems automatically perform some design tasks, such as selecting which views to materialize in order to provide quick response times. OLAP is a good tool for exploring the data in a human-driven fashion, when a person has a clear question in mind. Data mining is usually computer-driven, involving analysis of the data to create likely hypotheses that may be of interest to users. Data mining can bring to the forefront valuable and interesting structure in the data that would otherwise have gone unnoticed.

Tips and Insights for Database Professionals

Tip 1. To construct a data warehouse for a major application, use the four-step star schema dimensional data modeling (design) process by Kimball and Ross (2002): (1) select the business processes involved in satisfying a company's data warehouse information requirements; (2) for each business process, determine the granularity needed for drill-down operations; (3) determine the dimensions needed (attributes the users want to group by); and (4) identify the measures, or columns, to be aggregated when rows are grouped together.

Tip 2. When designing a fact table for a star schema, make the level of granularity the same as the most

detailed level available that any user would want to examine.

Tip 3. Normalization is not required for the fact table in a star schema. You want quick answers to queries, thus a single join away from the fact table to answer a query is highly desirable. To accomplish this, data is best stored in dimensional tables and hierarchies.

Tip 4. When designing for multiple business processes, use a data warehouse bus to present at a high level the organization of the dimensions across the business processes. Conform dimensions that are common across multiple business processes, thereby promoting consistent usage of terms and more meaningful discussions across business units.

Tip 5. If two business processes utilize mostly the same dimensions, consider whether it makes sense to implement the two into one star schema.

Tip 6. Use an OLAP system to store and maintain automatic summary tables as materialized views of commonly asked queries so future query response times will be minimized.

Tip 7. Use data warehousing and OLAP systems to obtain specific summary data from known detailed data. Use data mining techniques and systems to collect statistical data to support or disprove hypotheses (knowledge) about the data.

Literature Summary

The evolution and principles of data warehouses can be found in Barquin and Edelstein (1997), Cataldo (1997), Chaudhuri and Dayal (1997), Gray and Watson (1998), Kimball and Ross (1998, 2002), and Kimball and Caserta (2004). OLAP is discussed in Barquin and Edelstein (1997), Faloutsos, Matia, and Silberschatz (1996), Harinarayan, Rajaraman, and Ullman (1996), Kotidis and Roussopoulos (1999), Nadeau and Teorey (2002, 2003), and Thomsen (1997). Data mining principles and tools can be found in Han and Kamber (2001), Makridakis, Wheelwright, and Hyndman (1998), Mitchell (1997), The University of Waikato (2005), and Witten and Frank (2000), among many others.

11

CASE TOOLS FOR LOGICAL DATABASE DESIGN

Database design is just one part of the analysis and design phase of creating effective business application software (see Figure 11.1), but it is often the part that is the most challenging and the most critical to perform. In the previous chapters, we explored the classic ways of creating efficient and effective database designs, including ER modeling and the transformation of ER models into constructs by transformation rules. We also examined normalization, normal forms and denormalization, and specific topologies used in warehousing, such as star schema. All this information may leave your head spinning!

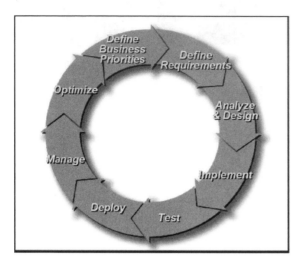

Figure 11.1 Business system life cycle. Courtesy of IBM Corp.

This chapter focuses on commercially available tools to simplify these design processes. These computer-aided system engineering, or CASE, tools provide functions that assist in system design. CASE tools are widely used in numerous industries and domains, such as circuit design, manufacturing, and architecture. Logical database design is another area where CASE tools have proven effective. This chapter explores the offerings of the major vendors in this space: IBM, Computer Associates, and Sybase. Each of these companies offers powerful, feature-rich technology for developing logical database designs and transitioning them into physical databases you can use.

Although it is impossible to present information on software products without some subjectivity and comment, we have sincerely attempted to discuss the capabilities of these products with minimal product bias or critique. Also, it is impossible to describe the features of these products in great detail in a chapter of this sort (a user manual of many hundred pages could be written describing each), so we have set the bar slightly lower, with the aim of surveying these products to give the reader a taste for the capabilities they provide. Further details can be obtained from the manufacturer's websites, which are listed in the "Literature Summary" section at the end of the chapter.

Introduction to the CASE Tools

In this chapter we will introduce some of the most popular and powerful products available for helping with logical database design: IBM's Rational Data Architect, Computer Associates' AllFusion ERwin Data Modeler, and Sybase's PowerDesigner. These CASE tools help the designer develop a well-designed database by walking through a process of conceptual design, logical design, and physical creation, as shown in Figure 11.2.

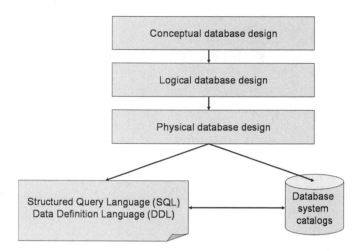

Figure 11.2 Database design process.

Computer Associates' AllFusion ERwin Data Modeler has been around the longest. A stand-alone product, AllFusion ERwin's strengths stem from relatively strong support of physical database modeling, the broadest set of technology partners, and third-party training. What it does it does well, but in recent years it has lagged in some advanced features. Sybase's PowerDesigner has come on strong in the past few years, challenging AllFusion ERwin. It has some advantages in reporting, and advanced features that will be described later in this chapter. IBM's Rational Data Architect is a new product that supplants IBM's previous product Rational Rose Data Modeler. Its strength lies in strong design checking; rich integration with IBM's broad software development platform, including products from their Rational, Information Management, and Tivoli divisions; and advanced features that will be described below.

In previous chapters, we have discussed the aspects of logical database design that CASE tools help design, annotate, apply, and modify. These include, for example, entity–relationship (ER) and Unified Modeling Language (UML) modeling, and how this modeling can be used to develop a logical database design. Within the ER design, there are several types of entity definitions and relationship modeling (unrelated, one-to-many, and many-to-many). These relationships are combined and normalized into schema patterns known as normal forms (e.g., 3NF, snowflake schema). An effective design requires the clear definition of keys, such as the primary key, the foreign key, and unique keys within relationships. The addition of constraints to limit the usage (and abuses) of the system within reasonable bounds or business rules is also critical. The effective logical design of the database will have a profound impact on the performance of the system, as well as the ease with which the database system can be maintained and extended.

There are several other CASE products that we will not discuss in this book. A few additional products worth investigating include Datanamic's DeZign for Databases, QDesigner by Quest Software, Visible Analyst by Standard, and Embarcadero ER/Studio. The Visual Studio .NET Enterprise Architect edition includes a version of Visio with some database design stencils that can be used to create ER models. The cost and function of these tools varies wildly, from open-source products up through enterprise software that costs thousands of dollars per license.

The full development cycle includes an iterative cycle of understanding business requirements; defining product requirements; analysis and design; implementation; test (component, integration, and system); deployment; administration and optimization; and change management. No single product currently covers that entire scope. Instead, product vendors provide, to varying degrees, suites of products that focus on portions of that cycle. CASE tools for database design largely focus on the analysis and design portion, and to a lesser degree, the testing portion of this iterative cycle.

CASE tools provide software that simplifies or automates some of the steps described in Figure 11.2. Conceptual design includes steps such as describing the business entities and functional requirements of the database; logical design includes definition of entity relationships and normal forms; and physical database design helps transform the logical design into actual database objects, such as tables, indexes, and constraints. The software tools provide significant value to database designers by:

1. Dramatically reducing the complexity of conceptual and logical design, both of which can be rather difficult to do well. This reduced complexity results in better database design in less time and with less skill requirements for the user.

2. Automating transformation of the logical design to the physical design (at least the basic physical design). This not only reduces time and skill requirements for the designer, but significantly removes the chance of manual error in performing the conversion from the logical model to the physical data definition language (DDL), which the database server will "consume" (i.e., as input) to create the physical database.

3. Providing the reporting, roundtrip engineering, and reverse engineering that make such tools invaluable in maintaining systems over a long period of time. System design can and does evolve over time due to changing and expanding business needs. Also, the people who design the system (sometimes teams of people) may not be the same as those charged with maintaining the system. The complexity of large systems combined with the need for continuous adaptability virtually necessitates the use of CASE tools to help visualize, reverse engineer, and track the system design over time.

You can find a broader list of available database design tools at the website Database Answers (*www.databaseanswers.com/ modelling_tools.htm*), maintained by David Alex Lamb at Queen's University in Kingston, Canada.

Key Capabilities to Watch for

Design tools should be able to help you with both data modeling and logical database design. Both processes are important. A good distinction between these appears on the Database Answers website.

For data modeling, the question you are asking is: What does the world being modeled look like? In particular, you are looking for similarities between things. Then you identify a "supertype" of a thing that may have subtypes—for example, Corporate Customers and Personal Customers. If, for example, supplier contacts are conceptually different things from customer contacts, then the answer is that they should be modeled separately. On the other hand, if they are merely subsets of the same thing, then treat them as the same thing.

For database design, you are answering a different question: How can I efficiently design a database that will support the functions of a proposed application or website? The key task here is to identify similarities between entities so that you can integrate them into the same table, usually with a "Type" indicator. For example, a **Customer** table, which combines all attributes of both Corporate Customers and Personal Customers. As a result, it is possible to spend a great deal of time breaking things out when creating a data model, and then collapsing them back together when designing the corresponding database.

Support for programmable and physical design attributes with a design tool can also expand the value a tool provides. In database terms, aspects to watch for will include support for indexes, uniqueness, triggers, and stored procedures.

The low-end tools (selling for less than U.S. $100 or available as open-source) provide the most basic functionality for ER modeling. The higher-end products provide the kinds of support needed for serious project design, such as:
- Complete roundtrip engineering
- UML design
- Schema evolution; change management
- Reverse engineering of existing systems
- Team support, allowing multiple people to work on the same project concurrently
- Integration with Eclipse and .NET and other tooling products
- Component and convention reuse (being able to reuse naming standards, domains, and logical models over multiple design projects)
- Reusable assets (e.g., extensibility, template)
- Reporting

The Basics

All of the products in question provide strong, easy-to-use functions for both data modeling and database design. All of these products provide the ability to graphically represent ER relationships. These tools also provide transformation processes to map from an ER model into an SQL design (DDL), using the transformation types described earlier in Chapter 5:
- Transform each entity into a table containing the key and nonkey attributes of the entity.

- Transform every many-to-many binary or binary recursive relationship into a relationship table with the keys of the entities and the attributes of the relationship.
- Transform every ternary or higher-level *n*-ary relationship into a relationship table.

Similarly, these tools produce the transformation table types described in Chapter 5:

- An entity table with the same information content as the original entity.
- An entity table with the embedded foreign key of the parent entity.
- A relationship table with the foreign keys of all the entities in the relationship.

Chapter 5 also described rules for null transformations that must apply, and the CASE tools typically enforce these.

These CASE tools also help with the modeling of normal forms and denormalization to develop a true physical schema for your database, as described in Chapter 5. The tools provide graphic interfaces for physical database design as well as basic modeling of uniqueness, constraints, and indexes. Figure 11.3 shows an example of IBM's Rational Data Architect's GUI for modeling ERs. Figure 11.4 shows a similar snapshot of the interface for Computer Associates' AllFusion ERwin Data Modeler.

After creating an ER model, the CASE tool enables easy modification of the model and its attributes through graphical interfaces. An example is shown in Figure 11.5 with IBM's Rational Data Architect, illustrating attribute editing. Of these CASE tools, Rational Data Architect has perhaps the most useful UML modeling function for data modeling and design. Its predecessor, Rational Rose Data Modeler, was the industry's first UML-based data modeler, and IBM has continued its development in this area with Rational Data Architect. UML provides a somewhat richer notation than information engineering (IE) entity–relationship diagram (ERD) notation, particularly for conceptual and logical data modeling. However, the IE-ERD notation is older and more commonly used. One of the nice aspects of Rational Data Architect is the ability to work with either UML or IE notation.

Figure 11.6 shows the AllFusion ERwin screen for defining the cardinality of entity relationships. It is worth noting that many relationships do not need to enter this dialog at all.

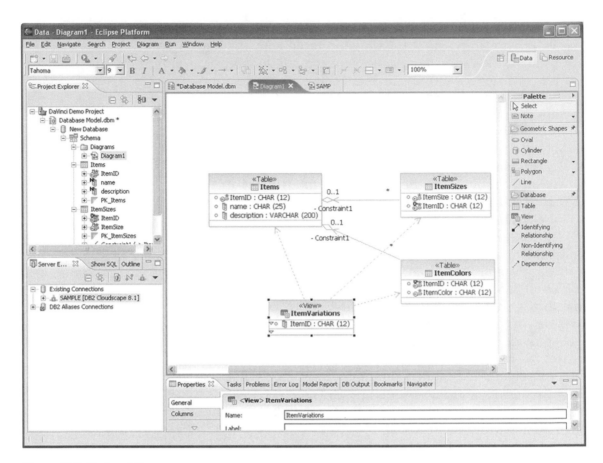

Figure 11.3 Rational Data Architect ER modeling. Courtesy of IBM Rational Division.

Generating a Database from a Design

To really take your design to the next level (i.e., a practical level) you will need a good design tool that can interact with the specific database product you use to actually create the DDL and associated scripts or commands that create and modify the basic database for you. For instance, using the example of Chapter 7, we have created an ER model containing sales relationships, shown in Table 11.1.

The CASE tools will automatically generate the required scripts, including the DDL specification to create the actual database, and will provide you with an option to apply those changes to an actual database, as follows:

```
create table customer (cust_no char(6),
    job_title varchar(256),
    primary key (cust_no),
```

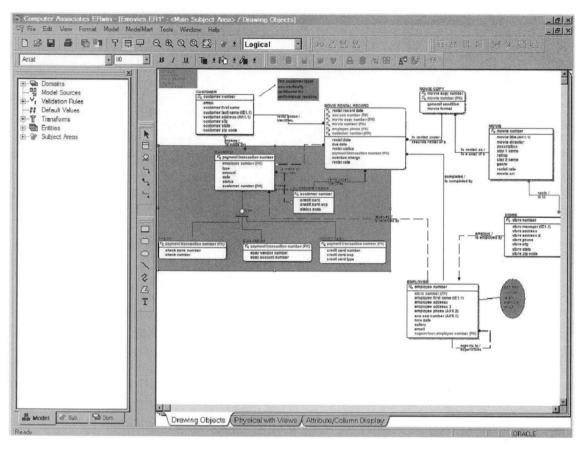

Figure 11.4 AllFusion ERwin Data Modeler ER modeling. Picture from Computer Associates.

```
    foreign key (job_title) references job
    on delete set null on update cascade);

create table job (job_title varchar(256),
    primary key (job_title));

create table order (order_no char(9),
    cust_no char(6) not null,
    primary key (order_no),
    foreign key (cust_no) references customer
    on delete cascade on update cascade);

create table salesperson (sales_name varchar(256),
    dept_no char(2),
    primary key (sales_name),
    foreign key (dept_no) references department
    on delete set null on update cascade);

create table department (dept_no char(2),
    primary key (dept_no));
```

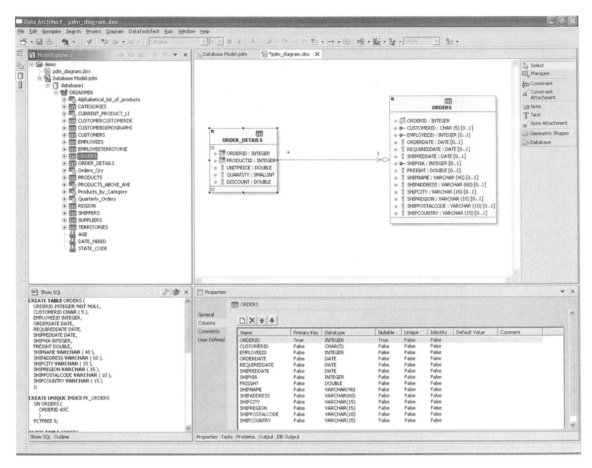

Figure 11.5 Property editing with IBM's Rational Data Architect. Courtesy of IBM Rational Division.

```
create table item (item_no char(6),
    dept_no char(2),
    primary key (item_no),
    foreign key (dept_no) references department
    on delete set null on update cascade);

create table order_item_sales (order_no char(9),
    item_no char(6),
    sales_name varchar(256) not null,
    primary key (order_no, item_no),
    foreign key (order_no) references order
    on delete cascade on update cascade,
    foreign key (item_no) references item
    on delete cascade on update cascade,
    foreign key (sales_name) references salesperson
    on delete cascade on update cascade);
```

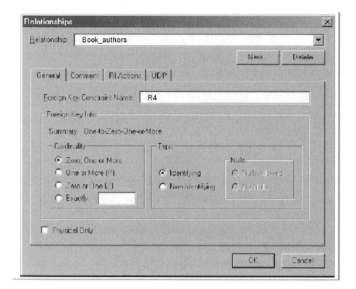

Figure 11.6 Specifying one-to-many relationships with ERwin. Courtesy of Computer Associates.

Table 11.1 ER Model Containing Sales Relationships

ER Construct	FDs
Customer(many): Job(one)	cust-no -> job-title
Order(many): Customer(one)	order-no -> cust-no
Salesperson(many): Department(one)	sales-name -> dept-no
Item(many): Department(one)	item-no -> dept-no
Order(many): Item(many): Salesperson(one)	order-no, item-no -> sales-name
Order(many): Department(many): Salesperson(one)	order-no, dept-no -> sales-name

```
create table order_dept_sales (order_no char(9),
    dept_no char(2),
    sales_name varchar(256) not null,
    primary key (order_no, dept_no),
    foreign key (order_no) references order
    on delete cascade on update cascade,
    foreign key (dept_no) references department
    on delete cascade on update cascade,
```

```
foreign key (sales_name) references salesperson
on delete cascade on update cascade);
```

It is worth noting that with all the CASE tools we discuss here, the conversion of the logical design to the physical design is quite rudimentary. These tools help create basic database objects, such as tables and, in some cases, indexes. However, the advanced features of the database server are often not supported—where they are supported, the CASE tool is usually behind by two or three software releases. Developing advanced physical design features, such as multidimensional clustering or materialized views, is far beyond the capabilities of the logical design tools we are discussing. Advanced physical database design is often highly dependant on data density and data access patterns. One feature of Rational Data Architect that stands out is that it provides linkages with the automatic computing (self-managing) capabilities within DB2 to provide semi-automated selection of advanced physical design attributes.

Figure 11.7 shows an example with ERwin schema generation, generating the DB2 DDL directly from the ER model designed within ERwin.

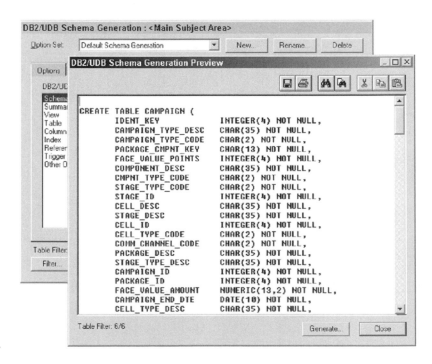

Figure 11.7 ERwin schema generation for a DB2 database. Picture from IBM (*www.redbooks.ibm.com/abstracts/redp3714.html?Open*).

Other very important capabilities shared by these tools include the ability to reverse-engineer existing databases (for which you may not have an existing ER or physical UML model), and the ability to automatically materialize the physical model or incremental changes of a model onto a real database. This capacity enables you to synchronize your database design with a real database as you make changes. This capability is massively useful for incremental application and database development, as well as for incremental maintenance.

Database Support

All of these products support a large array of database types. Certainly, all of the major database vendors are supported by each of these products (i.e., DB2 UDB, DB2 zOS, Informix IDS, Oracle, SQL Server), and a much larger set is supported through ODBC. However, what really matters most to the application developer is whether the database he or she is programming toward is directly supported by the CASE design tool. Database support is not equal between these products. Also, very significantly, each database product will have unique features of its own (such as reverse scan indexes, informational constraints, and so forth) that are not standard. One of the qualitative attributes of a good database design tool is whether it distinguishes and supports the unique extensions of individual database products. Each of the products has a strong history for doing so: in descending order, AllFusion ERwin Data Modeler, PowerDesigner, and Rational Data Architect. Notably, IBM's Rational Data Architect has a somewhat smaller range of supported databases than the other products, though it does support all the major database platforms. However, Rational Data Architect can be expected over time to have the tightest integration with the DB2 and Informix families, since all of these products are developed by IBM. Database designers are advised to investigate the level of support provided by a CASE tool for the database being developed toward, to ensure the level of support is adequate. Figure 11.8 shows an example of database server selection with the AllFusion ERwin Data Modeler.

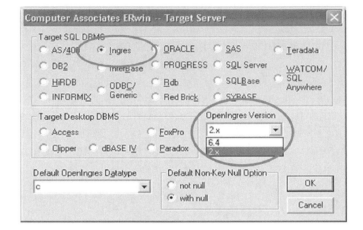

Figure 11.8 DBMS selection in AllFusion ERwin Data Modeler. Picture from Computer Associates (*http://iua.org.uk/conference/ Autumn%202003/Ruth% 20Wunderle.ppt#9*).

Collaborative Support

All three of these products are designed for collaborative development, so that multiple developers can work together to design portions of a database design, either supporting different applications or collaborating on the same portions. These collaboration features fall into two domains:

1. *Concurrency control.* This form of collaboration ensures that multiple designers do not modify the same component of the database design at the same time. This is comparable in software development terms to a source code control system.

2. *Merge and collaboration capabilities.* This form of collaboration enables designers to combine designs or merge their latest changes into a larger design project. These merging capabilities compare components between what is already logged into the project system and what a designer wishes to add or modify. The CASE tools identify the conflicting changes and visually identify them for the designer, who can decide which changes should be kept and which ones discarded in favor of the model currently defined in the project.

Figure 11.9 shows Sybase's PowerDesigner merge GUI, which identifies significant changes between the existing schema and the new schema being merged. In particular, notice how the merge tool has identified a change in **Table_1** Column_4, which has changed base types. The tool

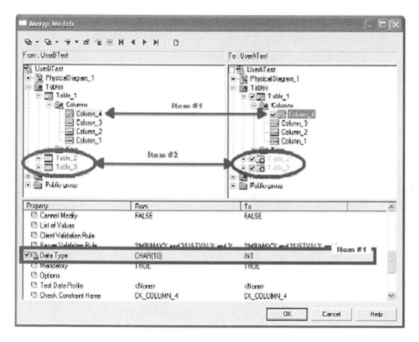

Figure 11.9 Merge process with PowerDesigner. Courtesy of Sybase.

also found that **Table_2** and **Table_3,** which exist in the merging design, were not present in the base design. AllFusion ERwin Data Modeler and Rational Data Architect have similar capabilities for merging design changes.

Distributed Development

Distributed development has become a fact of life for large enterprise development teams, in which groups of developers collaborate from geographically diverse locations to develop a project. The phenomenon is not only true across floors of a building, or between sites in a city, but now across states, provinces, and even countries. In fact, outsourcing of software development has become a *tour de force*, with many analysts projecting that the average enterprise will ultimately outsource 60% of application work, shifting aspects of project development to locations with cheaper labor. As the META Group said in its September 16, 2004 Offshore Market Milieu report: "With global resources costing one-third to one-fifth that of American employees—without accounting for hidden costs—and

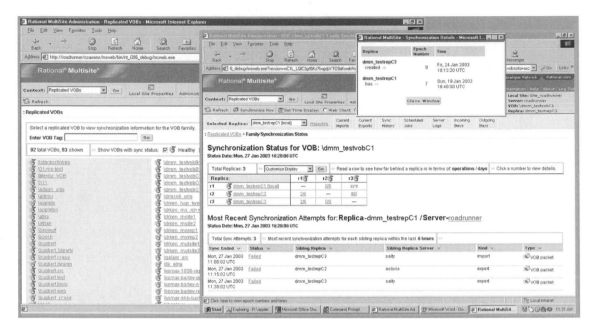

Figure 11.10 IBM's Rational MultiSite software for massively distributed software management. Courtesy of IBM Rational Division.

having higher process discipline, offshore strategies now pervade North American IT organizations."

Therefore, developers of database software working in a distributed collaborative environment need to consider the collaborative and distributed qualities of CASE tools for database design. The trend toward collaborative development and distributed development shows no sign of slowing; rather, it is on the increase. In the existing space, IBM's Rational MultiSite software, shown in Figure 11.10, allows the best administration across geographically diverse locations for replicating project software and data and subsequently merging the results. Rational MultiSite is a technology layered on top of Rational ClearCase and Rational ClearQuest (development and source code control products) to allow local replicas of Rational ClearCase and Rational ClearQuest repositories. Rational MultiSite also handles the automatic synchronization of the replicas. This is particularly useful for companies with distributed development who wish to have fast response times for their developers via access to local information, and such replication is often an absolute requirement for geographically distributed teams.

Application Life Cycle Tooling Integration

The best CASE tools for database design are integrated with a complete suite of application development tools that cover the software development life cycle. This allows the entire development team to work from an integrated tool platform, rather than the data modelers being off in their own world. Only the largest vendors offer this, and in fact true tooling integration across the development life cycle is somewhat rare. This solution is, in a very real way, the philosopher's stone of development infrastructure vendors. All the vendors who produce software development platforms have been working to develop this breadth during the past two decades. The challenge is elusive simply because it is hard to do well. The three companies we are discussing here all have broad offerings, and provide some degree of integration with their database design CASE technology.

For Computer Associates, the AllFusion brand is a family of development life cycle tools. It is intended to cover designing, building, deploying, and managing e-business applications. Sybase also has a broad product suite, and their strength is in the collaborative technology. From a design perspective, the ability to plug Sybase's PowerDesigner into their popular Sybase PowerBuilder application development tooling is a very nice touch, as seen in Figure 11.11. The IBM tooling is clearly the broadest based, and their new IBM Software Development Platform, which is built heavily but not exclusively from their Rational products, covers everything from requirements building to portfolio management, source code control, architectural design constraints, automated testing, performance analysis, and cross-site development. A representation of the IBM Software Development Platform is shown in Figure 11.12.

Design Compliance Checking

With all complex designs, and particularly when multiple designers are involved, it can be very hard to maintain the integrity of the system design. The best software architects and designers grapple with this by defining design guidelines and rules. These are sometimes called *design patterns* and *anti-patterns*.

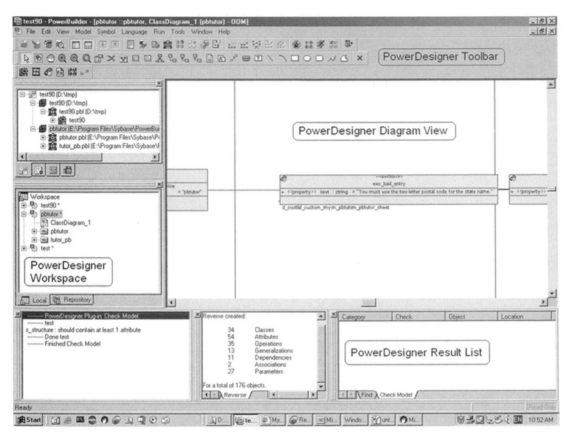

Figure 11.11 Sybase's PowerDesigner plug-in to Sybase PowerBuilder. Picture from Berndt Hambock (*www.isug.com/emea/PBUGG. html*).

A design pattern is a design principle that is expected to be generally adhered to within the system design. Conversely, an anti-pattern is precisely the opposite. It represents flaws in the system design that can occur either through violation of the design patterns or through explicit definition of an anti-pattern. The enforcement of design patterns and anti-patterns is an emerging attribute of the best CASE tools for systems design in general, and database design in particular. Figure 11.13 shows an example of the interface used in Rational Data Architect for compliance checking, which scans the system to enforce design patterns and check for anti-patterns. Some degree of support for design pattern and anti-pattern checking exists in AllFusion ERwin Data Modeler and Sybase's PowerDesigner as well. The compliance checking in IBM's Rational products is the most mature in general, with the notion of design patterns and

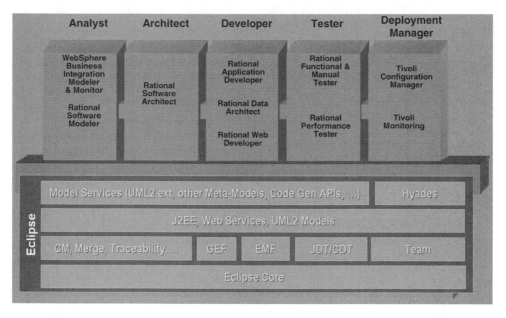

anti-patterns being a key philosophical point for IBM's Rational family of products. Some examples of things these compliance checkers will scan for include:

- Complete roundtrip engineering
- Design and normalization
  - Discover first, second, and third normal forms
- Index and storage
  - Check for excessive indexing
- Naming standards
- Security compliance
- Sarbanes-Oxley compliance
  - Check for valid data model and rules
- Model syntax checks

Reporting

Reporting capabilities are a very important augmentation of the design capabilities in CASE tools for database design. These reports allow you to examine your ER and UML modeling and database schema in both graphical and textual formats. The Sybase products have a superb reputation for reporting features; their products enable you to generate

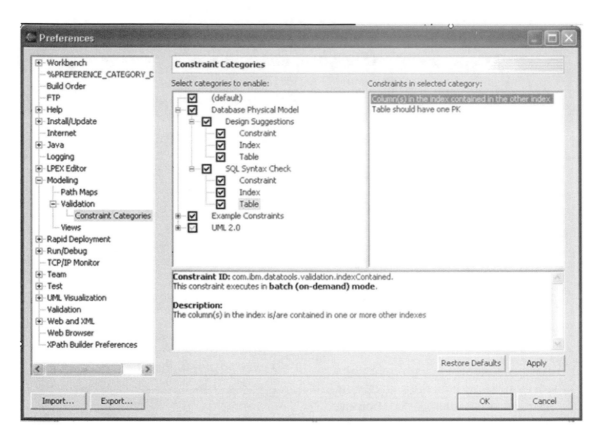

Figure 11.13 Modeling and database compliance checking. Courtesy of IBM Rational Division.

reports in common formats like Microsoft Word. Reporting can include both the modeling and the annotations that the designer has added. It can cover physical data models, conceptual data models, object-oriented models (UML), business process models, and semistructure data using XML. Notice in Figure 11.14 how the fourth page, which contains graphics, can be oriented in landscape mode, while the remaining pages are kept in portrait mode. AllFusion ERwin and Rational Data Architect also provide rich reporting features, though PowerDesigner has the richest capabilities.

Modeling a Data Warehouse

In Chapter 10 we discussed the unique design considerations required for data warehousing and decision support. Typically, warehouses are designed to support complex queries that provide analytic analysis of your data. As such, they exploit different schema topology models, such

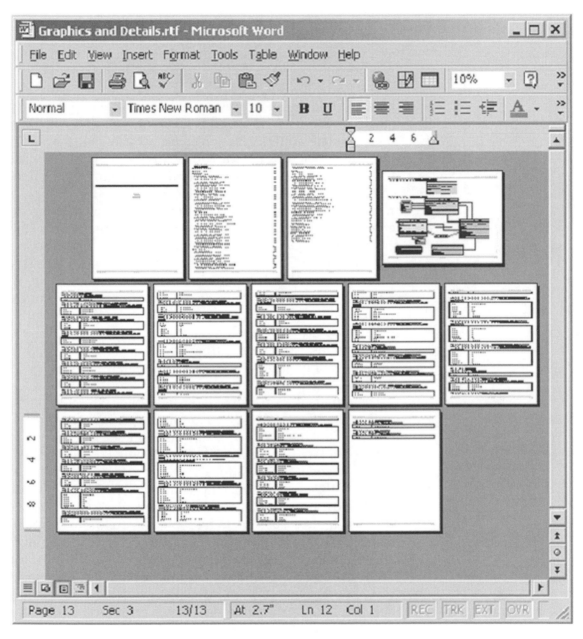

Figure 11.14 Reporting features with Sybase's PowerDesigner. Courtesy of Sybase.

as star schema and horizontal partitioning. They typically exploit data views and materialized data views, data aggregation, and multidimensional modeling far more extensively than other operational and transactional databases.

Traditionally, warehouses have been populated with data that is extracted and transformed from other operational databases. However, more and more companies are moving to consolidate system resources and provide real-time analytics by either feeding warehouses data in near-real-time (with a few minutes latency) or entirely merging their transactional data stores with their analytic warehouses into a single server or cluster. These trends are known as *active data warehousing*, and pose even more complex design challenges. There is a vast need for CASE tooling in this space.

Sybase offers a CASE tool known as Sybase Industry Warehouse Studio (IWS). Sybase IWS is really a set of industry-specific, prepackaged warehouses that require some limited customization. Sybase IWS tooling provides a set of wizards for designing star schemas and dimensional tables, and for implementing denormalization, summarization, and partitioning; as usual, the Sybase tools are strong on reporting facilities.

The industry domains covered by IWS are fairly reasonable—they include IWS for Media, IWS for Healthcare, IWS for Banking, IWS for Capital Markets, IWS for Life Insurance, IWS for Telco, IWS for Credit Cards, IWS for P&C Insurance, and IWS for CRA.

IBM's DB2 Cube Views (shown in Figure 11.15) provides OLAP and multidimensional modeling. DB2 Cube Views allows you to create metadata objects to dimensionally model OLAP structures and relational data. The graphical interface allows you to create, manipulate, import, or export cube models, cubes, and other metadata objects.

Sybase IWS uses standard database design constructs that port to many database systems, such as DB2 UDB, Oracle, Microsoft SQL Server, Sybase Adaptive Server Enterprise, and Sybase IQ. In contrast, IBM's DB2 Cube Views is designed specifically to exploit DB2 UDB. The advantage of DB2 Cube Views is that it can exploit product-specific capabilities in the DB2 database that may not be generally available in other databases. Some examples of this include materialized query tables (precomputed aggregates and cubes), multidimensional clustering, triggers, functional

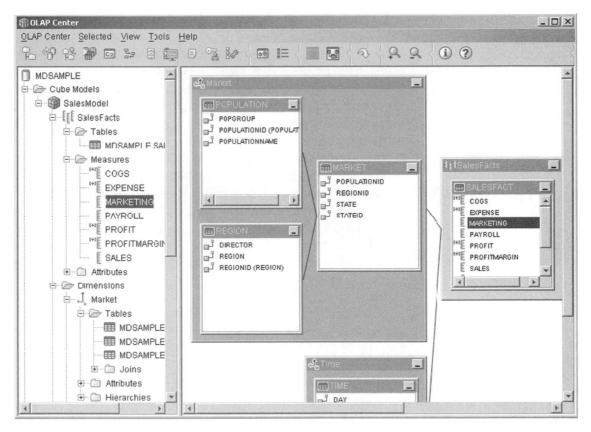

Figure 11.15 DB2 Cube Views interface. Courtesy of IBM Rational Division.

dependencies, shared-nothing partitioning, and replicated MQTs. The dependence of Sybase IWS on the lowest common denominator database feature provides flexibility when selecting the database server but may prove extremely limiting for even moderately sized marts and warehouses (i.e., larger than 100 GB), where advanced access and design features become critical.

To summarize and contrast, Sybase offers portable warehouse designs that require minimal customization and are useful for smaller systems, and DB2 Cube Views provides significantly richer and more powerful capabilities, which fit larger systems, require more customization, and necessitate DB2 UDB as the database server.

AllFusion ERwin Data Modeler has basic support to model OLAP and multidimensional databases, but does not have the same richness of tooling and wizards that the other companies offer to actually substantially simplify the design process of these complex systems.

Semistructured Data—XML

XML (eXtensible Markup Language) is a data model consisting of nodes of several types linked together with ordered parent–child relationships to form a hierarchy. One representation of that data model is textual—there are others that are not text! XML has increasingly become a data format of choice for data sharing between systems. As a result, increasing volumes of XML data are being generated.

While XML data has some structure it is not a fully structured format, such as the table definitions that come from a fully structured modeling using ER with IE or UML. XML is known in the industry as a semistructured format: It lacks the strict adherence of schema that structured data schemas have, yet it has some degree of structure that distinguishes it from completely unstructured data, such as image and video data.

Standards are forming around XML to allow it to be used for database style design and query access. The dominant standards are XML Schema and XML Query (also known as XQuery). Also worth noting is the OMG XMI standard, which defines a standard protocol for defining a structured format for XML interchange, based on an object model. Primarily for interfacing reasons, UML tools such as MagicDraw have taken XMI seriously and have therefore become the preferred alternatives in the open-source space.

XML data is text based and self-describing (meaning that XML described the type of each data point, and defines its own schema). XML has become popular for Internet-based data exchange based on these qualities as well as being "well-formed." Well-formed is a computer science term, implying XML's grammar is unambiguous through the use of mandated structure that guarantees terms are explicitly prefixed and closed. Figure 11.16 shows the conceptual design of a semistructured document type named "Recipe." Figure 11.17 shows an XML document for a hot dog recipe. Notice that the file is completely textual.

IBM's Rational Data Architect and Sybase's PowerDesigner have taken the lead in being early adopters of XML data modeling CASE tools. Both products support the modeling of semistructured data through XML and provide graphical tooling for modeling XML hierarchies.

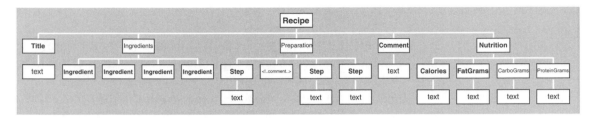

Figure 11.16 An XML schema for a recipe.

```
<?xml version="1.0" encoding="UTF-8" ?>
<Recipe TimeToPrepare="5" CookMethod="Grill" Difficulty="Easy" Serves="1"
Category="Entrees">
 <Title>Hot Dog with Onions</Title>
 <Ingredients>
  <Ingredient Name="Hot Dog" Amount="1"  />
  <Ingredient Name="Hot Dog Bun" Amount="1" />
  <Ingredient Name="Sliced Onion" Amount="1" Unit="tablespoon" />
  <Ingredient Name="Mustard" Amount="2" Unit="teaspoon" />
  <Ingredient Name="Relish" Amount="2" Unit="teaspoon" />
 </Ingredients>
 <Preparation>
  <Step>Preheat Grill to 350&#176; F. </Step>
  <!-- &#176; is the degree symbol -->
  <Step>Grill Hot dog for 5 Minutes, Turning frequently to avoid burning</Step>
  <Step>Put Hot Dog on bun, add mustard, onion, and relish</Step>
 </Preparation>
 <Comment>Some like to use spicy mustard,or replace mustard with
catsup</Comment>
 <Nutrition>
  <Calories>300</Calories>
  <FatGrams>18.5</FatGrams>
  <CarboGrams>12</CarboGrams>
  <ProteinGrams>9.5</ProteinGrams>
 </Nutrition>
</Recipe>
```

Figure 11.17 An XML document for a hot dog.

Summary

There are several good CASE tools available for computer-assisted database design. This chapter has touched on some of the features for three of the leading products: IBM's Rational Data Architect, Computer Associates' AllFusion ERwin Data Modeler, and Sybase's PowerDesigner. Each provides powerful capabilities to assist in developing ER models and transforming those models to logical database designs and physical implementations. All of these products support a wide range of database vendors, including DB2 UDB, DB2 zOS, Informix Data Server (IDS), Oracle, SQL Server, and many others through ODBC support. Each product has different advantages and strengths. The drawbacks a product may have now are certain to be improved over time, so discussing the relative merits of each product in a book can be somewhat of an injustice to a product that will deliver improved capabilities in the near future.

At the time of authoring this text, Computer Associates' AllFusion ERwin Data Modeler had advantages as a mature product with vast database support. The AllFusion products don't have the advanced complex feature support for XML and warehousing/analytics, but what they do support, they do well. Sybase's PowerDesigner sets itself apart with its superior reporting capabilities. IBM's Rational Data Architect has the best integration with a broad software application development suite of tooling, and the most mature use of UML. Both the Sybase and IBM tools are blazing new ground in their early support for XML semistructured data and for CASE tools for warehousing and OLAP. The best products provide the highest level of integration into a larger software development environment for large-scale collaborative, and possible geographically diverse, development. These CASE tools can dramatically reduce the time, cost, and complexity of developing, deploying, and maintaining a database design.

Tips and Insights for Database Professionals

Tip 1. Database designers are strongly encouraged to use one of the powerful and feature-rich CASE tools for developing logical database designs and

transitioning them into physical databases they can use. For a current list of tools, see *www.database answers.com/modeling_tools.htm*.

Tip 2. The chief motivations for selecting and using CASE tools are:

1. Desire to dramatically reduce the complexity of conceptual and logical designs.
2. Automatically transform a logical design into SQL table definitions or other data definition language constructs.
3. Obtain automatic reporting and reverse engineering capability.

Tip 3. Use lower-end tools (in the U.S. $100 range) if you only want to do ER modeling. Use higher-end tools for more complex tasks such as schema evaluation, UML design, reverse engineering, multiperson team support, integration with other software development tools, design compliance checking, or reporting

Tip 4. The best CASE tools for database design are those that are integrated with a complete suite of application tools that cover the entire software development life cycle. Examples of the most prominent of these tools, shown in this chapter, are:

1. IBM's Rational Data Architect
2. Computer Associates' AllFusion ERwin Data Modeler
3. Sybase's PowerDesigner

Tip 5. CASE tools for active data warehousing, decision support, and XML data modeling are available in today's marketplace.

Literature Summary

Current logical database design tools can be found in manufacturer websites, Database Answers, IBM Rational Software, Computer Associates, Sybase PowerDesigner, Directory of Data Modeling Resources (Infogoal), Objects by Design, Understanding Relational Databases: Referential Integrity, and Widom.

APPENDIX
THE BASICS OF SQL

Structured Query Language, or SQL, is the ISO-ANSI standard data definition language and data manipulation language for relational database management systems (DBMSs). Individual relational database systems use slightly different dialects of SQL syntax and naming rules, and these differences can be seen by consulting the SQL user guides for those systems. In this text, where we explore each step of the logical and design portion of the database life cycle, many examples of database table creation and manipulation make use of SQL syntax.

The basic use of SQL can be learned quickly and easily through reading this appendix. The more advanced features, such as statistical analysis and presentation of data, require more study and are beyond the reach of the typical nonprogrammer. However, SQL views can be set up by the database administrator (DBA) to help the nonprogrammer to set up repetitive queries, and other languages, such as forms, are being commercially sold for nonprogrammers. For the advanced database programmer, embedded SQL (in C programs, for instance) is widely available for the most complex database applications that need the power of procedural languages.

This appendix introduces the reader to the basic constructs for the SQL-99 (and SQL-92) database definition, queries, and updates through a sequence of examples with some explanatory text. We start with a definition of SQL terminology for data types and operators. This is followed by an explanation of the data definition language (DDL) constructs using the *create table* command and including a definition of the various types of integrity constraints such as foreign keys and referential integrity. Finally, we take a detailed look at the SQL-99 data manipulation language (DML) features through a series of both simple and more complex practical examples of database queries and updates.

The specific features of SQL as implemented by the major vendors IBM, Oracle, and Microsoft can be found in the references at the end of this appendix.

SQL Names and Operators

This section gives the basic rules for SQL-99 (and SQL-92) data types and operators.

- SQL names have no particular restrictions, but vendor-specific versions of SQL do have some restrictions. For example, in Oracle, names of tables and columns (attributes) can be up to 30 characters long, must begin with a letter, and can include the following symbols: a–z, 0–9, _, $, and #. Names should not duplicate reserved words or names for other objects (attributes, tables, views, indexes) in the database.
- Data types for attributes: character, character varying, numeric, decimal, integer, smallint, float, double precision, real, bit, bit varying, date, time, timestamp, interval.
- Logical operators: and, or, not, ( ).
- Comparison operators: =, <>, <, <=, >, >=, ( ), in, any, some, all, between, not between, is null, is not null, like.
- Set operators:
  - union—combines queries to display any row in each subquery
  - intersect—combines queries to display distinct rows common to all subqueries
  - except—combines queries to return all distinct rows returned by the first query but not the second (this is "minus" or "difference" in some versions of SQL)
- Set functions: count, sum, min, max, avg.
- Advanced value expressions: CASE, CAST, row value constructors. The CASE expression is similar to the CASE expressions in programming languages in which a *select* command needs to produce different results when there are different values of the search condition. The CAST expression allows you to convert data of one type to a different type, subject to some restrictions. Row value constructors allow one to set up multiple-column value comparisons with a much simpler expression than is normally required in SQL (see Melton and Simon, 1993, for detailed examples).

Data Definition Language

The basic definitions for SQL objects (tables and views) are:

- *create table*—defines a table and all its attributes
- *alter table*—adds new columns, drops columns, or modifies existing columns in a table
- *drop table*—deletes an existing table
- *create view, drop view*—defines/deletes a database view (see "SQL Views" section)

Some versions of SQL also have *create index/drop index*, which defines/deletes an index on a particular attribute or composite of several attributes in a particular table.

The following table creation examples are based on a simple database of three tables: **customer**, **item**, and **order**. (Reminder, we put table names in boldface throughout the book.)

```
create table customer
    (cust_num     numeric,
     cust_name    char(20),
     address      varchar(256),
     credit_level numeric,
     check (credit_level >= 1000),
     primary key (cust_num));
```

Note that the attribute cust_num could be defined as "numeric not null unique" instead of explicitly defined as the primary key, since they both have the same meaning. However, it would be redundant to have both forms in the same table definition. The check rule is an important integrity constraint that tells SQL to automatically test each insertion of credit_level value for something greater than or equal to 1000. If not, an error message should be displayed.

```
create table item
    (item_num     numeric,
     item_name    char(20),
     price        numeric,
     weight       numeric,
     primary key  (item_num));

create table order
    (ord_num      char(15),
     cust_num     numeric not null,
     item_num     numeric not null,
     quantity     numeric,
```

```
total_cost      numeric,
primary key     (ord_num),
foreign key     (cust_num) references customer
      on delete no action on update cascade,
foreign key     (item_num) references item
      on delete no action on update cascade);
```

SQL, while allowing for the above format for primary key and foreign key, recommends a more detailed format, shown below for table **order**.

```
constraint pk_constr primary key (ord_num),
constraint fk_constr1 foreign key (cust_num)
   references customer (cust_num)
   on delete no action on update cascade,
constraint fk_constr2 foreign key (item_num)
   references item (item_num)
   on delete no action on update cascade);
```

Here, pk_constr is a primary key constraint name, and fk_constr1 and fk_constr2 are foreign key constraint names. The word "constraint" is a keyword, and the object in parentheses after the table name is the name of the primary key in that table referenced by the foreign key.

The following constraints are common for attributes defined in the SQL *create table* commands:

- *Not null.* A constraint that specifies that an attribute must have a non-null value.
- *Unique.* A constraint that specifies that the attribute is a candidate key—that is, it has a unique value for every row in the table. Every attribute that is a candidate key must also have the constraint "not null." The constraint "unique" is also used as a clause to designate composite candidate keys that are not the primary key. This is particularly useful when transforming ternary relationships to SQL.
- *Primary key.* The primary key is a set of one or more attributes, which, when taken collectively, allows us to identify uniquely an entity or table. The set of attributes should not be reducible (see "Superkeys, Candidate Keys, and Primary Keys" section in Chapter 6). The designation "primary key" for an attribute implies that the attribute must be "not null" and "unique," but the SQL keywords NOT NULL and UNIQUE are redundant for

any attribute that is part of a primary key, and need not be specified in the *create table* command.

- *Foreign key.* The referential integrity constraint specifies that a foreign key in a referencing table column must match an existing primary key in the referenced table. The references clause specifies the name of the referenced table. An attribute may be both a primary key and a foreign key, particularly in relationship tables formed from many-to-many binary relationships or from *n*-ary relationships.

Foreign key constraints are defined for row deletion on the referenced table and for the update of the primary key of the referenced table. The referential trigger actions for delete and update are similar:

- *on delete cascade*—the delete operation on the referenced table "cascades" to all matching foreign keys.
- *on delete set null*—foreign keys are set to null when they match the primary key of a deleted row in the referenced table. Each foreign key must be able to accept null values for this operation to apply.
- *on delete set default*—foreign keys are set to a default value when they match the primary key of the deleted row(s) in the reference table. Legal default values include a literal value, "user," "system user," or "no action."
- *on update cascade*—the update operation on the primary key(s) in the referenced table "cascades" to all matching foreign keys.
- *on update set null*—foreign keys are set to null when they match the old primary key value of an updated row in the referenced table. Each foreign key must be able to accept null values for this operation to apply.
- *on update set default*—foreign keys are set to a default value when they match the primary key of an updated row in the reference table. Legal default values include a literal value, "user," "system user," or "no action."

The "cascade" option is generally applicable when either the mandatory existence constraint or the ID dependency constraint is specified in the ER diagram for the referenced table, and either "set null" or "set default" is applicable when optional existence is specified in the ER diagram for the referenced table (see Chapters 2 and 5).

Some systems, such as DB2, have an additional option on delete or update, called "restricted." "Delete restricted" means that the referenced table rows are deleted only if there are no matching foreign key values in the referencing table. Similarly, "update restricted" means that the referenced table rows (primary keys) are updated only if there are no matching foreign key values in the referencing table.

Various column and table constraints can be specified as "deferrable" (the default is "not deferrable"), which means that the DBMS will defer checking this constraint until you commit the transaction. Often this is required for mutual constraint checking.

The following examples illustrate the *alter table* and *drop table* commands. The first *alter table* command modifies the cust_name data type from char(20) in the original definition to varchar(256). The second and third *alter table* commands add and drop a column, respectively. The *add column* option specifies the data type of the new column.

```
alter table customer
modify (cust_name varchar(256));

alter table customer
add column cust_credit_limit numeric;

alter table customer
drop column credit_level;

drop table customer;
```

Data Manipulation Language

Data manipulation language commands are used for queries, updates, and the definition of views. These concepts are presented through a series of annotated examples, from simple to moderately complex.

SQL *Select* Command

The SQL *select* command is the basis for all database queries. We look at a series of examples to illustrate the syntax and semantics for the *select* command for the most frequent types of queries in everyday business applications. To illustrate each of the commands we assume the following set of data in the database tables:

customer table

cust_num	cust_name	address	credit_level
001	Kirk	Enterprise	10
002	Spock	Enterprise	9
003	Scotty	Enterprise	8
004	Bones	Enterprise	8
005	Gorn	PlanetoidArena	1
006	Khan	CetiAlphaFive	2
007	Uhura	Enterprise	7
008	Chekov	Enterprise	6
009	Sulu	Enterprise	6

item table

item_num	item_name	price	weight
125	phaser	350	2
137	beam	1500	250
143	shield	4500	3000
175	fusionMissile	2750	500
211	captainsLog	50	2
234	starShip	25,000	15,000
356	sensor	245	15
368	intercom	1200	75
399	medicalKit	75	3

order table

ord_num	cust_num	item_num	quantity	total_cost
10012	005	125	2	700
10023	006	175	20	55,000
10042	003	137	3	4500
10058	001	211	1	50
10232	007	368	1	1200
10266	002	356	50	12,250

(Continued)

order table—*Cont'd*

ord_num	cust_num	item_num	quantity	total_cost
10371	004	399	10	750
11070	009	143	1	4500
11593	008	125	2	700
11775	006	125	3	1050
12001	001	234	1	25,000

Basic Commands

1. Display the entire **customer** table. The asterisk (*) denotes that all records from this table are to be read and displayed.

   ```
   select *
   from customer;
   ```

   This results in a display of the complete **customer** table (as shown above).

2. Display customer name, customer number, and credit level for all customers on the Enterprise with credit level greater than 7. Order by ascending sequence of customer name (the order by options are asc, desc). Note that the first selection condition is specified in the "where" clause and succeeding selection conditions are specified by "and" clauses. Character type data and other nonnumeric data are placed inside single quotes, but numeric data is given without quotes. Note that useful column names can be created by using formatting commands (which are not shown here).

   ```
   select cust_name, cust_num, credit_level
   from customer
   where address = 'Enterprise'
   and credit_level > 7
   order by cust_name asc;
   ```

customer name	customer no.	credit level
Bones	004	8
Kirk	001	10
Scotty	003	8
Spock	002	9

3. Display all customer and order item information (all columns), but omitting customers with credit level above 6. In this query the "from" clause shows the definition of abbreviations c and o for tables **customer** and **order**, respectively. The abbreviations can be used anywhere in the query to denote their respective table names. This example also illustrates a "join" between table **customer** and table **order** using the common attribute name cust_num, as shown in the "where" clause. The join finds matching cust_num values from the two tables and displays all the data from the matching rows, except where the credit number is 7 or above, and ordered by customer number.

```
select c.*, o.*
from customer as c, order as o
where c.cust_num = o.cust_num
and c.credit_level < 7
order by cust_no asc;
```

cust. no.	cust. name	address	credit level	order no.	item no.	qty	total cost
005	Gorn	PlanetoidArena	1	10012	125	2	700
006	Khan	CetiAlphaFive	2	11775	125	3	1050
006	Khan	CetiAlphaFive	2	10023	175	20	55000
008	Chekov	Enterprise	6	11593	125	2	700
009	Sulu	Enterprise	6	11070	143	1	4500

Union and Intersection Commands

1. Which items are ordered by customer 002 or customer 007? This query can be answered in two ways, one with a set operator (union) and the other with a logical operator (or).

```
select item_num, item_name, cust_num, cust_name
from order
where cust_num = 002
union
select item_num, item_name, cust_num, cust_name
from order
where cust_num = 007;

select item_num, item_name, cust_num, cust_name
from order
where (cust_num = 002 or cust_num = 007);
```

item no.	item name	customer no.	customer name
356	sensor	002	Spock
368	intercom	007	Uhura

2. Which items are ordered by both customers 005 and 006? All the rows in table **order** that have customer 1 are selected and compared to the rows in **order** that have customer 3. Rows from each set are compared with all rows from the other set, and those that have matching item numbers have the item numbers displayed.

```
select item_num, item_name, cust_num, cust_name
from order
where cust_num = 005
intersect
select item_num, item_name, cust_num, cust_name
from order
where cust_num = 006;
```

item no.	item name	customer no.	customer name
125	phaser	005	Gorn
125	phaser	006	Khan

Aggregate Functions

1. Display the total number of orders. This query uses the SQL function "count" to count the number of rows in table **order**.

```
select count(*)
from order;
```

count (order)
11

2. Display the total number of customers actually placing orders for items. This is a variation of the count function and specifies that only the distinct number of customers are to be counted. The "distinct" modifier is required because duplicate values of customer numbers are likely to be found, because a customer can order many items and will appear in many rows of table **order**.

```
select count (distinct cust_num)
from order;
```

distinct count (order)
9

3. Display the maximum quantity of an order of item number 125. The SQL "maximum" function is used to search the table **order**, select rows where the item number is 125, and display the maximum value of quantity from the rows selected.

```
select max (quantity)
from order
where item_num = 125;
```

max (quantity)
3

4. For each type of item ordered, display the item number and total order quantity. Note that item_num and item_name in the *select* line must be in a "group by" clause. In SQL any attribute to be displayed in the result of the *select* command must be included in a "group by" clause when the result of an SQL function is also to be displayed. The "group by" clause results in a display of the aggregate sum of quantity values for each value of item_num and item_name. The aggregate sums will be taken over all rows with the same value of item_num.

```
select item_num, item_name, sum(quantity)
from order
group by item_num, item_name;
```

item no.	item name	sum(quantity)
125	phaser	7
137	beam	3
143	shield	1
175	fusionMissile	20
211	captainsLog	1

(Continued)

item no.	item name	sum(quantity)
234	starShip	1
356	sensor	50
368	intercom	1
399	medicalKit	10

5. Display item numbers for all items ordered more than once. This query requires the use of the "group by" and "having" clauses to display data that is based on a count of rows from table **order** having the same value for attribute item_num.

```
select item_num, item_name
from order
group by item_num, item_name
having count(*) >1;
```

item no.	item name
125	phaser

Joins and Subqueries

1. Display customer names for customers who order item number 125. This query requires a join (equijoin) of the **customer** and **order** tables in order to match customer names with item number 125. Including the item_num column in the output verifies that you have selected the item number you want. Note that the default ordering of output is typically ascending by the first column.

```
select c.cust_name, o.item_num
from customer as c, order as o
where c.cust_num = o.cust_num
and item_num = 125;
```

customer name	item no.
Chekov	125
Gorn	125
Khan	125

This query can be equivalently performed with a *sub-query* (sometimes called a *nested subquery*) with the following format. The *select* command inside the parentheses is a nested subquery and is executed first, resulting in a set of values for customer number (cust_num) selected from the **order** table. Each of those values are compared with cust_num values from the **customer** table, and matching values result in the display of the customer name from the matching row in the **customer** table. This is effectively a join between the **customer** and **order** tables with the selection condition of item number 125.

```
select cust_name, order_num
from customer
where cust_num in
       (select cust_num
        from order
        where item_num = 125);
```

2. Display customer names who order at least one item priced over 1000. This query requires a three-level nested subquery format. Note that the phrases "in," "= some," and "= any" in the "where" clauses are often used as equivalent comparison operators (see Melton and Simon, 1993).

```
select c.cust_name
from customer as c
where c.cust_num in
       (select o.cust_num
        from order as o
        where o.item_num = any
        (select i.item_num
         from item as i
         where i.price > 1000));
```

customer name
Khan
Kirk
Scotty
Sulu
Uhura

3. Which customers have not ordered any item priced over 100? Note that one can equivalently use "not in" instead of "not any." The query first selects the customer numbers

from all rows from the join of tables **order** and **item** where the item price is over 100. Then it selects rows from table **customer** where the customer number does not match any of the customers selected in the subquery, and displays the customer names.

```
select c.cust_name
from customer as c
where c.cust_num not any
        (select o.cust_num
        from order as o, item as i
        where o.item_num = i.item_num
        and i.price > 100);
```

customer name
Bones

4. Which customers have only ordered items weighing more than 1000? This is an example of the universal quantifier "all." First the subquery selects all rows from table **item** where the item weight is over 1000. Then it selects rows from table **order** where all rows with a given item number match at least one row in the set selected in the subquery. Any rows in **order** satisfying this condition are joined with the **customer** table and the customer name is displayed as the final result.

```
select c.cust_name
from customer as c, order as o
where c.cust_num = o.cust_num
and o.item_num = all
        (select i.item_num
        from item as i
        where i.weight > 1000);
```

customer name
Sulu

Note that Kirk has ordered one item weighing over 1000 (starShip), but he has also ordered an item weighing under 1000 (captainsLog), so his name does not get displayed.

SQL Update Commands

The following SQL update commands relate to our continuing example and illustrate typical usage of insertion, deletion, and update of selected rows in tables. The following command adds one more customer (klingon) to the **customer** table.

```
insert into customer
values (010,'klingon','rogueShip',4);
```

This next command deletes all customers with credit levels less than 2.

```
delete from customer
where credit_level < 2;
```

The following command modifies the credit level of any customer with level 6 to level 7.

```
update customer
set credit_level = 7
where credit_level = 6;
```

Referential Integrity

The following update to the **item** table resets the value of item_num for a particular item, but because item_num is a foreign key in the **order** table, SQL must maintain referential integrity by triggering the execution sequence named by the foreign key constraint "on update cascade" in the definition of the **order** table, as defined previously. This means that, in addition to updating a row in the **item** table, SQL will search the **order** table for values of item_num equal to 368 and reset each item_num value to 370.

```
update item
set item_num = 370
where item_num = 368;
```

If this update had been a "delete" instead, such as the following:

```
delete from item
where item_num = 368;
```

then the referential integrity trigger would have caused the additional execution of the foreign key constraint "on delete set default" in the **order** table (as defined previously), which finds every row in the **order** table with item_num equal to 368 and takes the action setup in the default. A typical action for this type of database might be to set item_num to either null or a predefined literal value to denote that the particular item has been deleted; this would then be a signal to the system that the customer needs to be contacted to change the order. Of course, the system would have to be set up in advance to check for these values periodically.

SQL Views

A view in SQL is a named, derived (virtual) table that derives its data from base tables, the actual tables defined by the *create table* command. While view definitions can be stored in the database, the views (derived tables) themselves are not stored, but derived at execution time when the view is invoked as a query using the SQL *select* command. The person who queries the view treats the view as if it were an actual (stored) table, unaware of the difference between the view and the base table.

Views are useful in several ways. First, they allow complex queries to be set up in advance in a view, and the novice SQL user is only required to make a simple query on the view. This simple query invokes the more complex query defined by the view. Thus, nonprogrammers are allowed to utilize the full power of SQL without having to create complex queries. Second, views provide greater security for a database because the DBA can assign different views of the data to different users and control what any individual user sees in the database. Third, views provide a greater sense of data independence—that is, even though the base tables may be altered by adding, deleting, or modifying columns, the view query may not need to be changed. While the view definition may need to be changed, that is the job of the DBA, not the person querying the view.

Views may be defined hierarchically—that is, a view definition may contain another view name as well as base table names. This allows for some views to become quite complex.

In the following example, we create a view called "orders" that shows which items have been ordered by each customer and how many. The first line of the view definition specifies the view name and (in parentheses) lists the attributes of that view. The view attributes must correlate exactly with the attributes defined in the *select* statement in the second line of the view definition:

```
create view orders (customer_name, item_name, quantity) as
    select c.cust_name, i.item_name, o.quantity
    from customer as c, item as i, order as o
    where c.cust_num = o.cust_num
    and o.item_num = i.item_num;
```

The *create view* command creates the view definition, which defines two joins among three base tables **customer**, **item**, and **order**; and SQL stores the definition to be executed later when invoked by a query. The following query selects all the data from the view "orders." This query causes SQL to execute the *select* command given in the preceding view definition, producing a tabular result with the column headings for customer_name, item_name, and quantity.

```
select *
from orders;
```

Views are usually not allowed to be updated, because the updates would have to be made to the base tables that make up the definition of the view. When a view is created from a single table, the view update is usually unambiguous, but when a view is created from the joins of multiple tables, the base table updates are very often ambiguous and may have undesirable side effects. Each relational system has its own rules about when views can and cannot be updated.

References

Bulger, B., Greenspan, J., & Wall, D. (2004). *MySQL/PHP Database Applications* (2nd ed.). Somerset, NJ: Wiley.

Gennick, J. (2004). *Oracle SQL*Plus: The Definitive Guide* (2nd ed.). Cambridge, MA: O'Reilly.

Gennick, J. (2010). *SQL Pocket Guide* (3rd ed.). Cambridge, MA: O'Reilly.

Melton, J., & Simon, A. R. (1993). *Understanding the New SQL: A Complete Guide*. San Francisco: Morgan Kaufmann.

Mullins, C. S. (2004). *DB2 Developer's Guide* (5th ed.). Upper Saddle River, NJ: Sams Publishing.

Neilson, P. (2009). *Microsoft SQL Server 2008 Bible*. Somerset, NJ: Wiley.

van der Lans, R. (2006). *Introduction to SQL: Mastering the Relational Database Language* (4th ed.). Boston: Addison-Wesley.

References

Ambler, S., & Sadalage, P. (2006). *Refactoring Databases: Evolutionary Database Design*. Boston: Addison-Wesley.

Armstrong, W. (1974). Dependency Structures of Data Base Relationships. *IFIP Congress, 580–583*.

Atkinson, M., Bancilhon, F., DeWitt, D., Dittrich, K., Maier, D., & Zdonik, S. (1989). The Object-Oriented Database System Manifesto. In *Proceedings of the First International Conference on Deductive and Object-Oriented Databases* (pp. 223–240). Kyoto, Japan. Also appears in F. Bancilhon, C. Delobel, & P. Kanellakis (Eds.), *Building an Object-Oriented Database System: The Story of O²*. San Francisco: Morgan Kaufmann.

Bachman, C. (1969). Data Structure Diagrams. *Database, 1*, 4–10.

Bachman, C. (1972). The Evolution of Storage Structures. *Communications of the ACM, 15*, 628–634.

Bachman, C. (1977, October 6). The Role Concept in Data Models. In *Proceedings of the 3rd International Conference on Very Large Data Bases* (pp. 464–476). IEEE.

Bagui, S. (2003). *Database Design Using Entity-Relationship Diagrams*. London: Tayler and Francis (Auerbach).

Barquin, R., & Edelstein, H. (Eds.). (1997). *Planning and Designing the Data Warehouse*. Upper Saddle River, NJ: Prentice-Hall.

Batini, C., Lenzerini, M., & Navathe, S. (1986, December). A Comparative Analysis of Methodologies for Database Schema Integration. *ACM Computing Surveys, 18*, 323–364.

Batini, C., Ceri, S., & Navathe, S. (1992). *Conceptual Database Design: An Entity-Relationship Approach*. Menlo Park, CA: Benjamin/Cummings.

Beeri, C., Bernstein, P., & Goodman, N. (1978). A Sophisticated Introduction to Database Normalization Theory. In *Proc. 4th Intl. Conf. on Very Large Data Bases* (pp. 113–124). IEEE.

Bernstein, P. (1976). Synthesizing 3NF Tables from Functional Dependencies. *ACM Transactions on Database Systems, 1*, 272–298.

Briand, H., Habrias, H., Hue, J., & Simon, Y. (1985). Expert System for Translating E-R Diagram into Databases. In *Proceedings of the 4th International Conference on Entity-Relationship Approach* (pp. 199–206). IEEE Computer Society Press.

Brodie, M., Mylopoulos, J., & Schmidt, J. (Eds.). (1984). *On Conceptual Modeling: Perspectives from Artificial Intelligence, Databases, and Programming Languages*. New York: Springer-Verlag.

Bruce, T. (1992). *Designing Quality Databases with IDEF1X Information Models*. New York: Dorset House.

Bulger, B., Greenspan, J., & Wall, D. (2004). *MySQL/PHP Database Applications* (2nd ed.). Somerset, NJ: Wiley.

Cardenas, A. (1975, May). Analysis and Performance of Inverted Database Structures. *Communications of the ACM, 18*, 253–264.

Cataldo, J. (1997, December). Care and Feeding of the Data Warehouse. *Database Programming and Design, 10*, 36–42.

Cattell, R. G. G., Barry, D. K., Berler, M., Eastman, J., Jordan, D., & Russell, C., et al. (Eds.). (2000). *The Object Data Management Standard: ODMG 3.0*. San Francisco: Morgan Kaufmann.

Chaudhuri, S., & Dayal, U. (1997, March). An Overview of Data Warehousing and OLAP Technology. *SIGMOD Record, 26*, 65–74.

Chen, P. (1976, March). The Entity-Relationship Model—Toward a Unified View of Data. *ACM Transactions on Database Systems, 1,* 9–36.

Churcher, C. (2009). *Beginning Database Design: From Novice to Professional.* New York: Springer-Verlag.

Cobb, R., Fry, J., & Teorey, T. (1984, February). The database designer's workbench. *Information Sciences, 32,* 33–45.

Codd, E. (1970, June). A Relational Model for Large Shared Data Banks. *Communications of the ACM, 13,* 377–387.

Codd, E. (1974). Recent Investigations into Relational Data Base Systems. In *Proceedings of the IFIP Congress.* Amsterdam: North-Holland.

Codd, E. (1979, December). Extending the Database Relational Model to Capture More Meaning. *ACM Transactions on Database Systems,* 397–434.

Codd, E. (1990). *The Relational Model for Database Management, Version 2.* Boston: Addison-Wesley.

Computer Associates. *AllFusion ERwin Data Modeler.* Retrieved from http://www3.ca.com/Solutions/Product.asp?ID=260.

Database Answers. *Modeling tools.* Retrieved from http://www.databaseanswers.com/modelling_tools.htm.

Date, C. (2003). *An Introduction to Database Systems* (Vol. 1, 8th ed.). Boston: Addison-Wesley.

Directory of Data Modeling Resources. Retrieved from http://www.infogoal.com/dmc/dmcdmd.htm.

Dittrich, K., Gotthard, W., & Lockemann, P. (1986). Complex Entities for Engineering Applications. In *Proceedings of the 5th ER Conference.* Amsterdam: North-Holland.

Dutka, A., & Hanson, H. (1989). *Fundamentals of Data Normalization.* Boston: Addison-Wesley.

Elmasri, R., & Navathe, S. (2010). *Fundamentals of Database Systems* (6th ed.). Boston: Addison-Wesley.

Fagin, R. (1977). Multivalued Dependencies and a New Normal Form for Relational Databases. *ACM Transactions on Database Systems, 2,* 262–278.

Faloutsos, C., Matias, Y., & Silberschatz, A. (1996). Modeling skewed distributions using multifractal and the "80-20 law." In *Proceedings of the 22nd VLDB Conference* (pp. 307–317).

Feldman, P., & Miller, D. (1986, August). Entity Model Clustering: Structuring a Data Model by Abstraction. *Computer Journal, 29,* 348–360.

Gennick, J. (1999). *Oracle SQL*Plus: The Definitive Guide.* Cambridge, MA: O'Reilly.

Gennick, J. (2004). *SQL Pocket Guide.* Cambridge, MA: O'Reilly.

Goldberg, A., & Robson, D. (1983). *Smalltalk-80: The Language and Its Implementation.* Boston: Addison-Wesley.

Gray, P., & Watson, H. (1998). *Decision Support in the Data Warehouse.* Upper Saddle River, NJ: Prentice-Hall.

Halpin, T., & Morgan, T. (2008). *Information Modeling and Relational Databases: From Conceptual Analysis to Logical Design* (2nd ed.). San Francisco: Morgan Kaufmann.

Han, J., & Kamber, M. (2001). *Data Mining: Concepts and Techniques.* San Francisco: Morgan Kaufmann.

Harinarayan, V., Rajaraman, A., & Ullman, J. (1996). Implementing Data Cubes Efficiently. In *Proceedings of the 1996 ACM-SIGMOD Conference* (pp. 205–216).

Harriman, A., Hodgetts, P., & Leo, M. (2004). Emergent Database Design: Liberating Database Development with Agile Practices. In *Agile Development Conference.* Salt Lake City, 2004. Retrieved from http://www.agiledevelopmentconference.com/files/XR2-2.pdf.

Harrington, J. (2002). *Relational Database Design Clearly Explained* (2nd ed.). San Francisco: Morgan Kaufmann.

Hawryszkiewycz, I. (1984). *Database Analysis and Design.* Chicago: SRA.

Hernandez, M., & Getz, K. (2003). *Database Design for Mere Mortals: A Hands-On Guide for Relational Databases* (2nd ed.). Boston: Addison-Wesley.

Hoberman, S. (2009). *Data Modeling Made Simple: A Practical Guide for Business and IT Professionals* (2nd ed.). Bradley Beach, NJ: Technics-Publications.

Hull, R., & King, R. (1987, September). Semantic Database Modeling: Survey, Applications, and Research Issues. *ACM Computing Surveys, 19,* 201–260.

IBM Rational Software. Retrieved from http://www-306.ibm.com/software/rational/DEF1X. Retrieved from http://www.idef.com.

Jajodia, S., & Ng, P. (1984). Translation of Entity-Relationship Diagrams into Relational Structures. *Journal of Systems and Software, 4,* 123–133.

Jensen, C., & Snodgrass, R. (1996). Semantics of Time-Varying Information. *Information Systems, 21,* 311–352.

Kent, W. (1983, February). A Simple Guide to Five Normal Forms in Relational Database Theory. *Communications of the ACM, 26,* 120–125.

Kimball, R., & Caserta, J. (2004). *The Data Warehouse ETL Toolkit* (2nd ed.). Somerset, NJ: Wiley.

Kimball, R., & Ross, M. (2002a). *The Data Warehouse Lifecycle Toolkit* (2nd ed.). Somerset, NJ: Wiley.

Kimball, R., & Ross, M. (2002). *The Data Warehouse Toolkit: The Complete Guide to Dimensional Modeling* (2nd ed.). Somerset, NJ: Wiley.

Kirkerud, B. (1989). *Object-Oriented Programming with Simula.* Boston: Addison-Wesley (International Computer Science Series).

Kotidis, Y., & Roussopoulos, N. (1999). DynaMat: A Dynamic View Management System for Data Warehouses. In *Proceedings of the ACM SIGMOD 1999* (pp. 371–382).

Lightstone, S., Teorey, T., & Nadeau, T. (2007). *Physical Database Design.* San Francisco, CA: Morgan Kaufmann Publishers.

Maier, D. (1983). *Theory of Relational Databases.* Rockville, MD: Computer Science Press.

Makridakis, S., Wheelwright, C., & Hyndman, R. (1998). *Forecasting Methods and Applications* (3rd ed.). Somerset, NJ: Wiley.

Mannino, M. (2008). *Database Design, Application Development, and Administration* (4th ed.). New York: ediyu.

Martin, J. (1982). *Strategic Data-Planning Methodologies.* Upper Saddle River, NJ: Prentice-Hall.

Martin, J. (1983). *Managing the Data-Base Environment.* Upper Saddle River, NJ: Prentice-Hall.

McGee, W. (1974). A Contribution to the Study of Data Equivalence. In J. W. Klimbie & K. L. Koffeman (Eds.), *Data Base Management* (pp. 123–148). Amsterdam: North-Holland.

McLeod, D., & King, R. (1979). Applying a Semantic Database Model. In *Proceedings of the 1st International Conference on the*

Entity-Relationship Approach to Systems Analysis and Design (pp. 193–210). Amsterdam: North-Holland.

Melton, J., & Simon, A. (1993). *Understanding the New SQL: A Complete Guide*. San Francisco: Morgan Kaufmann.

Mitchell, T. (1997). *Machine Learning*. Boston: WCB/McGraw-Hill.

Muller, R. (1999). *Database Design for Smarties: Using UML for Data Modeling*. San Francisco: Morgan Kaufmann Pub.

Mullins, C. (2004). *DB2 Developer's Guide* (5th ed.). Upper Saddle River, NJ: Sams Publishing.

Naiburg, E., & Maksimchuk, R. (2001). *UML for Database Design*. Boston: Addison-Wesley.

Nadeau, T., & Teorey, T. (2002). Achieving Scalability in OLAP Materialized View Selection. In *Proceedings of DOLAP '02* (pp. 28–34).

Nadeau, T., & Teorey, T. (2003). A Pareto Model for OLAP View Size Estimation. *Information Systems Frontiers, 5*, 137–147. New York: Kluwer Academic Publishers.

Neilson, P. (2003). *Microsoft SQL Server Bible*. Somerset, NJ: Wiley.

Nijssen, G., & Halpin, T. (1989). *Conceptual Schema and Relational Database Design: A Fact Oriented Approach*. Upper Saddle River, NJ: Prentice-Hall.

Objects by Design: UML modeling tools. Retrieved from http://www.objectsbydesign.com/tools/umltools_byCompany.html.

Peckham, J., & Maryanski, F. (1988, September). Semantic Data Models. *ACM Computing Surveys, 20*, 153–190.

Powell, G. (2005). *Beginning Database Design*. Somerset, NJ: Wiley.

Quatrani, T. (2003). *Visual Modeling with Rational Rose 2002 and UML* (3rd ed.). Boston: Addison-Wesley.

Ramakrishnan, R., & Gehrke, J. (2004). *Database Management Systems*. (3rd ed.). Boston: McGraw-Hill.

Rumbaugh, J., Jacobson, I., & Booch, G. (2004). *The Unified Modeling Language User Guide* (2nd ed.). Boston: Addison-Wesley.

Rumbaugh, J., Jacobson, I., & Booch, G. (2005). *The Unified Modeling Language Reference Manual* (2nd ed.). Boston: Addison-Wesley.

Sakai, H. (1983). Entity-Relationship Approach to Logical Database Design. In C. G. Davis, S. Jajodia, P. A. Ng & R. T. Yeh (Eds.), *Entity-Relationship Approach to Software Engineering* (pp. 155–187). Amsterdam: Elsevier, North-Holland.

Scamell, R., & Umanath, N. (2007). *Data Modeling and Database Design*. Florence, KY: Cengage Learning.

Scheuermann, P., Scheffner, G., & Weber, H. (1980). Abstraction Capabilities and Invariant Properties Modeling within the Entity-Relationship Approach. In P. Chen (Ed.), *Entity-Relationship Approach to Systems Analysis and Design* (pp. 121–140). Amsterdam: Elsevier, North-Holland.

Senko, M., et al. (1973). Data Structures and Accessing in Data-base Systems. *IBM Systems Journal, 12*, 30–93.

Silberschatz, A., Korth, H., & Sudarshan, S. (2010). *Database System Concepts* (6th ed.). Boston: McGraw-Hill.

Silverston, L. (2001). *The Data Model Resource Book, Vol. 1: A Library of Universal Data Models for All Enterprises*. Somerset, NJ: Wiley.

Simon, A. (1995). *Strategic Database Technology: Management for the Year 2000*. San Francisco: Morgan Kaufmann.

Simsion, G. (2007). *Data Modeling Theory and Practice*. Bradley Beach, NJ: Technics Publicatons.

Simsion, G., & Witt, G. (2004). *Data Modeling Essentials: Analysis, Design, and Innovation* (3rd ed.). Scottsdale, AZ: Coriolis.

Smith, H. (1985, August). Database Design: Composing Fully Normalized Tables from a Rigorous Dependency Diagram. *Communications of the ACM, 28,* 826–838.

Smith, J., & Smith, D. (1977, June). Database Abstractions: Aggregation and Generalization. *ACM Transactions on Database Systems, 2,* 105–133.

Snodgrass, R. (2000). *Developing Time-Oriented Database Applications in SQL.* San Francisco: Morgan Kaufmann.

Stephens, R., & Plew, R. (2000). *Database Design.* Upper Saddle River, NJ: Sams.

Stephens, R. (2008). *Beginning Database Design Solutions.* Somerset, NJ: Wrox.

Sybase PowerDesigner. Retrieved from http://www.sybase.com/products/developmentintegration/powerdesigner.

Teichroew, D., & Hershey, E. (1977). PSL/PSA: A Computer Aided Technique for Structured Documentation and Analysis of Information Processing Systems. *IEEE Transactions on Software Engineering, SE-3,* 41–48.

Teorey, T., & Fry, J. (1982). *Design of Database Structures.* Upper Saddle River, NJ: Prentice-Hall.

Teorey, T., Yang, D., & Fry, J. (1986, June). A Logical Design Methodology for Relational Databases Using the Extended Entity-Relationship Model. *ACM Computing Surveys, 18,* 197–222.

Teorey, T., Wei, G., Bolton, D., & Koenig, J. (1989, August). ER Model Clustering as an Aid for User Communication and Documentation in Database Design. *Communications of the ACM, 32,* 975–987.

Thomsen, E. (2002). *OLAP Solutions* (2nd ed.). Somerset, NJ: Wiley.

Tsichritzis, D., & Lochovsky, F. (1982). *Data Models.* San Francisco: Prentice-Hall.

Ubiquiti Inc. Retrieved from http://www.ubiquiti.com/.

UML Overview. Developer.com. Retrieved from http://www.developer.com/design/article.php/1553851.

University of Waikato. *Weka 3—Data Mining with Open Source Machine Learning Software in Java.* Retrieved from http://www.cs.waikato.ac.nz/ml/weka.

Understanding Relational Database: Referential Integrity. Retrieved from http://www.miswebdesign.com/resources/articles/wrox-beginning-php-4-chapter-3-5.html.

van der Lans, R. (2000). *Introduction to SQL: Mastering the Relational Database Language* (3rd ed.). Boston: Addison-Wesley.

Widom, J. Data Management for XML. Retrieved from http://www-db.stanford.edu/~widom/xml-whitepaper.html.

Witten, I., & Frank, E. (2000). *Data Mining: Practical Machine Learning Tools and Techniques with Java Implementations.* San Francisco: Morgan Kaufmann.

Wong, E., & Katz, R. (1979). Logical Design and Schema Conversion for Relational and DBTG Databases. In *Proceedings of the International Conference on the Entity-Relationship Approach* (pp. 311–322).

XML Database Products (Ronald Bourret, 2010). Retrieved from http://www.rpbourret.com/xml/XMLDatabaseProds.htm.

XML Design Patterns Index. Retrieved from http://www.xmlpatterns.com/patterns.shtml.

XML Technology. Retrieved from http://www.w3.org/standards/xml/.

XML Tutorials. Retrieved from http://www.w3schools.com/xml/default.asp.

Yao, S. (Ed.), (1985). *Principles of Database Design.* Upper Saddle River, NJ: Prentice-Hall.

Zachmann, J. (1987). A Framework for Information Systems Architecture. *IBM Systems Journal, 26,* 3. IBM Pub. G321-5298.

Zachman Institute for Framework Advancement. Retrieved from http://www.zifa.com.

EXERCISES

ER and UML Conceptual Data Modeling

Problem 2.1. Draw a detailed ER diagram for a car rental agency database (e.g., Hertz). Keep track of the current rental location of each car and its current condition and history of repairs, along with information for a local office, including customer information, expected return date, return location, and car status (ready, being-repaired, currently-rented, being-cleaned). Select attributes from your intuition about the situation and list them separately from the diagram, but in association with a particular entity or relationship in the ER model.

Problem 2.2. Given the following assertions for a relational database that represents the current term enrollment at a large university, draw an ER diagram for this schema that takes into account all the assertions given. There are 2000 instructors, 4000 courses, and 30000 students. Use as many ER constructs as you can to represent the true semantics of the problem.

Assertions:

- An instructor may teach one or more courses in a given term (average = 2.0 courses).
- An instructor must direct the research of at least one student (average = 2.5 students).
- A course may have none, one, or two prerequisites (average = 1.5 prerequisites).
- A course may exist even if no students are currently enrolled.
- All courses are taught by exactly one instructor.
- The average enrollment in a course is 30 students.
- A student must select at least one course per term (average = 4.0 course selections).

Problem 3.1. Draw a detailed UML diagram for a car rental agency database (e.g., Hertz). Keep track of the current rental location of each car and its current condition and history of repairs, along with information for a local office, including customer information, expected return date, return location, and car status (ready, being-repaired, currently-rented, being-cleaned). Select attributes from your intuition about the situation, and list them separately from the diagram, but in association with a particular class in the UML diagram.

Problem 3.2. Given the following assertions for a relational database that represents the current term enrollment at a large university, draw a UML diagram for this schema that takes into account all the assertions given. There are 2000 instructors, 4000 courses, and 30000 students. Use as many UML constructs as you can to represent the true semantics of the problem. Assertions:

- An instructor may teach none, one, or more courses in a given term (average = 2.0 courses).
- An instructor must direct the research of at least one student (average = 2.5 students).
- A course may have none, one, or two prerequisites (average = 1.5 prerequisites).
- A course may exist even if no students are currently enrolled.
- All courses are taught by only one instructor.
- The average enrollment in a course is 30 students.
- A student must select at least one course per term (average = 4.0 course selections).

Conceptual Data Modeling and Integration

Problem 4.1. The following ER diagrams represent two views of a video store database as described to a database designer. Show how the two views can be integrated in the simplest and most useful way by making all necessary changes on the two diagrams. State any assumptions you need to make.

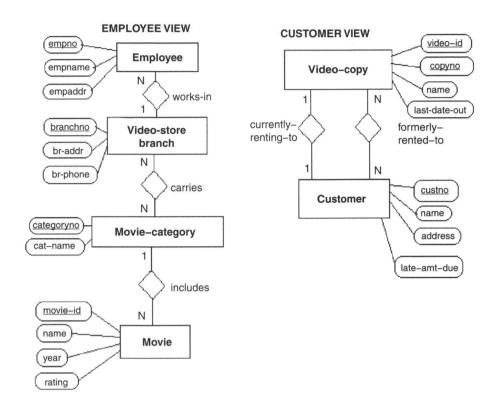

Transformation of the Conceptual Model to SQL

Problem 5.1.

a. Transform your integrated ER diagram from Problem 4.1 into an SQL database with five to ten rows per table of data you can make up to fit the database schema.

b. Demonstrate your database by displaying all the following queries:

  1. Which video store branches have *Shrek* in stock (available) now?

  2. In what section of the store (film category) can you find *The Terminator*?

  3. For customer Annika Sorenstam, what titles are currently being rented and what are the overdue charges, if any?

  4. (Any query of your choice—show what your system can really do!)

Normalization and Minimum Set of Tables

Problem 6.1. Given the table **R1**(A, B, C) with FDs A -> B and B -> C:

a. Is A a superkey for this table?

b. Is B a superkey for this table?

c. Is this table in 3NF, BCNF, or neither?

Problem 6.2. Given the table **R1**(A,B,C,D) with FDs AB -> C and BD -> A:

a. What are all the superkeys of this table?

b. What are all the candidate keys for this table?

c. Is this table in 3NF, BCNF, or neither?

Problem 6.3. The following FDs represent a set of airline reservation system database constraints. Design a minimum set of BCNF tables, preserving all FDs, and express your solution in terms of the code letters given below (a time-saving device for your analysis). Is the set of tables you derived also BCNF?

```
reservation_no -> agent_no, agent_name,
  airline_name, flight_no, passenger_name
reservation_no -> aircraft_type, departure_date,
  arrival_date, departure_time, arrival_time
reservation_no -> departure_city, arrival_city,
  type_of_payment, seating_class, seat_no
airline_name, flight_no -> aircraft_type,
  departure_time, arrival_time
airline_name, flight_no -> departure_city,
  arrival_city, meal_type
airline_name, flight_no, aircraft_type -> meal_type
passenger_name -> home_address, home_phone,
  company_name
aircraft_type, seat_no -> seating_class
company_name -> company_address, company_phone
company_phone -> company_name
```

```
A: reservation_no         E: flight_no
B: agent_no               F: passenger_name
C: agent_name             G: aircraft_type
D: airline_name           H: departure_date
```

```
I: arrival_date          Q: seat_no
J: departure_time        R: meal_type
K: arrival_time          S: home_address
L: departure_city        T: home_phone
M: arrival_city          U: company_name
N: type_of_payment       V: company_address
P: seating_class         W: company_phone
```

Problem 6.4. Given the following set of FDs, find the minimum set of 3NF tables. Designate the candidate key attributes of these tables. Is the set of tables you derived also BCNF?
a. J -> KLMNP
b. JKL -> MNP
c. K -> MQ
d. KL -> MNP
e. KM -> NP
f. N -> KP

Logical Database Design (Generic Problem)

Problem 7.1. Design and implement a small database that will be useful to your company or student organization.
a. State the purpose of the database in a few sentences.
b. Construct an ER or UML class diagram for the database.
c. Transform your ER or UML diagram into a working database with five to ten rows per table of data you can make up to fit the database schema. You should have at least four tables, enough to have some interesting queries. Use Oracle, DB2, SQL Server, Access, or any other database system.
d. Show that your database is normalized (BCNF) using FDs derived from your ER diagram and from personal knowledge of the data. Analyze the FDs for each table separately (this simplifies the process).
e. Demonstrate your working database by displaying the results of four queries. Pick interesting and complex queries (impress us!).

OLAP

Problem 10.1. As mentioned in Chapter 10, hypercube lattice structures are a specialization of product graphs. Figure 10.16 shows an example of a three-dimensional hypercube lattice structure. Figure 10.13 shows an example of a two-dimensional product graph. Notice the two figures are written using different notations. Write the hypercube lattice structure in Figure 10.16 using the product graph notation introduced with Figure 10.13. Keep the same dimension order. Don't worry about carrying over the view sizes. Assume the Customer, Part, and Supplier dimensions are keyed by customer id, part id, and supplier id, respectively. Shade the nodes representing the fact table and the views selected for materialization as indicated in the "Selection of Materialized Views" section in Chapter 10.

SOLUTIONS TO SELECTED EXERCISES

Problem 2.2.

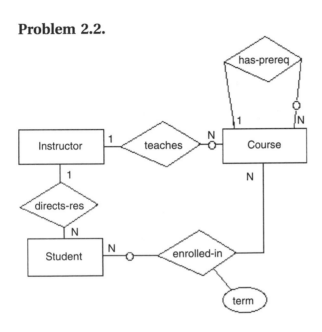

Problem 3.2.

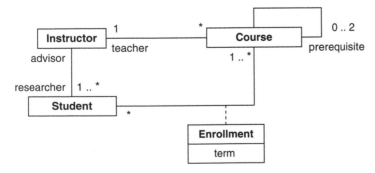

Problem 4.1. Connect Movie to Video-copy as a 1-to-*n* relationship (Video-copy at the *n* side), or use a generalization from Movie to Video-copy with Movie as the supertype and Video-copy as the subtype.

Problem 6.1. Given the table **R1**(A, B, C) with FDs A -> B and B -> C:
a. Is A a superkey for this table? *Yes*
b. Is B a superkey for this table? *No*
c. Is this table in 3NF, BCNF, or neither? *Neither 3NF nor BCNF.*

Problem 6.3. Minimum set of 3NF (and BCNF) tables:
R1: ABCDEFHINQ with key A and FD A -> BCDEFHINQ (and A -> P optional).
R2: DEGJKLMR with key DE and FD DE -> GJKLMR.
R3: FSTU with key F and FD F -> STU.
R4: UVW with keys U and W and FDs U -> VW and W-> U.
R5: GQP with key GQ and FD GQ -> P.

Problem 6.4. Given these FDs, begin Step 1 (LHS reduction):
a. J -> KLMNP
b. JKL -> MNP *First, eliminate K and L since J -> KL in (a), merge with (a).*
c. K -> MQ
d. KL -> MNP *Third, eliminate L since K -> MNP from merged (c), (d) is redundant.*
e. KM -> NP *Second, eliminate M since K -> M in (c), merge with (c).*
f. N -> KP

End of Step 1; begin Step 2 (RHS reduction for transitivities):
a. J -> KLMNP *First, reduce by eliminating MNP since K -> MNP.*
b. K -> MQNP *Second, reduce by eliminating P since N -> P.*
c. N -> KP

End of Step 2 and consolidation in Step 3:
a. J -> KL
b. K -> MNQ (or K -> MNPQ) *First, merge (b) and (c) for Superkey Rules 1 and 2.*
c. N -> KP (or N -> K)

Steps 4 and 5:
a. J -> KL *Candidate key is J (BCNF).*
b. K -> MNPQ and N -> K *Candidate keys are K and N (BCNF).*

Problem 10.1.

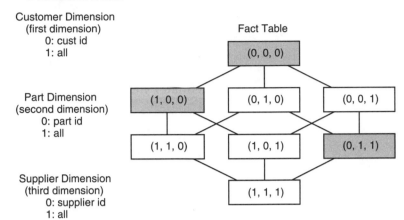

Customer Dimension
(first dimension)
   0: cust id
   1: all

Part Dimension
(second dimension)
   0: part id
   1: all

Supplier Dimension
(third dimension)
   0: supplier id
   1: all

Fact Table

(0, 0, 0)

(1, 0, 0)   (0, 1, 0)   (0, 0, 1)

(1, 1, 0)   (1, 0, 1)   (0, 1, 1)

(1, 1, 1)

Glossary

activity diagram (UML)—a process workflow model (diagram) showing the flow from one activity to the next.

aggregation—a special type of abstraction relationship that defines a higher-level entity that is an aggregate of several lower-level entities; a "part-of" relationship. For example, a Bicycle entity is an aggregate of Wheel, Handlebar, and Seat entities.

association—a relationship between classes (in UML). Associations can be binary, *n*-ary, reflexive, or qualified.

attribute—a primitive data element that provides descriptive detail about an entity; a data field or data item in a record. For example, lastname would be an attribute for the entity Customer. Attributes may also be used as descriptive elements for certain relationships among entities.

automatic summary table (AST)—materialized (summary) views or aggregates of data saved by OLAP for future use to reduce query time.

binary recursive relationship—a relationship between one occurrence of an entity with another occurrence of the same entity.

binary relationship—a relationship between occurrences of two entities.

BLOB—binary large object, often containing multimedia types of data or images.

Boyce-Codd normal form (BCNF)—a table is in Boyce-Codd normal form if and only if for every functional dependency X -> A, where X and A are either simple or composite attributes (data items), X must be a superkey in that table. This is a strong form of 3NF and is the basis for most practical normalization methodologies.

candidate key—any subset of the attributes (data items) in a superkey that is also a superkey and is not reducible to another superkey.

CASE tool—computer-aided software engineering tool, or software design tool, to assist in the logical design of large or complex databases. For example, AllFusion ERwin Data Modeler, Rational Data Architect, or PowerDesigner.

class—a concept in a real-world system, represented by a noun in UML; similar to an entity in the ER model.

class diagram (UML)—a conceptual data model; a model of the static relationships between data elements of a system (similar to an ER diagram).

completeness constraint—double line symbol connecting a supertype entity with the subtypes to designate that the listed subtype entities represent a complete set of possible subtypes.

composition—a relationship between one class and a group of other classes in UML; the class at the diamond (aggregate) end of the relationship is composed of the class(es) at the small (component) end; similar to aggregation in the ER model.

conceptual data model—an organization of data that describes the relationships among the primitive data elements. For example, in the ER model, it is a diagram of the entities, their relationships, and their attributes.

connectivity of a relationship—a constraint on the count of the number of associated entity occurrences in a relationship, either one or many.

data item—the basic component of a data record in a file or database table; the smallest unit of information that has meaning in the real world. For example, customer last name, address, identification number.

data mining—a way of extracting knowledge from a database by searching for correlations in the data in order to present promising hypotheses to the user for analysis and consideration.

data model—an organization of data that describes the relationships among the primitive and composite data elements.

data warehouse—a large repository of historical data that can be integrated for decision support.

database—a collection of interrelated stored data that serves the needs of multiple users; a collection of tables in the relational model.

database administrator (DBA)—person in a software organization who is in charge of designing, creating, and maintaining the databases of an enterprise. The DBA makes use of a variety of software tools provided by a DBMS.

database life cycle—an enumeration and definition of the basic steps in the requirements analysis, design, creation, and maintenance of a database as it evolves over time.

database management system (DBMS)—a generalized software system for storing and manipulating databases. For example, Oracle, IBM's DB2, and Microsoft SQL Server or Access.

DBA—see database administrator.

degree of a relationship—the number of entities associated in the relationship: recursive binary (1 entity), binary (2 entities), ternary (3 entities), n-ary (n entities).

denormalization—the consolidation of database tables to increase performance in data retrieval (query), despite the potential loss of data integrity. Decisions on when to denormalize tables are based on cost–benefit analysis by the DBA.

deployment diagram (UML)—shows the physical nodes on which a system executes. This is more closely associated with physical database design.

dimension table—the smaller tables used in a data warehouse to denote the attributes of a particular dimension such as time, location, customer characteristics, product characteristics, etc.

disjointness constraint (d)—symbol in an ER diagram to designate that the lower-level entities in a generalization relationship have nonoverlapping (disjoint) occurrences. If the occurrences overlap, then use the designation (o) instead of (d) in the ER diagram.

entity—a data object that represents a person, place, thing, or event of informational interest; corresponds to a record in a file when stored. For example, you could define Employee, Customer, Project, Team, and Department as entities.

entity cluster—the result of a grouping operation on a collection of entities and relationships in an ER model to form a higher-level abstraction that can be used to more easily keep track of the major components of a large-scale global schema.

entity instance (or occurrence)—a particular occurrence of an entity. For example, an instance of the entity Actor would be Johnny Depp.

entity–relationship (ER) model—a conceptual data model involving entities, relationships among entities, and attributes of those entities.

entity–relationship (ER) diagram—a diagram (or graph) of entities and their relationships, and possibly the attributes of those entities.

exclusion constraint—a symbol (+) between two relationships in the ER model that have a common entity that implies that either one relationship must hold at a given point in time, or the other must hold, but not both.

existence dependency—there exists a dependency between two entities such that one is dependent for its existence on the other and cannot exist alone. For example, an Employee Work-history entity cannot exist without the corresponding Employee entity. Also refers to the connectivity between two entities as being mandatory or optional.

fact table—the dominating table in a data warehouse and its star schema, containing dimension attributes and data measures at the individual data level.

file—a collection of records of the same type. For example, an employee file is a collection of employee records.

first normal form (1NF)—a table is in first normal form if and only if there are no repeating columns of data taken from the same domain and having the same meaning.

foreign key—any attribute in an SQL table (key or nonkey) that is taken from the same domain of values as the primary key in another SQL table and can be used to join the two tables (without loss of data integrity) as part of an SQL query.

functional dependency (FD)—the property of one or more attributes (data items) that uniquely determines the value of one or more other attributes (data items). Given a table **R**, a set of attributes B is functionally dependent on another set of attributes A if, at each instant of time, each A value is associated with only one B value.

generalization—a special type of abstraction relationship that specifies that several types of entities with certain common attributes can be generalized (or abstractly defined) with a higher-level entity type, a supertype entity; an "is-a" relationship. For example, Employee is a generalization of Engineer, Manager, and Administrative-assistant based on the common attribute job-title. A tool often used to make view integration possible.

global schema—a conceptual data model that shows all the data and their relationships in the context of an entire database.

key—a generic term for a set of one or more attributes (data items) that, taken collectively, allows one to identify uniquely an entity or a record in an SQL table; a superkey.

logical design—the steps in the database life cycle involved with the design of the conceptual data model (schema), schema integration, transformation to SQL tables, and table normalization; the design of a database in terms of how the data is related, but without regard to how it will be stored.

lossless decomposition—a decomposition of an SQL table into two or more smaller tables is lossless if and only if the cycle of table decomposition (normalization) and the recomposition through joining the tables back through common attributes can be done without loss of data integrity.

mandatory existence—a connectivity between two entities that has a lower bound of one. For example, for the "works-in" relationship between an Employee and a Department, every Department has at least one Employee at any given time. *Note:* If this is not true, then the existence is optional.

multiplicity—in UML, the multiplicity of a class is an integer that indicates how many instances of that class are allowed to exist.

normalization—the process of breaking up a table into smaller tables to eliminate problems with unwanted loss of data (the egregious side effects of losing data integrity) from the deletion of records, and inefficiencies associated with multiple data updates.

object-relational database—a relational database with object-oriented concepts added. While not fully object oriented, object-relational database systems still successfully compete with object-oriented database systems.

online analytical processing (OLAP)—a query service that overlays a data warehouse by creating and maintaining a set of summary views (automatic summary tables, or ASTs) to allow for quick access to summary data.

optional existence—a connectivity between two entities that has a lower bound of zero. For example, for the "occupies" relationship between an Employee and an Office, there may exist some Offices that are not currently occupied.

package—in UML, a package is a graphical mechanism used to organize classes into groups for better readability.

physical design—the step in the database life cycle involved with the physical structure of the data—that is, how it will be stored, retrieved, and updated efficiently. In particular, it is concerned with issues of table indexing and data clustering on secondary storage devices (disks).

primary key—a key that is selected from among the candidate keys for an SQL table to be used to create an index for that table.

qualified association—in UML, an association between classes may have constraints specified in the class diagram.

record—a group of data items treated as a unit by an application; a row in a database table.

reflexive association—in UML, a reflexive association relates a class to itself.

referential integrity—a constraint in an SQL database that requires that for every foreign key instance that exists in a table, the row (and thus the primary key instance) of the parent table associated with that foreign key instance must also exist in the database.

relation—a table in a relational database.

relationship—real-world association among one or more entities. For example, "purchased" could be a relationship between Customer and Product.

requirements specification—a formal document that defines the requirements for a database in terms of the data needed, the major users and their applications, the physical platform and software system, and any special constraints on performance, security, and data integrity.

row—a group of data items treated as a unit by an application; a record; a tuple in relational database terminology.

schema—a conceptual data model that shows all the relationships among the data elements under consideration in a given context; the collection of table definitions in a relational database.

second normal form (2NF)—a table is in second normal form if and only if each nonkey attribute (data item) is fully dependent on the primary key—that is, either the left side of every functional dependency (FD) is a primary key or can be derived from a primary key.

star schema—the basic form of data organization for a data warehouse, consisting of a single large fact table and many smaller dimension tables.

subtype entity—the higher-level abstract entity in a generalization relationship.

superkey—a set of one or more attributes (data items) that, taken collectively, allows one to identify uniquely an entity or a record in a relational table.

supertype entity—the lower-level entity in a generalization relationship.

table—in a relational database, the collection of rows (or records) of a single type (similar to a file).

ternary relationship—a relationship that can only be defined among occurrences of three entities.

third normal form (3NF)—a table is in third normal form if and only if for every functional dependency $X \rightarrow A$, where X and A are either simple or composite attributes (data items), either X must be a superkey or A must be a member attribute of a candidate key in that table.

tuple—a row in a relational table; a record.

UML—Unified Modeling Language; a popular form of diagramming tools used to define data models and processing steps in a software application.

view integration—a step in the logical design part of the database life cycle that collects individual conceptual data models (views) into a single unified global schema. Techniques such as generalization are used to consolidate the individual data models.

XML—the eXtensible Markup Language used to represent data and transfer it between systems, particularly for Web technologies.

INDEX

Note: Page numbers followed by *f* indicate figures and *t* indicate tables.

Looking for more information on Database Design?

If you've enjoyed this book, take a look at these bonus chapters from *Physical Database Design*, another book from Morgan Kaufmann.

3

QUERY OPTIMIZATION AND PLAN SELECTION

It is a capital mistake to theorize before one has the data. Insensibly one begins to twist facts to suit theories, instead of theories to suit facts.

—Sir Arthur Conan Doyle (1859–1930)

If you ever wanted to learn to play the piano, there are many different approaches that people have tried over the past three centuries. The traditional recommended way is to sign up with a professional teacher and take lessons one-on-one. Others have tried a variety of methods of self-instruction, such as using books like *Piano for Dummies*, watching videos, or just getting some sheet music and starting to play. Regardless of which method you choose, there is another variable, namely how to proceed to learn the piece you want to play: hands separate and then together, hands together from the beginning, learning in sections, etc. Therefore, to get to the final goal, there are literally dozens and possibly hundreds of paths one can take to get the final "correct" result. The quality of the result may vary, but you can get there many different ways. For database queries there are also multiple paths leading to the same result, and it is important to be able to analyze the different paths for the quality of the result; that is, to be able to analyze the performance of the system for each path to the correct result and choose the best path to get you there.

This chapter focuses on the basic concepts of query optimization needed to understand the interactions between physical database design and query processing. We start with a simple example of query optimization and illustrate how input/output (I/O) time estimation techniques can be applied to determining which query execution plan would be best. We focus here on the practical trade-off analysis needed to find the best query execution plan to illustrate the process.

3.1 Query Processing and Optimization

The basic steps of query processing are:

1. *Scanning, parsing, and decomposition of an SQL query.* This step checks for correct SQL query syntax and generates appropriate error messages when necessary. The output of this step is an intermediate form of the query known as a query tree or query execution plan.

2. *Query optimization.* This step includes both local and global optimization. Global optimization determines the order of joins and the order of selections and projections relative to the joins. It also involves restating (recasting) nested join queries into flat queries involving the same joins. This is the main concept described in this chapter. Local optimization determines the index method for selections and joins. Both kinds of optimization are based on estimates of cost (I/O time) of the various alternative query execution plans generated by the optimizer. The cost model is based on a description of the database schema and size, and looks at statistics for the attribute values in each table involved in queries.

3. *Query code generation and execution.* This step uses classical programming language and compiler techniques to generate executable code.

3.2 Useful Optimization Features in Database Systems

In addition to the basics of query processing and optimization described above, there are many useful features in database management systems today that aid the database administrator, application developer, and database system itself to process queries more efficiently.

3.2.1 Query Transformation or Rewrite

Modern databases (e.g., Oracle, DB2, SQL Server) transform (rewrite) queries into more efficient forms before optimization takes place. This helps tremendously with query execution plan selection. Examples of the more popular query rewrites are transforming subqueries into joins or semi-joins, pushing down the group by operations below joins, the elimination of joins on foreign keys when the tables containing the results of the join are no longer used in the query, converting outer joins to inner joins when they produce equivalent results, and replacing a view reference in a query by the actual view definition (called *view merging*).

A very common transformation is the materialized view rewrite. If some part of a query is equivalent to an existing materialized view, then the code is replaced by that view. Oracle, for instance, performs a materialized view transformation, then optimizes both the original query and the rewritten query and chooses the more efficient plan between the two alternatives.

Rewrites are especially common in data warehouses using the star schema format. In Oracle, for instance, joins of the fact table with one or more dimension tables are replaced by subqueries involving both tables, using special (bitmap) indexes on the fact table for efficiency.

3.2.2 Query Execution Plan Viewing

How do you know what plan your database chose for the most recent query? All modern database products provide some facility for the user to see the access plan. In DB2 and Oracle it is called Explain or Explain Plan (the graphical version is called Visual Explain). This facility describes all the steps of the plan, the order in which tables are accessed for the query, and whether an index is used to access a table. The optimizer selects the best plan from among the candidate plans generated.

3.2.3 Histograms

Many database systems (e.g., DB2, SQL Server, Oracle) make use of stored histograms of ranges of attribute values from the actual database to help make better estimates of selectivities for selection and join operations, so costs for query execution plans can be estimated more accurately.

3.2.4 Query Execution Plan Hints

Along with Explain, plan hints have become a major fixture in the database industry, allowing application programmers (users) to force certain plan choices, removing uncertainty in many cases. Hints are programmer directives to an SQL query that can change the query execution plan. They are supported by all of the major database systems. While made widely available, they should be used only when major performance problems are present. As an example of the use of a hint, a user can set up an experiment to compare a suboptimal index with an optimal index (and therefore an optimal plan) and see if the performance difference is worth the overhead to use the optimal index, especially if it is used only for this query.

3.2.5 Optimization Depth

Different database products have different search depth, the simplest being greedy search, but there are usually more advanced dynamic programming-based approaches as well. Often the search depth is a configurable parameter.

3.3 Query Cost Evaluation—An Example

The example in this section assumes that we have a basic query execution plan to work with, and focuses on query cost evaluation to minimize I/O time to execute the query whose plan we are given. It illustrates the benefit of applying well-known query optimization strategies to a simple real-life problem. Although the problem is elementary, significant improvements in query time can still be achieved using heuristic rules, and the definition of those rules can be clearly illustrated.

Let us assume a simple three-table database (Date, 2003) with the following materialization of tables: part, supplier, and the intersection table shipment.

Part (P)				Supplier (S)				Shipment (SH)			
pnum	pname	wt	snum	sname	city	status	snum	snum	pnum	qty	shipdate
p1	bolt	3	s1	brown	NY	3	s1	s1	p2	50	1-4-90
p2	nail	6	s2	garcia	LA	2	s1	s1	p3	45	2-17-90
p3	nut	2	s3	kinsey	NY	3	s2	s2	p1	100	11-5-89
								s2	p3	60	6-30-91
								s3	p3	50	8-12-91

Attribute name and size (bytes), and table name and size:
supplier: snum(5), sname(20), city(10), status(2) => 37 bytes in one record in supplier
part: pnum(8), pname(10), wt(5) => 23 bytes in one record in part
shipment: snum(5), pnum(8), qty(5), shipdate(8) => 26 bytes in one record in shipment
Note: Assumed block size (bks) = 15,000 bytes.

3.3.1 Example Query 3.1

"What are the names of parts supplied by suppliers in New York City?" If we translate the query to SQL we have

```
SELECT p.pname
FROM P, SH, S
WHERE P.pnum = SH.pnum
AND SH.snum = S.snum
AND S.city = 'NY';
```

Possible join orders of three tables = 3! = 6:
1. S join SH join P
2. SH join S join P
3. P join SH join S
4. SH join P join S
5. S × P join SH
6. P × S join SH

There are six possible join orders of these three tables, given the two joins specified in the query. Orders 1 and 2 are equivalent because of the commutativity of joins: A join B is equivalent to B join A. By the same rule, orders 3 and 4 are equivalent, and orders 5 and 6 are equivalent. Orders 5 and 6 are to be avoided if at all possible because they involve the Cartesian product form of join when there are no overlapping columns. When this occurs the size of the resulting table is the product of the rows in the individual tables and can be extremely large. Also, the data in the new table is arbitrarily connected.

We are left with orders 1 and 3 as the reasonable options to consider. Within these two orders, we can also consider doing the joins first or doing the selections first. We can also consider doing the queries with indexes and without indexes. We now do a cost estimate for these four among the eight possible alternatives:

- Option 1A: Order 1 with joins executed first, selections last, without indexes.
- Option 1B: Order 1 with selections executed first, joins last, without indexes.
- Option 3A: Order 3 with joins executed first, selections last, without indexes.
- Option 3B: Order 3 with selections executed first, joins last, without indexes.

Intuitively we know that option 1B improves on 1A because joins are by far the most costly operations, and if we can reduce the size of the tables before joining them, it will be a lot faster than joining the original larger tables. In option 1B we also explore the possibility of using indexes.

In these examples we only consider queries and not updates to illustrate the efficiency of executing selections first and using indexes. In practice, query optimizers must consider updates.

Finally, we use sequential block accesses (SBA) and random block accesses (RBA) as estimators for I/O time since there is a linear relationship between SBA or RBA and I/O time, and I/O time is a generally accepted form of cost comparison in database operations.

Option 1A Cost Estimation: Brute-Force Method of Doing All Joins First, with No Indexes

We summarize the basic sizes of records, counts of records, and counts of blocks accessed sequentially in the following table. The tables TEMPA, TEMPB, and so on, are temporary tables formed as the result of intermediate operations during the course of the query.

This approach is detailed below and summarized in Figure 3.1 using the query execution plan notation of Roussopoulos (1982). The query execution plan dictates that the joins are executed first, then the selections. We use merge joins, so no indexes are used in this option.

Table	Row Size	No. Rows	BF	Scan Table (no. Blocks)
supplier (S)	37 bytes	200	405	1
part (P)	23 bytes	100	652	1
shipment (SH)	26 bytes	100K	576	174
TEMPA (S join SH)	58 bytes	100K	258	388
TEMPB (TEMPA join P)	73 bytes	100K	205	488
TEMPC (select TEMPB)	73 bytes	10K	205	49

BF is the blocking factor or rows per block (estimated with average row size).

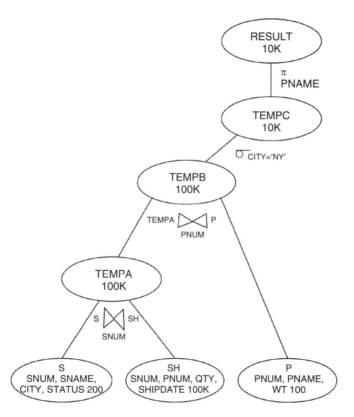

Figure 3.1 Query execution plan for option 1A.

For each step we first estimate the number of records accessed, then sequential blocks accesses, then take a sum of SBAs. We assume each table is stored on disk after each operation and then must be read from disk to do the next operation.

Step 1. Join S and SH over the common column snum forming TEMPA (snum, sname, city, status, pnum, qty, shipdate) at 58 bytes per row (record). If a sort of a table is required before executing a merge join, the estimated cost of an M-way sort is approximately $2 \times nb \times \log_M nb$ (O'Neil, 2001; Silberschatz, 2006) where nb is the number of blocks (pages) in the table to be sorted. In these examples, $M = 3$. However, in this case we don't need to sort SH since table S is very small, less than one block, so we only need to scan SH and compare in fast memory with one block of S.

> Number of block accesses (step 1)
> $=$ read S $+$ read SH $+$ write TEMPA
> $=$ ceiling(200/405) $+$ ceiling(100K/576)
> $+$ceiling(100K/258)
> $= 1 + 174 + 388$
> $= 563.$

Step 2. Join P and TEMPA over the common column pnum forming TEMPB.

> Number of block accesses (step 2)
> $=$ read P $+$ sort TEMPA $+$ read TEMPA
> $+$write TEMPB
> $= 1 + 2 \times 388 \times \log_3 388 + 388 + 488$
> $= 1 + 4214 + 388 + 488$
> $= 5,091.$

Step 3. Select TEMPB where city $=$ 'NY' forming TEMPC (same attributes as TEMPB) at 73 bytes per row. Assume NY has 10% of all suppliers.

> Number of block accesses (step 3)
> $=$ read TEMP $+$ write TEMPC
> $= 488 + 49 = 537.$

Step 4. Project TEMPC over pname forming RESULT (pname) at 10 bytes per row.

Number of rows = 10K (read TEMPC)
Number of block accesses (step 4)
  = read TEMPC
  = 49.

In summary, for the entire query (option 1A) we have
the following totals:

Number of block accesses for query (option 1A)
  = 563 + 5, 091 + 537 + 49 = 6, 240.

*Option 1B Cost Estimation: Do All Selections (Including
Projections) before Joins, without Indexes (and an
Exploration of the Potential Use of Indexes)*

Table	Row Size	No. Rows	BF	Scan Table (no. Blocks)
supplier (S)	37 B	200	405	1
part (P)	23 B	100	652	1
shipment (SH)	26 B	100K	576	174
TEMP1 (select from S)	37 B	20	405	1
TEMP2 (project over SH)	13 B	100K	1,153	87
TEMP3 (project over P)	18 B	100	833	1
TEMP4 (TEMP1 semi-join TEMP2)	13 B	10K	1,153	9
TEMP5 (TEMP4 semi-join TEMP3)	18 B	10K	833	13

This approach is detailed below and summarized in
Figure 3.2.
Step 1. We first select S where city = 'NY' forming
TEMP1 (snum, sname, city, status) at 37 bytes per row.
Because this is a very small table, we avoid creating an
index and just scan the table instead.

Number of block accesses (step 1)
  = read S + write 10% of rows to TEMP1
  = 1 + 1
  = 2.

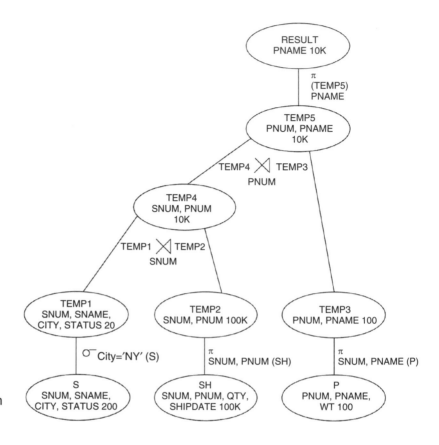

Figure 3.2 Query execution plan for option 1B.

Step 2. We then project SH over snum, pnum forming TEMP2 (snum, pnum) at 13 bytes per row. No indexes are required since a projection operation requires a full table scan.

$$\begin{aligned} &\text{Number of block accesses (step 2)}\\ &= \text{read SH} + \text{write TEMP2}\\ &= 174 + 87\\ &= 261. \end{aligned}$$

Step 3. Next we project P over pnum, pname forming TEMP3 (pnum, pname) at 18 bytes per row. Again, no index is required for a projection operation.

$$\begin{aligned} &\text{Number of block accesses (step 3)}\\ &= \text{read P} + \text{write TEMP3}\\ &= 1 + 1\\ &= 2. \end{aligned}$$

Step 4. Now we want to do a semi-join (a combined join and projection) with TEMP1 with TEMP2 (essentially joining smaller versions of S and SH), forming TEMP4 (snum, pnum) at 13 bytes per row, which has the same scheme as TEMP2. Note that sorting of TEMP2 is not required here because TEMP1 is a very small table (much less than one block). Even with 10% hit rates of records in TEMP2, virtually every block will be accessed because of the very large blocking factor. Therefore, we don't need an index in this situation.

$$
\begin{aligned}
&\text{Number of block accesses (step 4)}\\
&= \text{read TEMP1} + \text{read TEMP2}\\
&\quad + \text{write TEMP4}\\
&= 1 + 87 + 9\\
&= 97.
\end{aligned}
$$

Step 5. Now we have TEMP4 (snum, pnum) and TEMP3 (pnum, pname) that need to be joined over pnum. To accomplish this with a minimum of I/O cost we do a semi-join with TEMP4 projected over pnum before joining with TEMP3 and forming TEMP5 (pnum, pname) with 18 bytes per row. No sorting of TEMP4 is required because TEMP3 is very small (less than one block).

$$
\begin{aligned}
&\text{Number of block accesses (step 5)}\\
&= \text{read TEMP4} + \text{read TEMP3}\\
&\quad + \text{write TEMP5}\\
&= 9 + 1 + 13\\
&= 23.
\end{aligned}
$$

Step 6. Finally we project TEMP5 over pname for the final result.

$$
\begin{aligned}
&\text{Number of rows} = 10\text{K (read TEMP5)}\\
&\text{Number of block accesses (step 6)}\\
&= \text{read TEMP5}\\
&= 13.
\end{aligned}
$$

In summary, the total cost of answering the query using this approach is as follows:

$$
\begin{aligned}
&\text{Number of block accesses for the query (option 2A)}\\
&= 2 + 261 + 2 + 97 + 23 + 13\\
&= 398.
\end{aligned}
$$

We now compare the two approaches:

	Block Accesses
Option 1A	6,240 executing joins first
Option 1B	398 executing joins last

It is clearly seen that the use of table reduction techniques (early selections and projections) has the potential of greatly reducing the I/O time cost of executing a query. Although in this example indexes were not required, in general they can be very useful to reduce I/O time further.

3.4 Query Execution Plan Development

A query execution plan is a data structure that represents each database operation (selections, projections, and joins) as a distinct node. The sequence of operations in a query execution plan can be represented as top down or bottom up. We use the bottom-up approach, and Figures 3.1 and 3.2 are classic examples of the use of query execution plans to denote possible sequences of operations needed to complete SQL queries. An SQL query may have many possible execution sequences, depending on the complexity of the query, and each sequence can be represented by a query execution plan. Our goal is to find the query execution plan that finds the correct answer to the query in the least amount of time. Since the optimal solution to this problem is often too difficult and time consuming to determine relative to the time restrictions imposed on database queries by customers, query optimization is really a process of finding a "good" solution that is reasonably close to the optimal solution, but can be quickly computed.

A popular heuristic for many query optimization algorithms in database systems today involves the simple observation from Section 3.3 that selections and projections should be done before joins because joins tend to be by far the most time-costly operations. Joins should be done with the smallest segments of tables possible, that is, those segments that have only the critical data needed to satisfy the query. For instance in Example Query 3.1, the supplier records are requested for suppliers in New York, which represents only 10% of the supplier table. Therefore, it makes sense to find those records first, store them in a temporary table, and use that table as the supplier table for the join between supplier and shipment. Similarly, only the columns of the tables in a join that have meaning to the join, the subsequent joins, and the final display of results need to be carried along to the join operations. All other columns should be projected out of the table before the join operations are executed.

To facilitate the transformation of a query execution plan from a random sequence of operations to a methodical sequence that does selections and projections first and joins last, we briefly review the basic transformation rules that can be applied to such an algorithm.

3.4.1 Transformation Rules for Query Execution Plans

The following are self-evident rules for transforming operations in query execution plans to reverse the sequence and produce the same result (Silberschatz, 2006). Allow different query trees to produce the same result.

Rule 1. Commutativity of joins: R1 join R2 = R2 join R1.

Rule 2. Associativity of joins: R1 join (R2 join R3) = (R1 join R2) join R3.

Rule 3. The order of selections on a table does not affect the result.

Rule 4. Selections and projections on the same table can be done in any order, so long as a projection does not eliminate an attribute to be used in a selection.

Rule 5. Selections on a table before a join produce the same result as the identical selections on that table after a join.

Rule 6. Projections and joins involving the same attributes can be done in any order so long as the attributes eliminated in the projection are not involved in the join.

Rule 7. Selections (or projections) and union operations involving the same table can be done in any order.

This flexibility in the order of operations in a query execution plan makes it easy to restructure the plan to an optimal or near-optimal structure quickly.

3.4.2 Query Execution Plan Restructuring Algorithm

The following is a simple heuristic to restructure a query execution plan for optimal or near-optimal performance.

1. Separate a selection with several AND clauses into a sequence of selections (rule 3).
2. Push selections down the query execution plan as far as possible to be executed earlier (rules 4, 5, 7).
3. Group a sequence of selections as much as possible (rule 3).
4. Push projections down the plan as far as possible (rules 4, 6, 7).
5. Group projections on the same tables, removing redundancies.

Figure 3.1 illustrates a query execution plan that emphasizes executing the joins first using a bottom-up execution sequence. Figure 3.2 is the same plan, transformed to a plan that executes the joins last using this heuristic.

3.5 Selectivity Factors, Table Size, and Query Cost Estimation

Once we are given a candidate query execution plan to analyze, we need to be able to estimate the sizes of the intermediate tables the query optimizer will create during query execution. Once we have estimated those table sizes, we can compute the I/O time to execute the query using that query execution plan as we did in Section 3.3. The sizes of the intermediate tables were given in that example. Now we will show how to estimate those table sizes.

Selectivity (S) of a table is defined as the proportion of records in a table that satisfies a given condition. Thus, selectivity takes on a value between zero and one. For example, in Example Query 3.1, the selectivity of records in the table supplier that satisfies the condition WHERE city 'NY' is 0.1, because 10% of the records have the value NY for city.

To help our discussion of selectivity, let us define the following measures of data within a table:

- The number (cardinality) of rows in table R: card(R).
- The number (cardinality) of distinct values of attribute A in table R: $card_A(R)$
- Maximum value of attribute A in a table R: $max_A(R)$
- Minimum value of attribute A in a table R: $min_A(R)$

3.5.1 Estimating Selectivity Factor for a Selection Operation or Predicate

The following relationships show how to compute the selectivity of selection operations on an SQL query (Ozsu, 1991).

The selectivity for an attribute A in table R to have a specific value a in a selected record applies to two situations. First, if the attribute A is a primary key, where each value is unique, then we have an exact selectivity measure

$$S(A = a) = 1/card_A(R). \qquad 3.1$$

For example, if the table has 50 records, then the selectivity is 1/50 or 0.02.

On the other hand, if attribute A is not a primary key and has multiple occurrences for each value a, then we can also use Equation 3.1 to estimate the selectivity, but we must acknowledge that we are guessing that the distribution of values is uniform. Sometimes this is a poor estimate, but generally it is all we can do without actual distribution data to draw upon. For example, if there are 25 cities out of 200 suppliers in the supplier table in Example Query 3.1, then the number of records with 'NY' is estimated to be $card_{city}(supplier) = 200/25 = 8$. The selectivity of 'NY' is $1/card_{city}(supplier) = 1/8 = 0.125$. In reality, the number of records was given in the example to be 10%, so in this case our estimate is pretty good, but it is not always true.

The selectivity of an attribute A being greater than (or less than) a specific value a also depends on a uniform distribution (random probability) assumption for our estimation:

$$S(A > a) = (max_A(R) - a)/(max_A(R) - min_A(R)). \qquad 3.2$$

$$S(A < a) = (a - min_A(R))/(max_A(R) - min_A(R)). \qquad 3.3$$

The selectivity of two intersected selection operations (predicates) on the same table can be estimated exactly if the individual selectivities are known:

$$S(P \text{ and } Q) = S(P) \times S(Q), \qquad 3.4$$

where P and Q are predicates.

So if we have the query

```
SELECT city, qty
FROM shipment
WHERE city = 'London'
AND qty = 1000;
```

where P is the predicate city = 'London' and Q is the predicate qty = 1000, and we know that

$S(\text{city} = \text{'London'}) = .3,$ and
$S(\text{qty} = 1000) = .6,$ then the selectivity of the
entire query,
$S(\text{city} = \text{'London' AND qty} = 1000) = .3 \times .6 = .18.$

The selectivity of the union of two selection operations (predicates) on the same table can be estimated using the well-known formula for randomly selected variables:

$$S(P \text{ or } Q) = S(P) + S(Q) - S(P) \times S(Q) \qquad 3.5$$

where P and Q are predicates.

So if we take the same query above and replace the intersection of predicates with a union of predicates, we have:

```
SELECT city, qty
FROM shipment
WHERE city = 'London'
OR qty = 1000;
```

$S(\text{city} = \text{'London'}) = .3$
$S(\text{qty} = 1000) = .6$
$S(\text{city} = \text{'London' OR qty} = 1000) = .3 + .6 - .3 \times .6 = .72.$

3.5.2 Histograms

The use of average values to compute selectivities can be reasonably accurate for some data, but for other data it may be off by significantly large amounts. If all databases only used this approximation, estimates of query time could be seriously misleading. Fortunately, many database management systems now store the actual distribution of attribute values as a *histogram*. In a histogram, the values of an attribute are divided into ranges, and within each range, a count of the number of rows whose attribute falls within that range is made.

In the example above we were given the selectivity of qty = 1000 to be .6. If we know that there are 2,000 different quantities in the shipment table out of 100,000 rows, then the average number of rows for a given quantity would be 100,000/2,000 = 50. Therefore, the selectivity of qty = 1000 would be 50/100,000 = .0005. If we have stored a histogram of quantities in ranges consisting of integer values: 1, 2, 3, 4, ..., 1,000, 1,001,.....2,000, and found that we had 60,000 rows containing quantity values equal to 1,000, we would estimate the selectivity of qty = 1000 to be .6. This is a huge difference in accuracy that would have dramatic effects on query execution plan cost estimation and optimal plan selection.

3.5.3 Estimating the Selectivity Factor for a Join

Estimating the selectivity for a join is difficult if it is based on nonkeys; in the worst case it can be a Cartesian product at one extreme or no matches at all at the other extreme. We focus here on the estimate based on the usual scenario for joins between a primary key and a nonkey (a foreign key). Let's take, for example, the join between a table R1, which has a primary key, and a table R2, which has a foreign key:

$$\text{card}(R1 \text{ join } R2) = S \times \text{card}(R1) \times \text{card}(R2), \qquad 3.6$$

where S is the selectivity of the common attribute used in the join, when that attribute is used as a primary key. Let's illustrate this computation of the selectivity and then the size of the joined table, either the final result of the query or an intermediate table in the query.

3.5.4 Example Query 3.2

Find all suppliers in London with the shipping date of June 1, 2006.

```
SELECT supplierName
  FROM supplier S, shipment SH
```

```
WHERE S.snum = SH.snum
AND S.city = 'London'
AND SH.shipdate = '01-JUN-2006';
```

Let us assume the following data that describes the three tables: supplier, part, and shipment:

- card(supplier) = 200
- $\text{card}_{\text{city}}$(supplier) = 50
- card(shipment) = 100,000
- $\text{card}_{\text{shipdate}}$(shipment) = 1,000
- card(part) = 100

There are two possible situations to evaluate:

1. The join is executed before the selections.

2. The selections are executed before the join.

Figure 3.3 Query execution plan for cases 1 and 2.

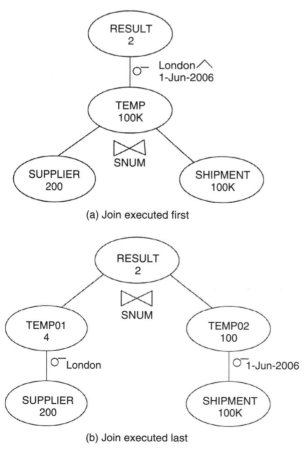

(a) Join executed first

(b) Join executed last

Case 1: Join Executed First

If the join is executed first we know that there are 200 suppliers (rows in the supplier table) and 100,000 shipments (rows in the shipment table), so the selectivity of supplier number in the supplier table is 1/200. Now we apply Equation 3.6 to find the cardinality of the join, that is, the count of rows (records) in the intermediate table formed by the join of supplier and shipment:

$$
\begin{aligned}
\text{card}&(\text{supplier join shipment}) \\
&= S(\text{snum}) \times \text{card}(\text{supplier}) \\
&\quad \times \text{card}(\text{shipment}) \\
&= (1/200) \times 200 \times 100,000 \\
&= 100,000.
\end{aligned}
$$

This is consistent with the basic rule of thumb that a join between a table R1 with a primary key and a table R2 with the corresponding foreign key results in a table with the same number of rows as the table with the foreign key (R2). The query execution plan for this case is shown in Figure 3.3(a). The result of the two selections on this joined table is:

$$\begin{aligned}
\text{card(result)} &= \text{S(supplier.city} = \text{`London')} \\
&\quad \times \text{S(shipment.shipdate} = \\
&\quad \text{`01-JUN-2006')} \times \text{card} \\
&\quad \text{(supplier join shipment)} \\
&= (1/50) \times (1/1,000) \times 100,000 \\
&= 2 \text{ rows.}
\end{aligned}$$

Case 2: Selections Executed First

If the selections are executed first, before the join, the computation of estimated selectivity and intermediate table size is slightly more complicated, but still straightforward. We assume there are 50 different cities in the supplier table and 1,000 different ship dates in the shipment table. See the query execution plan in Figure 3.3(b).

$\text{S(supplier.city} = \text{`London')} = 1/\text{card}_{\text{city}}(\text{supplier}) = 1/50.$
$\text{S(shipment.shipdate} = \text{`01-JUN-2006')}$
$\quad = 1/\text{card}_{\text{shipment}}(\text{shipment})$
$\quad = 1/1,000.$

We now determine the sizes (cardinalities) of the results of the two selections on supplier and shipment:

$$\begin{aligned}
&\text{card(supplier.city} = \text{`London')} \\
&\quad = (1/50) \times (200 \text{ rows in supplier}) = 4 \text{ rows.}
\end{aligned}$$

$$\begin{aligned}
&\text{card(shipment.shipdate} = \text{`01-JUN-2006')} \\
&\quad = (1/1,000) \times (100,000) = 100 \text{ rows.}
\end{aligned}$$

These two results are stored as intermediate tables, reduced versions of supplier and shipment, which we will now call 'supplier' and 'shipment':

$$\begin{aligned}
\text{card('supplier')} &= 4(\text{Note: `supplier' has 4 rows with city} \\
&= \text{`London'.})
\end{aligned}$$

$$\begin{aligned}
\text{card('shipment')} &= 100(\text{Note: `shipment' has 100 rows} \\
&\quad \text{with shipdate} = \text{`01-JUN-2006'.})
\end{aligned}$$

Now that we have the sizes of the two intermediate tables we can apply Equation 3.6 to find the size of the final result of the join:

$$\text{card('supplier' join 'shipment')}$$
$$= S(\text{snum}) \times \text{card('supplier')} \times \text{card('shipment')}$$
$$= (1/200) \times 4 \times 100$$
$$= 2.$$

The final result is 2 rows, that is, all the suppliers in London with the ship date of 01-JUN-2006.

We note that both ways of computing the final result have the same number of rows in the result, but the number of block accesses for each is quite different. The cost of doing the joins first is much higher than the cost for doing the selections first.

3.5.5 Example Estimations of Query Execution Plan Table Sizes

We now revisit Figures 3.1 and 3.2 for actual table sizes within the query execution plan for Example Query 3.1.

Option 1A (Figure 3.1)

For the query execution plan in Figure 3.1 we first join supplier (S) and shipment (SH) to form TEMPA. The size of TEMPA is computed from Equation 3.6 as

$$\text{card(TEMPA)} = S \times (\text{card(supplier)} \times \text{card(shipment)})$$
$$= 1/200 \times 200 \times 100,000 = 100,000 \text{ rows},$$

where $S = 1/200$, the selectivity of the common attribute in the join, snum.

Next we join TEMPA with the part table, forming TEMPB.

$$\text{card(TEMPB)} = S \times (\text{card(TEMPA)} \times \text{card(part)})$$
$$= 1/100 \times 100,000 \times 100 = 100,000 \text{ rows},$$

where $S = 1/100$, the selectivity of the common attribute in the join, pnum.

Finally we select the 10% of the rows from the result that have city = 'NY', giving us 10,000 rows in TEMPC and the final result of the query. We note that the 10% ratio holds through the joins as long as the joins involve primary key–foreign key pairs (and do not involve the attribute city).

Option 1B (Figure 3.2)

In Figure 3.2 we look at the improved query execution plan for option 1B.

TEMP1 is the result of selecting city = 'NY' rows from supplier, with selectivity .1 using Equation 3.1, giving us 200 rows (supplier) × .1 = 20 rows in TEMP1.

TEMP2 is the result of projecting columns snum and pnum from shipment, and therefore has the same number of rows as shipment, 100,000. Similarly, TEMP3 is the result of a projection of pnum and pname from the part table, and has the same number of rows as part, 100.

TEMP4 is shown as the semi-join of TEMP1 and TEMP2 over the common attribute, snum. We note that a semi-join can be represented by a join followed by a projection of pnum and snum from the result. Applying Equation 3.6 to this join:

$$
\begin{aligned}
\text{card(TEMP4)} &= S \times \text{card(TEMP1)} \times \text{card(TEMP2)} \\
&= 1/200 \times 20 \times 100,000 \\
&= 10,000 \text{ rows,}
\end{aligned}
$$

where S = 1/200, the selectivity of the common attribute of the join, snum.

TEMP5 is shown as the semi-join of TEMP4 and TEMP3 over the common attribute, pnum. Again we apply Equation 3.6 to this join:

$$
\begin{aligned}
\text{card(TEMP5)} &= S \times \text{card(TEMP4)} \times \text{card(TEMP3)} \\
&= 1/100 \times 10,000 \times 100 \\
&= 10,000 \text{ rows,}
\end{aligned}
$$

where S = 1/100, the selectivity of the common attribute of the join, pnum.

The final result, taking a projection over TEMP5, results in 10,000 rows.

3.6 Summary

This chapter focused on the basic elements of query optimization: query execution plan analysis and selection. We took the point of view of how the query time can be estimated from the sequential and random block accesses needed to execute a query. We also looked at the estimation of intermediate table size in a query made up of a series of selections, projections, and joins. Table size is a critical measure of how long merge joins take, whereas index definitions help determine how long indexed or hash joins take to execute.

Tips and Insights for Database Professionals

- **Tip 1. Indexes can greatly improve query time and should be an integral part of a query optimizer.** Automated tools used by Microsoft and IBM integrate index design with query optimization. Some basic estimates for query time for a given query execution plan can be manually estimated, with or without indexes.

3.7 Literature Summary

Burleson, D. (2005). *Physical Database Design Using Oracle.* Boca Raton, FL: Auerbach Publishers.

Date, C. J. (2003). *An Introduction to Database Systems* (vol. 1, 8th ed.). Boston: Addison-Wesley.

Elmasri, R., & Navathe, S. B. (2010). *Fundamentals of Database Systems* (6th ed.). Boston and Redwood City, CA: Addison-Wesley.

Garcia-Molina, H., Ullman, J., & Widom, J. (2008). *Database Systems: The Complete Book* (2nd ed.). Englewood Cliffs, NJ: Prentice-Hall.

O'Neil, P., & O'Neil, E. (2001). *Database: Principles, Programming, and Performance* (2nd ed.). San Francisco: Morgan Kaufmann.

Ozsu, M. T., & Valduriez, P. (1991). *Principles of Distributed Database Systems.* Englewood Cliffs, NJ: Prentice-Hall.

Roussopoulos, N. (1982). View Indexing in Relational Databases. *ACM Transactions Database Systems, 7*(2), 258–290.

Ramakrishnan, R., & Gehrke, J. (2004). *Database Management Systems* (3rd ed.). New York: McGraw-Hill.

Selinger, P. G., Astrahan, M. M., Chamberlin, D. D., Lorie, R. A., & Price, T. G. (1979). Access Path Selection in a Relational Database Management System. In *ACM SIGMOD Conference* (pp. 23–34).

Silberschatz, A., Korth, H. F., & Sudarshan, S. (2010). *Database System Concepts* (6th ed.). New York: McGraw-Hill.

A

A SIMPLE PERFORMANCE MODEL FOR DATABASES

Performance is your reality. Forget everything else.
—Harold Geneen

This appendix presents a simple performance cost model for evaluating physical design methods and tradeoffs among various designs. The model includes estimations for input/output (I/O) time and network delays.

A.1 I/O Time Cost—Individual Block Access

A block (or page) has been traditionally the basic unit of I/O from disk to fast memory (RAM). It can range in size from 2 to 16 KB, although 4,096 bytes (4 KB) is the most typical size in many systems. Blocks usually include many rows in a table, but occasionally a large row can span several blocks. In recent years, prefetch buffers have been used more often in operational systems to increase I/O efficiency. Prefetch buffers are typically 64 KB (in DB2, for instance). In some systems the disk track is the I/O transfer size of choice.

Block access cost
= disk access time to a block from a random starting location $\qquad$ A.1
= average disk seek time + average rotational delay + block transfer.

Disk access time is becoming much faster with new technologies, and currently we can estimate the access time to a 4 KB block to be well below 10 ms in a shared-disk environment. For example, an IBM U320 146 GB hard drive has an average seek time of 3.6 ms, average rotational delay of 2 ms for a half rotation (at 15,000 RPM), and a transfer rate of 320 MB/sec. For this disk, the expected block access cost in a shared-disk environment is:

I/O time(4 KB block access in a shared disk)
$= 3.6\,\text{ms} + 2\,\text{ms} + 4\,\text{KB}/320\,\text{MB}/\text{sec} = 5.6\,\text{ms}.$

I/O time(64 KB prefetch buffer in a shared disk)
$= 3.6\,\text{ms} + 2\,\text{ms} + 64\,\text{KB}/320\,\text{MB}/\text{sec} = 5.8\,\text{ms}.$

In a dedicated disk environment, the disk-seek component is rarely needed, so the time is considered negligible.

I/O time(4 KB block access in a dedicated disk)
$= 2\,\text{ms} + 4\,\text{KB}/320\,\text{MB}/\text{sec} = 2.0\,\text{ms}.$

I/O time(64 KB prefetch buffer access in a dedicated disk)
$= 2\,\text{ms} + 64\,\text{KB}/320\,\text{MB}/\text{sec} = 2.2\,\text{ms}.$

A.2 I/O Time Cost—Table Scans and Sorts

Disk technologies that create higher speeds plus special prefetching hardware can also make table scans and sorting operations extremely efficient. The total I/O time for a full table scan is computed simply as the I/O time for a single block or prefetch buffer, whichever applies, times the total number of those I/O transfers in the table.

Sorting, which is a part of many queries, especially those needing a sort-merge join, has progressed well beyond the simple two-way sorts of the past. The estimated cost of an M-way sort is approximately $2 \times nb \times \log_M nb$, where nb is the number of blocks in the table to be transferred to memory from disk (O'Neil, 2001; Silberschatz, 2006). In the examples in this book, we use $M = 3$ to represent three-way sorts.

A.3 Network Time Delays

Network delays can be significant compared to I/O delays, and when data is accessed across a network, the following model can be used, which is very similar to the disk I/O model.

Network delay = propagation time + transmission time,

A.2

where

Propagation time = network distance/propagation speed,

A.3

and

Transmission time = packet size/network transmission rate.

A.4

The propagation speed is estimated to be 200,000 km/sec, which is approximately two-thirds of the speed of light, taking into account normal degradations of transmission media from the theoretical speed of light of approximately 300,000 km/sec. The network distance is given in kilometers (km). If the network media you are using has a known propagation delay, then substitute the known value for 200 km/ms in the equation. Rough approximations are considered reasonable here to get "ballpark" estimates of total time.

The transmission time for a packet on a network is the time to get the packet on or off the network to or from the controlling device in the local computer system. It is analogous to the transfer time for a block on a disk. The transmission rate is given in bits/second and packet size is given in bytes. We assume an 8-bit per byte conversion factor.

For example, the time to send one packet of 1,500 bytes (let's say its one block of data) over an Ethernet with a transmission rate of 1 Gb/sec in a wide area network (WAN) at a network distance of 1,000 kilometers would be:

Network time = 1, 000 km/200, 000 km/sec + 1, 500 bytes
        × 8 bits/byte/1 Gb/sec
     = .005 sec + .000012 sec
     = .005012 sec(or 5.012 ms).

For a local area network (LAN) with a network distance of .1 km, we get:

$$\begin{aligned}
\text{Network time} &= .1\,\text{km}/200,000\,\text{km/sec} + 1,500\,\text{bytes}\\
&\quad \times 8\,\text{bits/byte}/1\,\text{Gb/sec}\\
&= .0000005\,\text{sec} + .000012\,\text{sec}\\
&= .0000125\,\text{sec}\,(\text{or }.0125\,\text{ms}).
\end{aligned}$$

Putting these numbers in perspective, higher-speed Ethernet networks have very small transmission times, and for longer distances of WANs, the total network time is dominated by the propagation time. In this case, the typical values for network time (that is, the propagation time) are in the same range as disk I/O times, and need to be considered in the estimate of total response time.

For LANs where network distances may be less than .1 km, the dominating delay is transmission time, but neither time in this example is significant compared to typical disk I/O times. Thus, in LANs we can consider network delays to be negligible unless there are extremely large packets or trains of packets.

A.4 CPU Time Delays

CPU time delays are mainly dependent on the processing required by the database application, and are largely independent of the I/O operations. Those CPU delays caused by the software to manage the I/O are usually negligible compared to the I/O times, and are even further diminished when they overlap the I/O operations. Our model assumes database systems to be I/O-bound and considers CPU delays as negligible.

References

O'Neil, P., & O'Neil, E. (2001). *Database Principles, Programming, and Performance* (2nd ed.). San Francisco, CA: Morgan Kaufmann Publishers.

Silberschatz, A., Korth, H., & Sudarshan, S. (2010). *Database System Concepts* (6th ed.). Boston, MA: McGraw-Hill.